D1388111

Sports Medicine in Primary Care

Robert C. Cantu, M.D., F.A.C.S.

Associate Chairman, Department of Surgery
Chief, Neurosurgical Service
Director, Service of Sports Medicine
Emerson Hospital
Concord, Massachusetts

with contributions by

Roseanna Hemenway Means, M.D.
Lyle J. Micheli, M.D.
Arthur J. Siegel, M.D.
Paul Vinger, M.D.

The Collamore Press
D. C. Heath and Company
Lexington, Massachusetts
Toronto

Published simultaneously in Canada and the United Kingdom.

Printed in the United States of America

International Standard Book Number: 0–669–04593–4 Casebound

International Standard Book Number: 0–669–05429–1 Paperbound

Library of Congress Catalog Card Number: 81–0925

Library of Congress Cataloging in Publication Data

Cantu, Robert C.
    Sports medicine in primary care.

    Includes index.
    1. Sports medicine.   2. Family medicine.
I. Title.
RC1210.C34   617′.1027   81-70166
ISBN 0-669-04593-4 Casebound   AACR2
ISBN 0-669-05429-1 Paperbound

Contents

iii

Contributing Authors

Roseanna H. Means, M.D.
Department of Medicine
Brigham and Women's Hospital
Boston

Lyle J. Micheli, M.D.
Instructor in Orthopaedic Surgery,
Harvard Medical School
Director, Division of Sports Medicine,
Children's Hospital Medical Center
Boston

Arthur J. Siegel, M.D.
Assistant Professor of Medicine
Harvard Medical School
Boston

Paul F. Vinger, M.D.
Assistant Clinical Professor in Ophthalmology,
Harvard Medical School
Department of Ophthalmology
Emerson Hospital and Massachusetts Eye and Ear Infirmary
Concord and Boston

Foreword

Office practice is a dynamic adventure that undergoes continual change in the ways physicians address current health problems of patients. Sports medicine is an area in which changing life-style creates new needs for treatment and strategies to preserve health. The role of the office practitioner as healer and dispenser of competent care for injury involves helping to promote safety in sports participation and skill in treating injuries.

Sports Medicine in Primary Care is a primer of preventive and direct care. The first section addresses basic concepts that apply to all patients whether young or old, male or female. These chapters provide a concise summary of important information in the areas of exercise, nutrition, conditioning, and practical exercise guidance. Complex information is distilled into meaningful form for the physician, who can in turn impart sound concepts to patients.

Part two addresses the specific needs of selected patient groups such as younger athletes and women. An internist's view of medical complications during sport provides some diagnostic strategies and is followed by a chapter on practical advice to the physician as team doctor.

The third section focuses on sports injuries with an emphasis on prevention and on complications requiring specialty referral. Each chapter, beginning with head injuries, highlights immediate treatment and special precautions germane to specific sequelae of injury.

Overall, this book provides in one concise volume relevant information on exercise and practical guidelines for treatment of sports-related injuries. It is a valuable resource for office and team physicians alike. I am pleased to have participated in its preparation and heartily recommend it to my colleagues.

Arthur J. Siegel, M. D.

Acknowledgments

I would like to express my special thanks to Art Siegel, Roseanna Hemenway Means, Paul Vinger, and Lyle Micheli for their invaluable contributions to this book, and to my secretary, Pat Blackey, who somehow managed a busy office and manuscript typing with equal alacrity. I also wish to acknowledge my sincere appreciation to Sarah Boardman, whose initial suggestions resulted in this project.

Robert C. Cantu, M.D., F.A.C.S.

I / Well-Patient Sports Medicine

1/Conditioning the Cardiovascular System

To a certain extent, fortune dictates the basic state of our health at birth. During the first years of our lives, our health is partially determined by the care given by parents and others. Parents dictate what we eat, and their good and bad examples affect our personal health habits. Teachers also influence us, as do our classmates and, sometimes unfortunately, TV commercials that promote various products. Eventually, as we grow older and wiser, we exert increasingly greater control over our own bodies. It is at this point that we become aware of our biological clock.

What is a biological clock? It is a time machine, ticking within each individual. This time machine, set before birth, dictates the maximum length of every person's life. One of the most important factors governing our basic health is heredity. We are what our parents make us. We remain alive only while our vital organs function. Although medical science has recently made significant progress in transplanting hearts, kidneys, and other parts of the body necessary to life, we can only survive as long as the least of these vital parts survive.

The sad fact is that people, because of individual abuses (such as excessive alcohol consumption and cigarette smoking), weaken their own organs. In addition, because of lack of physical activity (hypokinesia), people also fail to maintain their body in optimum condition to guarantee not merely long life, but good health as well.

We are never too old to begin a program of cardiovascular improvement. At birth, our vascular system is largely free of fatty deposits, but with each day of life deposits accumulate in our arteries threatening our health and survival. The English researcher Osborne showed that early signs of disease can be detected in the coronary arteries of children as young as 5 years of age [11]. Between 16 and 20 years of age, over one-half the population has atherosclerosis of the coronary arteries. Autopsy studies of Korean War casualties showed that many of our soldiers had significant arteriosclerosis before the age of 25.

Research showing the early occurrence of coronary-artery disease demonstrates the desirability of a total fitness program from cradle to grave. While playing, most young children run. As children grow older, they should never stop running—although most do. However, even for those who have abandoned exercise, it is never too late to begin a fitness program. Heart patients now complete full-distance (26-mile, 385-yard) marathons. Recent studies have shown a reduction in previous arteriosclerosis with endurance cardiovascular training[1]. The buildup of plaques deposited in coronary arteries apparently can be reversed. Health and physical fitness can be regained even by those who seem hopelessly out of shape.

What is Physical Fitness?

To understand fitness, it is necessary to know something about the physiology of exercise, particularly as it involves the cardiovascular system. The cardiovascular system—consisting of the heart, arteries, capillaries, and veins—conducts blood, containing life-essential oxygen and nutrients, to our body cells. The road to vigorous health begins with a fit cardiovascular system. Physically disadvantaged individuals usually suffer from some impairment of their cardiovascular system. Frequently, the disruption is sudden and severe, perhaps a major blockage of a coronary artery or a cerebral-artery occlusion or rupture. Other individuals may recognize the deterioration of their cardiovascular system by certain telltale signs: excessive fatigue, dyspnea, or angina following physical activity. Heart attacks kill and disable more people in the Western world than any other affliction; as the affluent life spreads to the non-Western world, the incidence of heart attack is climbing there as well.

The root cause of cardiovascular impairment is related to family history. A tendency toward heart attack is built into our genes. If our father or mother suffered early cardiovascular impairment, the odds are that we will too—particularly if we mimic their health habits. Because we did not select our parents, our biological clock lies outside our initial control. However, knowing our family's health history will help us understand our bodies better. Physically disadvantaged persons with a family history of cardiovascular disease should begin an exercise program immediately in order to resist the genetic weakness they have inherited. This is true regardless of their age.

One of the great tributes to good health is the Boston Marathon, run each April from Hopkinton to downtown Boston. Thousands of healthy (and some nonhealthy) runners participate in this 26-mile event that is usually witnessed by more than one million people lining the route. Ironically, the Boston Marathon passes through (at about the 6-mile mark) Framingham, Massachusetts, a town of about 70,000 people that has been the site of several classic public studies on the health of large groups of people.

One recent Framingham study, begun in 1968 and sponsored by the United States Public Health Service, closely followed 5,000 residents (2,336 men and 2,873 women) and focused on coronary disease [6–10]. The study determined that men with elevated cholesterol levels, who had hypertension or diabetes and who smoked, had ten times more coronary-artery disease than average individuals. With these four factors absent, the likelihood of death from heart disease was reduced to one-third the standard risk.

Clearly, the elevation of blood cholesterol, hypertension, and diabetes, as well as being a man, greatly increased one's chances of heart attack. (After menopause, women are at equal risk for heart attack as men of the same age.)

Cigarette smoking should be included in this discussion because it is so important to our health, or lack of health. Cigarette smoking has been identified as a principal cause of certain types of cancer, but smokers stand an even greater risk of suffering a heart attack because of their smoking habits. That smoking significantly increases the risk of coronary disease has been proved by epidemiologic studies in the United States, Canada, Great Britain, and elsewhere. In fact, the incidence of sudden death during a heart attack, if it occurs, is nearly 400% greater in cigarette smokers.

Consider one example involving heart patients who attempted to improve their health by becoming involved in physical-fitness programs. At the Toronto Rehabilitation Centre, Dr. Terence Kavanagh supervises a walking and jogging endurance program for post-heart-attack patients, several of whom have progressed to running the Boston Marathon [11]. The incidence of recurring fatal heart attacks among patients at the center is only 1.3%, an impressive record. The vast majority of deaths, according to Dr. Kavanagh, occurred in patients who, despite admonitions, had not stopped smoking cigarettes.

There are other factors that increase the risk of heart attack, one of which is obesity. However, obesity is usually only a risk factor in association with one or more of the other risk factors such as diabetes, hypertension, high blood cholesterol, or inactivity. Usually there is no single reason why people fail to live to the potential programmed on their biological clock.

Another factor of heart attack risk is emotional stress and the so-called type-A personality. A type-A individual is characterized by Friedman and Rosenman as a person who is competitive, excessively ambitious, impatient with delay, compulsive, and never satisfied with achievement[5]. The findings of Friedman and Rosenman are far from conclusive, however. Multiple studies in the United States and abroad indicate no correlation between responsibility at work and coronary disease. So perhaps the type-A personality is merely associated with other risk factors such as smoking. Dr. Kavanagh comments: "I am constantly impressed by the wide spectrum of personalities attending postcoronary rehabilitation and, in my experience, the coronary-disease population is not at all homogeneous"[2].

Also among the risk factors closely identified with heart attacks is inactivity. Professor Jeremy Morris of the British Research Council first drew attention to this fact in 1953[12]. He studied the incidence of heart disease in London Transport Department workers and found that bus conductors, who averaged 24 trips per hour up and down the winding staircase of the moving double-decker bus, had one-third less heart disease than the more sedentary bus drivers. In 1973 Morris reported the beneficial effects of leisure-time exercise in 17,000 British civil servants[13]. He concluded: "Habitual vigorous exercise during leisure time reduces the incidence of coronary heart disease in middle-age among sedentary male workers. Vigorous activities which are normal for such men are sufficient. Training of the heart and cardiovascular system is one of the mechanisms of protection against common risk factors and the disease."

More recently, in 1977, Dr. Ralph S. Paffenbarger, Jr. reported that the risk of heart attack was significantly reduced in men engaged in strenuous sports, while casual sports seemed to have no beneficial effect [14, 15]. His research involved 17,000 male alumni of Harvard University aged 35 to 74 years who had been studied for six to ten years. Heart-attack rates declined among these men in proportion to their degree of physical activity. This trend was true for all ages and for both nonfatal and fatal attacks. The message came through loud and clear: the more calories the men spent in total activity in a week, the less risk of heart attack.

The number of kilo calories for those observed in the Harvard study was 2,000. It appeared that 2,000 kilocalories expended per week in exercise protected an individual against heart attack. This protective effect for active men seemed to hold regardless of other risk factors such as cigarette smoking, hypertension, obesity, or parental heart-attack history. Among the strenuous sports affording the most protection, Dr. Paffenbarger listed running, swimming, basketball, handball, and squash. Casual sports that afforded no protection included golf, bowling, baseball, softball, and volleyball.

When considering the benefits of daily physical activity, we should reflect on the three regions of the world most renowned for longevity: the Ecuadorian Andes, the Karamoran mountains in Kashmir, and the Agkazia region of the southern Soviet Union. In these regions, people often live to the age of 100 years or more, and heart attacks are rare. Researchers have noted that diets vary, and that partaking of "local spirits" is common among the aged. In all three regions, the people assume they will live to an old age and work literally until they drop. Their work involves heavy labor and frequent sustained walking over hilly terrain. These people expend 400 to 800 calories a day while working, and objective physical examination shows a very high degree of cardiovascular fitness. Therefore, substantial evidence now exists that cardiovascular fitness (attained either by work or by a formal exercise program for sedentary workers) prevents heart attack and increases longevity.

Consider how the body's cardiovascular system works. Our atmosphere contains 21% oxygen and our body requires a constant supply of this oxygen to survive. Within a few minutes of oxygen deprivation, the cells of our body begin to die, commencing with our most sensitive organ, the brain. Our lungs extract oxygen from the atmosphere. Breathing is controlled automatically by a feedback system from our brain. Specific cells in the brain respond to the blood levels of oxygen, and when the content falls below a critical level, the brain sends impulses through its nerves to the chest wall, diaphragm, and heart. This causes us to breathe more deeply and rapidly and it is why we get out of breath when running or exercising vigorously. The increased heart rate pumps more blood to the lungs to acquire the increased oxygen being supplied.

Our lungs consist of ever-smaller air passages, beginning with the major bronchi, then the smaller bronchioles, and terminating in tiny terminal air sacs known as alveoli. The walls of the aveoli contain fine hairlike capillary blood vessels that are part of the lung's circulation. In accordance with the laws of physics, gases pass through the walls of our capillary blood vessels, from a region of high concentration to a region of lower concentration. Thus, oxygen passes from the alveoli to the capillary blood vessels, and carbon dioxide passes in the opposite direction.

In the capillary blood vessel, most of the oxygen combines with the protein hemoglobin in the red blood cells. In this form, it is carried away from the lungs to the left side of the heart. From there it is pumped through the arterial system. The arteries branch into smaller and smaller vessels until they end in capillaries, in muscles and in other tissues of the body. In this way, oxygen-rich blood is delivered to active oxygen-poor muscles. There, the oxygen separates from the hemoglobin under the influence of various environmental conditions, including heat of muscle contraction, acidity, and presence of myoglobin. The net result is that the muscle receives oxygen. The deoxygenated blood returns through the veins to the right side of the heart from which, again, it is pumped to the lungs to repeat the entire cycle (figure 1–1).

Muscles contract, or shorten in length, through an interlocking action by which their two component protein fibrils, actin and myosin, slide together. Energy is required to begin and continue this work. The immediate source of energy is adenosine triphosphate (ATP), which releases energy when converted to adenosine diphosphate (ADP), but the

Figure 1–1   Schematic of the cardiovascular system.

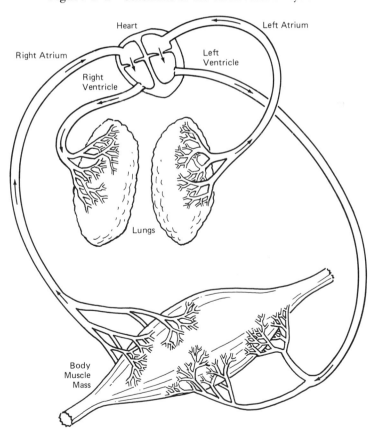

actual source of energy is the food we eat. The major source of short-term energy involves the breakdown of glycogen to glucose, which is oxidized to carbon dioxide and water (aerobic metabolism = glycogen and FFA + P + ADP + O_2 → CO_2 + H_2O + ATP). Long-distance runners sometimes follow a specific dietary regimen known as carbohydrate loading in an attempt to increase the glycogen stores of their body before a marathon race.

In order to oxidate glucose, the body requires a plentiful supply of oxygen. In the absence of sufficient oxygen, breakdown of glycogen is incomplete, and less ATP is synthesized. This is one reason that distance runners run much slower at high altitudes, as at Mexico City (7,300 feet) in the 1968 Olympics. In addition, a toxic substance, lactic acid, accumulates in the muscles and the bloodstream. High lactic-acid levels block the formation of more ATP, are associated with the sensation of fatigue, and eventually lead to the cessation of muscle contraction.

Exercises in which the effort outstrips the body's ability to supply oxygen include underwater swimming and sprinting. These are oxygen-deficient, or anaerobic, activities, as opposed to aerobic activities, where ample oxygen is present. They can be done for only a few minutes (anaerobic metabolism = (1) ATP ⇄ ADP + P + free energy; (2) CP + ADP ⇄ creatine + ATP; (3) glycogen or glucose and FFA + P + ADP + O_2 → CO_2 + H_2O + ATP). Some individuals can sustain higher levels of anaerobic activity than others. World champions, whether sprinters or distance performers, are born, not made—or maybe born as well as made. Training will improve both speed and the ability to incur large oxygen debts, but the potential world-record holder possesses a greater potential for anaerobic metabolism before beginning to train.

The more oxygen one can use per minute, the higher one's ability to sustain aerobic, or endurance, exercise. The maximal oxygen a person can use per minute is that person's maximal oxygen consumption. *Fitness is defined in terms of maximal oxygen consumption, sometimes referred to by physiologists as VO_2 max.* Included in the oxygen-transport system determining this are the lungs, adequate hemoglobin in the blood, an efficient chemical system in the muscles, and the movement of blood by the heart. With absence of lung disease and anemia, from a practical point of view one can say that maximal oxygen consumption is primarily a measure of maximal cardiac output. Thus, physical fitness is determined by the efficiency of the heart and is measured by the ability to consume oxygen. Maximum oxygen consumption is the measurement of one's greatest capacity to consume oxygen. In endurance athletics, the VO_2 max is a number the athletes seem to focus on. Crew and cross-country ski-team members, when asked what kind of shape they are in, will answer that they are a 74 or 76. In Scandinavia, that number is known as the condition number. The highest score ever recorded was 94, by Sveno-Oke Lundbeck, the great Swedish cross-country-ski racer. The United States national cross-country team members are in the low 80s. Marathon runner Bill Rodgers is a 78 and Frank Shorter is a 70. The population at large is in the 40s and Alpine ski racers are in the 50s.

To determine maximum oxygen consumption (the best overall assessment of cardiovascular fitness) we must find how effectively muscle is able to extract oxygen from the blood going by. The sum total of the heart, lungs, blood vessels, and muscle interaction is reflected in the maximum oxygen consumption. In figure 1–2, the author is being tested on a treadmill. The nose is blocked, so that he is able to inhale through a top valve and exhale through a bottom valve. The exhaled air is continuously monitored for oxygen and carbon-dioxide concentration. Knowing the oxygen concentration being inspired, a computer gives a continuous readout of the oxygen consumed. The heart rate is also monitored and fed through an analog-digital converter. The computer has eliminated the need for five, six, or even seven laboratory technicians to collect exhaled air bags and sample the concentrations of gases in them.

A rowing ergometer, bicycle ergometer, or cross-country-ski simulator using the arms and legs together can be used with the same computer setup. This affords the opportunity to assess conductance. An example is a cross-country skier whose oxygen consumption for legs alone is 70 and arms alone is 50. When looked at together, they are not simply additive. When this individual exercises with arms and legs together, there is a tremendous increase in total peripheral resistance. We find the oxygen consumption to be 66, so there is not an increase in oxygen consumption but a decrease in power. While this is an indirect method, it is nonetheless a good way of getting relatively precise information with which to plan training regimens for athletes. The Scandinavians and East Germans have designed swimming flumes where the water runs through at a known speed, and the swimmer's oxygen consumption is calculated.

The specific muscle groups involved in a given activity must be the ones tested. If an athlete uses only arms, he or she could have a tremendously large heart, large lungs, and a great total peripheral resistance, yet such a small muscle mass would be involved that he or she would not have a very high oxygen consumption. There is a wide variety

Figure 1–2   Treadmill test to determine maximum oxygen consumption

of different combinations of arms, legs, trunk, and abdomen that will be used by an elite-class athlete.

What are the best cardiovascular exercises? The best exercise is probably one you will enjoy and will, therefore, be most likely to puruse continuously. But some exercises provide certain characteristics that make them more advantageous than others.

First, from a cardiovascular standpoint, the primary objective for good health is sustained vigorous exercise pursued long enough to burn more than 400 calories. The activity should increase the heart rate to approximately 75% to 80% of its potential in order to experience cardiovascular improvement. On the average, this translates into a pulse rate of around 120 to 150 beats per minute to achieve this increased endurance fitness. This also translates, practically speaking, into a 75% to 80% maximal oxygen consumption. To exceed 80% of maximal cardiac output as measured by pulse rate may lead to inadequate oxygenation causing anaerobic metabolism and tissue damage. Unless one is a competitive athlete training for victory rather than fitness, this should be avoided. Most beneficial fitness exercises occur at lower pulse rates. Ideally, exercise should be continuous for 30 or more minutes. Tennis, with delays between points, or football, with a huddle before every play, rank low as fitness exercises.

The second desirable characteristic for a fitness exercise is that it be rhythmical, the muscles alternately contracting and relaxing. This implies steady free-flowing movements that, once underway, contain no stops or starts. Such exercises include walking, jogging, running, hiking, cross-country skiing, swimming, bicycle riding, and rowing a boat. In comparison, golf, baseball, football, tennis, and other sports with stop-and-go activity rate poorly.

The third feature of efficient exercise involves the ability to increase the work load as the level of fitness increases. With increased fitness, the same activity that initially caused a pulse rate of 140 may now produce an increase to only 100. Thus, the activity must progressively be made more difficult. This can be accomplished in several ways. One can slowly increase the effort of the exercise. If one has been jogging a mile in 10:00, speed can be increased to cover that mile in 9:00, or 8:00, or faster. Or, one can run further at the same pace. Most beginning joggers, consciously or not, employ both methods. Similar changes occur as physical condition improves in other endurance sports such as cycling or swimming.

The final feature of effective exercise is endurance. Exercise should be sustained for at least 30 minutes and, if possible, up to one hour to produce maximum results. It also should be done at least four days a week, preferably more. The added advantage of exercising every day is only another percent or two of fitness, but enjoyment may be increased by regular daily exercise.

Effects of Endurance Training on the Heart

The first sign of increased cardiovascular fitness is slowing of the heart rate. This bradycardia is experienced both at rest and at exercise. Thus, with a specific amount of exertion, a fit person's heart rate will increase, but may still be slower than that of a nonfit individual at rest. The second effect of cardiovascular fitness is that the heart pumps more blood with each contraction, so the volume of blood pumped per heartbeat, the stroke volume, is increased. The heart works more powerfully and efficiently.

The precise physiologic explanation for this bradycardia remains unknown. The heart rate is the net effect of the impulses of two sets of nerves to this muscle: the sympathetic nerves, which speed up the heart rate, and the parasympathetic nerves, which slow the heart rate. These nerves are part of the autonomic nervous system, which operates automatically without any conscious thought. The digestive tract, various internal glands, and the heart and blood vessels, are innervated by this part of the nervous system that operates automatically. At times of fear or anxiety, the sympathetic nervous system predominates, increasing the heart rate with a resultant increase in blood pressure. With certain unfit individuals, this can trigger a heart attack. Regular endurance exercise resulting in cardiovascular fitness means an increase in parasympathetic activity at rest and a decrease in sympathetic activity with exertion. Thus there is a slowing of the heart rate and lowering of blood pressure both at rest and with exercise. This means the heart is less susceptible to the noxious influence of the sudden shocks, stresses, and anxiety-provoking situations that confront us daily. In other words, it may be possible to overcome the supposedly bad effect of the type-A personality if one is fit.

The heart increases in strength as it enlarges. The young endurance athlete, long-distance runner, swimmer, or cyclist will experience an enlargement of the heart. In years past many ultrafit young endurance athletes were labeled as abnormal and kept from competing in sports because, it was said, their hearts were too big. This enlargement is normal, involves primarily the left ventricle, and bears no resemblance to the dilation of a failing heart. Such youths should be encouraged to continue their training. Now that many people in their forties and older are seriously training, we may see some cardiac enlargement in this age group as well. So far, however, no good studies have been done to determine whether the middle-aged jogger can develop a beneficial increase in heart size.

Today we realize that the observed training changes have less to do with the heart than initially thought. The cardiac changes that occur in a 12- or 13-year-old child beginning an endurance program such as long-distance running, are different from those who enter a pressure sport such as wrestling or weight lifting. These changes require about eight years of training, so that 12- and 13-year-old children will be around 20 or 21 years of age before their cardiac systems are fully developed. The training effects that we see remain controversial. Some exercise physiologists contend that the heart increases in contractility, and it is certainly true that when a trained heart is in a hypoxic situation under a tremendous pressure load, it is able to maintain a greater contractility than an untrained heart. The biggest changes in the heart are seen in the volume of the main pumping chamber, the left ventricle. The left-ventricular mass also increases, but compared with that of the pressure-sport athlete, the ventricular wall is thinner and the chamber is larger.

Controversy remains as to whether the coronary arteries enlarge in response to endurance training. Since not many athletes have been autopsied, we are really not certain. It is interesting to note that Clarence DeMar, who won the Boston Marathon seven times and who died at age 66 from cancer of the stomach, had very large coronary arteries at autopsy. Interestingly, he had considerable coronary-artery atherosclerotic disease. Thus, the unequivocal training effects on the heart are three: an increase in end diastolic volume, increased left-ventricular mass, and perhaps an increase in contractility. The increase in left-ventricular mass is greatest for the pressure athlete. Imagine a wrestler trying to hold an individual for 30 or 40 seconds or a weight lifter trying to lift 300 or 400 pounds; the heart has an obligation to maintain a tremendous pressure head, and the effect is the development of a very thick left-ventricular wall without an increase in chamber size.

On x-ray, the pressure athlete's heart is no larger than that of the sedentary nonathlete. However, endurance athletes have been noted to have hearts larger than those of the population at large. In the 1930s scientists in Shanghai noticed that rickshaw drivers had larger hearts than their businessmen passengers. Forty years later it was apparent that the rickshaw drivers long outlived the businessmen they pulled around.

The heart receives its own blood flow between contractions during diastole. The slower the heart rate, the longer the resting period; or the greater the length of diastole, the greater the blood flow to the heart muscle. Therefore, another advantage of exercise is a greater supply of blood to the heart. Fitness also produces a reduction in the oxygen requirements of the heart. Therefore, fit individuals live well within their cardiac reserve. They are afforded a great margin of safety and protection from the daily stresses of life that may challenge a less fit heart.

Perhaps the greatest recent advances have been in learning what happens to the cardiac output after it leaves the heart. There are two very dramatic findings. The first regards vascular conductance. The sedentary individual has a very high peripheral resistance as exercise begins. The well-conditioned athlete, on the other hand, has a very low peripheral resistance or very high conductance. An example is the runner or cross-country skier who has well-trained lower extremities. The sympathetic control of the peripheral vasculature has released a certain amount of tone so that there is an increase in conductance. There is also an increase in capillarization. The main effect of endurance training is a decrease in sympathetic tone and resultant increase in conductance. Thus there is a low peripheral resistance and a relatively low work load on the heart in terms of the pressure against which it has to pump. A runner who does no upper-body work will have high conductance in the legs only. This same individual shoveling snow with untrained upper extremities will experience a tremendous increase in pressure. That is why coronary-care units often fill up after a snowstorm with individuals who might walk or perhaps even jog. They have subjected their hearts to pressure loads far surpassing accustomed levels.

As mentioned previously, increased cardiovascular fitness is associated with a decrease in blood pressure both at rest and with exertion. High blood pressure increases the deposition of atheromatous material, literally blows plaque material into the walls of the blood vessels. Increased blood pressure increases the likelihood of a stroke or heart attack. Frequently a heart attack can be traced to a specific unaccustomed heavy physical exertion or a great anxiety-provoking situation. Each of these situations increases heart rate and, thus, blood pressure. If preexisting disease is present, the work load on the heart may outstrip the ability of the heart to adequately supply itself with oxygen via its own circulation during diastole. The result is a heart attack.

Isometric muscle contractions, such as straining to lift a heavy object, can prove especially hazardous to the unfit individual, since the rise in blood pressure is disproportionately high. Fit individuals, however, can carry out heavy physical tasks or be exposed to anxiety-provoking situations with very little increase in heart rate or blood pressure. Numerous studies show that people who regularly engage in heavy physical exercise have less increase in blood pressure with advancing years. Too little physical activity, on the other hand, can cause several forms of hypertension.

Other Effects of Endurance Training

Endurance fitness brings benefits other than those to the heart (table 1–1). Fitness also lengthens clotting times of the blood and makes the blood less viscous. This means that occlusion of blood vessels is less likely, and circulation is improved, since the blood can pass through the vessels with greater ease. In addition, heavy exercise lowers the serum blood cholesterol level, raises the high-density lipoprotein/low-density lipoprotein (HDL/LDL) ratio, and offers protection against a diet relatively high in saturated fats. Studies have shown a reversal of the size of atherosclerotic plaques when the previously elevated blood pressure and blood cholesterol are reduced to normal levels by exercise [1].

Endurance exercise produces dramatic changes in the muscle, the site where oxygen is extracted and used. We now recognize two muscle-fiber types: the fast-twitch and the slow-twitch fibers. The proportion of fast-twitch fibers is characteristic of a sprint athlete, while the slow-twitch fibers predominate in the endurance athlete. The general sedentary population has approximately 50% slow-twitch, 50% fast-twitch, as do power-sport athletes, such as, discus throwers, javelin throwers, shot-putters, and weight lifters. The slow-twitch fibers are used to control and direct and the fast-twitch for power and extreme acceleration.

These patterns are probably present from birth. Identical twins have identical fiber types. In fact, looking at the entire cardiopulmonary system, we find almost no difference between monozygous twins except for the muscular system, where developmental differences are seen to depend on training. Superior sprinters are born with 70% or even 80% fast-twitch fibers. They have a relatively low capacity to consume oxygen but high capacity to do speed work. Such an individual may be able to run a 100-meter dash but would probably never finish a marathon. With power training, fast-twitch fibers become even larger. The latest evidence indicates that they will even split, so that an increase in fast-twitch fibers and muscle bulk occurs. Individuals with primarily slow-twitch fibers can lift weights with a resultant very modest increase in muscle bulk, while one with primarily fast-twitch fibers rapidly takes on a Charles Atlas figure in response to weight lifting. The fast-twitch fiber can increase in size dramatically; the slow-twitch fiber cannot.

Superior endurance athletes are born with a high percentage of slow-twitch endurance fibers. If they start training in their early teens, a maximal heart size will be achieved

Table 1–1   Positive Influences of Endurance Exercise

Blood Vessels and Chemistry
Increase blood oxygen content
Increase blood-cell mass and blood volume
Increase fibrinolytic capability
Increase efficency of peripheral blood distribution and return
Increase blood supply to muscles and more-efficient exchange of oxygen and carbon dioxide
Reduce serum triglycerides and cholesterol levels
Reduce platelet cohesion or stickiness
Reduce systolic and diastolic blood pressure, especially when elevated
Reduce glucose intolerance

Heart
Increase strength of cardiac contraction (myocardial efficiency)
Increase blood supply (collateral) to heart
Increase size of coronary arteries
Increase size of heart muscle
Increase blood volume (stroke volume) per heartbeat
Increase heart-rate recovery after exercise
Reduce heart rate at rest
Reduce heart rate with exertion
Reduce vulnerability to cardiac arrythmias

Lungs
Increase blood supply
Increase diffusion of O_2 and CO_2
Increase functional capacity during exercise
Reduce nonfunctional volume of lung

Endocrine (Glandular) and Metabolic Function
Increase tolerance to stress
Increase glucose tolerance
Increase thyroid function
Increase growth-hormone production
Increase lean-muscle mass
Increase enzymatic function in muscle cells
Increase functional capacity during exercise (muscle oxygen-uptake capacity)
Reduce body-fat content
Reduce chronic catecholamine production
Reduce neurohumeral overreaction

Neural and Psychic
Reduce strain and nervous tension resulting from psychological stress
Reduce tendency for depression
Increase euphoria or joie de vivre

by the age of 20 or 21 years. The specific training effects realized over the ensuing 10 to 20 years occur almost entirely in the muscle. The endurance fibers of the elite endurance athlete may actually become a little smaller, decreasing the distance oxygen must travel to get to that cell. There is a dramatic increase in the number of capillaries, so the blood flow to the muscle is increased. It is not certain whether there is an increase in capillaries or whether they actually double back on themselves. This greatly enlarges the capacity of the muscle to extract oxygen. More capillaries, smaller muscle cells, and an increase in the number of mitochondrial enzymes to extract that oxygen are the major changes in response to years of endurance training.

Although everyone is born with a certain fiber type, some changes do occur in fast-twitch fibers in response to volume training. Although they do not turn into slow-twitch fibers, they do increase their ability to consume oxygen and thus accomplish an endurance event. This happens with distance or tempo training. Recently, further advances have come with the use of the electron microscope and analysis of individual muscle enzymes. The slow-twitch fiber or endurance fiber has many mitochondria. As an individual trains, the cell becomes slightly smaller and the mitochondria increase dramatically in size. In contrast, the fast-twitch fibers have few mitochondria and thus a very low ability to consume oxygen. They may have large glycogen stores that they can rapidly utilize but only at the expense of a buildup of lactic acid that stops contraction of the muscle. The mitochondria limit the ability of the muscle cell to work aerobically, and their increase in response to endurance training is of paramount importance. In summary, the beneficial effects of endurance training on the normal middle-aged person include a slowing of the heart rate (bradycardia), prolongation of diastole causing increased blood flow to the heart muscle, increase in stroke volume causing a more efficient and powerful heart muscle, reduced blood pressure, reduced clotting time and viscosity of the blood, and a decrease in blood fats and their deposition in the body's blood vessels.

Quantifying Exercise

In his books on aerobics, Kenneth A. Cooper, M. D., presents a readily understood method of quantifying exercise [2–4]. He provides charts that give point values for different types of exercise. For example, swimming 250 yards in five minutes is worth 2 points, while playing handball for thirty minutes earns 4½ points. Dr. Cooper contends that if people accumulate 30 to 34 points in a week, they can consider themselves physically fit. He believes that total physical fitness can be achieved if one exercises 12 to 20 minutes per day, vigorously enough to sustain a heart beat of 150 beats minute. If the exercise fails to reach that level, it must be sustained for a longer time to be equally beneficial. Dr. Cooper also believes that cardiovascular fitness is realized only by a sustained steady increase in heart rate for periods of at least 30 minutes four times a week. Ideally, the activity should be rhythmical and the intensity increased as fitness improves.

If the objective of exercise is to achieve a sustained increase in heart rate, any activity done at an accelerated rate can be used, from running to vacuuming the floor. However, not all sports meet this criterion. Doubles tennis, for example, rates quite poorly as physical exercise because of the frequent inactivity between points. Likewise golf, walking, baseball, football, weight lifting, and even calisthenics do not achieve a sustained increase in heart rate unless maintained for regular periods with short rest intervals. Downhill skiing, squash, handball, and racquetball generate a moderate level of cardiovascular exercise, but the activity is not continuous. The activities that achieve maximal cardiovascular exercise levels include running, stationary running, cross-country skiing, roller skating, swimming, rowing, and cycling.

The amount of exercise required for good cardiovascular fitness varies with the exercise pursued and how vigorously it is pursued. It can be achieved by strenuous continuous exercise for as short as 30 minutes three or four times a week. The same degree of cardiovascular fitness requires 60 minutes or more three or four times a week if the pursuit is less taxing and is intermittent. Regardless of the activity, one should push it to the point of breathing deeply but not gasping for breath. The primary goal of any exercise program should be a fit cardiovascular system. Chapter 4 shows how to write precise exercise prescriptions involving all recreational pursuits based on these principles.

References

1. Barndt, R. Jr., Blankenhorn, D. H., Crawford, D. W., and Brooks, S. H. Regression and progression of early femoral atherosclerosis in treated hyperlipoproteinemic patients. *Ann. Intern. Med.* 86:139–146, 1977.
2. Cooper, K. H. *Aerobics.* New York: M. Evans & Co., Inc., 1968.
3. Cooper, K. H. *The New Aerobics.* New York: Bantam, 1970.
4. Cooper, K. H. *The Aerobics Way.* New York: M. Evans & Co., Inc., 1977.
5. Friedman, M. and Rosenman, R. H. *Type A Behavior and Your Heart,* New York: Alfred A. Knopf, 1974.
6. Kannel, W. B., Brand, N., Skinner, S. S., et al. The relationship of adiposity to blood pressure and development of hypertension: The Framingham Study. *Ann. Intern. Med.* 67:48–59, 1967.
7. Kannel, W. B., Dawber, T. R., Friedman, G. D., Glennon, W. E., and MacNamara, P. M. Risk factors in coronary heart disease: An evaluation of several serum lipids as predictors of coronary heart disease: The Framingham Study. *Ann. Intern. Med.* 61:888–899, 1964.
8. Kannel, W. B., Gordon, T., Sorlie P., and MacNamara, P. M. Physical activity and coronary vulnerability: The Framingham Study. *Cardiology Digest* 6:24–40, 1971.
9. Kannel, W. B. and Gordon, T. (eds.) *The Framingham Study: An Epidemiological Investigation of Cardiovascular Disease.* Section 30. Washington D. C.: Department of Health, Education, and Welfare (National Institutes of Health) 74–599, 1974.
10. Kannel, W. B. and Gordon, T. (eds.) *The Framingham Study: An Epidemiological Investigation of Cardiovascular Disease.* Sections 1–3. Washington, D. C.: Department of Health, Education, and Welfare (National Institutes of Health) 1968–1978.
11. Kavanagh, T. *Heart Attack? Counterattack!* Toronto: Van Nostrand Reinhold Ltd., 1976.
12. Morris, J. W., Heady, J. A., Raffle, P. A., et al. Coronary heart disease and physical activity of work. Lancet 11:1053, 1953.
13. Morris, J. N., Chave, S. P., Adam, C., et al. Vigorous exercise in leisure time and the incidence of coronary heart disease. Lancet 1:333–339, 1973.

14. Paffenbarger, R. S., Jr.: Hard work makes the heart grow safer. *New York Times,* 24 March, 1977, p. 20.
15. Paffenbarger, R. S., Jr., Wing, A. L., and Hyde, R. T. Physical activity as an index of heart risk in college alumni. *Am. J. Epidemiol.* 108:1161–1175, 1978.

2 / Nutrition for Sports

Food fads are more prominent in the area of athletics than in any other sphere of nutrition [8, 18]. It appears that special dietary schemes and ergogenic aids to improve performance and endurance have been advocated by trainers, coaches, and athletes since competitions first were held. The early Greek athletes consumed a vegetarian diet until 520 B.C., when Eurymenes of Samos decided that if animals ran fast, so too might humans who ate their flesh [3]. An overzealous disciple, Milo of Croton, is said to have consumed up to twenty pounds of meat a day.

More recent, but equally invalid, schemes include supplemental dietary wheat-germ oil (a potent source of vitamin E and polyunsaturated fatty acids), gelatin (a source of glycine), and phosphate and alkalinizing agents [18]. Also fallacious is the practice of withholding certain foods. For example, milk is considered to cause cotton mouth, curdles in the stomach, and a lower respiratory quotient decreasing efficiency [20].

It is obvious that a close relationship exists between diet, nutrition, and physical exercise. First, an individual who exercises regularly makes heavy demands on the body's reserves of fluid and energy. One must be aware of the special dietary and nutritional needs created as a result of an exercise program. The ordinary diet must be supplemented and adjusted if one is to realize the maximum benefit from an exercise program. Before discussing the special dietary requirements of exercise, a few basic comments about general dietary objectives are appropriate.

The McGovern Committee studied American dietary habits and concluded that Americans eat too much and eat the wrong things. They consume too much meat, saturated fat, cholesterol, sugar, and salt. At the same time, they do not eat enough fruit, grain (especially whole-grain products), vegetables, and unsaturated fat. The committee urged American leaders to educate the public to increase consumption of fruits, vegetables, and whole-grain cereals and to sharply reduce intake of fat and sugar.

Although new research constantly changes our perceptions about what we eat, the U. S. dietary goals, first issued in 1977, still serve as informed guidelines for managing our diets. The goals include:

1. Consume only as much energy (calories) as expended.
2. Increase complex carbohydrate consumption to about 48% of total calories.
3. Reduce overall fat consumption to 30% of calories.
4. Reduce saturated fat consumption, and balance it with other fats.
5. Reduce cholesterol consumption to about 300 milligrams a day.
6. Reduce refined sugar consumption to about 10% of total calories.
7. Reduce salt consumption to 5 grams a day.

The suggestions of the committee, although physiologically sound, will not be easily implemented in this country. They run counter to long standing ethnic and cultural patterns of eating. Implementation may also cause heavy financial losses to major food producers and manufacturers who control food advertising, especially advertising of sugar-laden cereals that appeal to children. These companies may not welcome an attempt to change the financially successful status quo.

Despite the expected resistance from cultural habits and big business, the recommended dietary changes will ultimately be realized. Today, Americans are more fitness-conscious than ever before, and the enthusiasm is far from cresting.

Weight Loss through Diet and Exercise

Body weight is lost when one or more of the body's substances is decreased, thus reducing total body mass. It is a fundamental law of nature that energy can neither be created nor destroyed, rather only transformed from one kind of mechanical energy to another. Fat is stored energy. The body's fundamental energy equation is

$$\text{Calories in} = \text{calories used at rest by the body} \\ + \text{calories used in exertion} \\ + \text{calories stored as fat.}$$

Weight loss is achieved when caloric intake is less than caloric expenditure. Short-term weight loss can be effected by loss of water, fat, protein, or glycogen. Such weight loss occurs frequently during periods of strenuous exercise. Longer-term weight loss also depletes minerals from the bone and soft tissues of the body. Actually, weight loss is a simple biologic process that is related to the protein, glycogen, and water that exist in the body. For every gram of protein or glycogen in the body, there are approximately three to four grams of water. When a deficit of protein or glycogen occurs, water loss follows. Presently, it is not established that there is any water loss when triglycerides are mobilized from adipose cells.

Until recently, it was thought that on average, one pound (0.45 kilograms) of body-weight loss corresponded to the burning of about 3,500 kilocalories. This figure was derived from a value that suggested that 98% of the calories burned were derived from body fat. Studies now show that during the first several weeks of dietary restriction, weight loss is far in excess of the caloric deficit and reflects primarily water loss. Much of this initial water loss is due to a poorly understood diuresis that occurs with loss of sodium and water. However, the remainder is the obligatory water loss that accompanies the depletion of body glycogen stores. Later in a calorie-restricted diet, the water diuresis stops entirely, and in some instances, a water gain can occur while net losses of fat and protein continue.

It is of interest to note that different diets can produce an acceleration of weight loss due to greater water loss. For instance, a diet low in carbohydrate (the extreme being a fast) will cause a greater water diuresis and more precipitous weight loss. During a prolonged, partial, or total caloric restriction, the body gradually adapts by conserving protein and water and increasingly burning fat to make up the energy deficit. Studies show that obese individuals accomplish this adaptation more rapidly than lean people. However, the key finding is that the body's fat loss is essentially proportional to its energy deficit. So in the end, the type of diet is relatively unimportant. What ultimately determines fat loss is the degree of caloric deprivation. Because of this, most nutritionists now recommend a balanced diet that combines smaller portions of the basic foods with a reduction or elimination of refined sugars and desserts. Such a diet not only accomplishes weight reduction but also instills eating habits that promote the maintenance of desired weight.

As surely as the sun rises and sets, there will always be one more diet that promises quick weight loss without effort. The latest fad is the last-chance diet, or protein-supplemented fasting, a nearly no-carbohydrate diet that supplies nutrition by a mixture of liquid proteins, vitamins, and minerals. The promoters of the last-chance diet claim that when protein is provided in the diet, the body does not use its own protein, thus minimizing muscle waste and the depletion of protein stores. Is this really so? Not according to an article in *The New England Journal of Medicine* that reported "although some consider a low-caloric diet consisting entirely of protein to be uniquely advantageous in preserving body nitrogen, it has yet to be demonstrated convincingly that protein alone is more effective in this regard than an isocaloric mixture of protein and carbohydrate" [21]. Whenever carbohydrate intake is severly restricted, as it is in the last-chance diet, fat is mobilized, and rapid mobilization of fat may cause serious side effects, including liver damage. Also, low potassium levels may result, and even cardiac-arrhythmia deaths have been attributed to this diet. The chemical imbalance created by the loss of salt, water, and other minerals may lead to weakness, faintness, and other side effects. Even more tragic (because these diets do not encourage proper eating), only one-third of those who follow them are able to keep fat off 18 months after abandoning them.

Influence of Diet and Exercise on Cholesterol, Cardiovascular Disease, and Atherosclerosis

The knowledge acquired over the past few decades about cholesterol, cardiovascular disease, and atherosclerosis indicates that a carefully combined program of diet and exercise can greatly retard these diseases. Arteriosclerosis is a process by which the walls of the blood vessels become infiltrated with fat, which in time calcifies and forms plaques that can occlude an artery. It is seldom localized. When it develops in a major vessel to the brain or lower extremities, for example, there is nearly always similar impairment of the coronary arteries of the heart. In fact, the major cause of death in patients following surgery for localized atherosclerosis is heart attack[7].

The precise mechanism by which cholesterol is deposited in the walls of arteries and an advanced plaque evolves is still being unraveled. It is apparent though, that multiple defects in the cellular cholesterol metabolism, as well as smooth-muscle-cell proliferation, are involved. While the means by which even normal cells proliferate and build up cholesterol remain an enigma, certain correlations regarding cholesterol are apparent.

Blood contains two classes of fats that are essential to life: cholesterol and triglycerides. Elevated levels of cholesterol and/or triglycerides are associated with accelerated atherosclerosis and increased probability of heart attack. Of the multiple factors that influence the blood levels of these fats, diet, heredity, and exercise are the most important. A reduction in blood triglycerides and cholesterol occurs with exercise and with a diet low in saturated fats.

Cholesterol is transported by protein compounds called lipoproteins. Recent investigations have shown that the total level of cholesterol is of less importance than the ratio of high-density lipoprotein (HDL) to low-density lipoprotein (LDL) [12]. Low-density lipoproteins are the harmful transport vehicles that carry cholesterol into the tissues and increase the buildup of fatty atherosclerotic plaques. Conversely, high-density lipoproteins are capable of transporting cholesterol out of arteries and tissues and into the liver, where it is broken down and eliminated. A high level of HDL to LDL correlates with a low risk for atherosclerosis and heart disease. Vigorous sustained exercise will raise HDL levels and lower LDL levels. A diet low in saturated fats will achieve the same result. Triglycerides are also lowered by exercise and correlate with the HDL to LDL ratio. Elevated triglyceride levels are seen with increased LDL levels, while normal or low triglyceride levels are seen with elevated HDL levels.

Is the Cholesterol Theory in Trouble?

In a *New England Journal of Medicine* article, Dr. George Mann of Vanderbilt University Medical School wrote:

> A generation of research on the diet-heart question has ended in disarray. The official line since 1950 for management of the epidemic of coronary heart disease had been a dietary treatment. Foundations, scientists, and the media, both lay and scientific, have promoted low-fat, low-cholesterol polyunsaturated diets, and the epidemic continues unabated, cholesterolemia in the population is unchanged, the clinicians are unconvinced of efficacy. . . . This litany of failures must lead the clinician to wonder where the proper research and solutions lie. The problem of coronary heart disease is real enough here, and yet it is rare in less-developed societies. What aspect of life-style here makes atherosclerosis so malignant, its clinical consequences so fearsome?[16]

The cholesterol theory is traced back to 1808, when a Russian named I. A. Ignatovski demonstrated experimentally that a high-protein, high-fat, high-cholesterol diet in rabbits rapidly caused arteriosclerosis. His results were quickly confirmed, but his assumption that protein played a major role was never accepted. In 1813, when Anitsch-kow and Chalatow produced rapid arteriosclerosis in rabbits by feeding them high-cholesterol diets alone, the basic model that high dietary cholesterol causes atherosclero-sis was off and winging and has been popular ever since. It made no difference that other investigators later showed that feeding rabbits little or no cholesterol—but high-protein diets—produced atherosclerosis even more rapidly; the cholesterol theory remained in popular acceptance.

Why is the cholesterol theory being reevaluated now? Several very large long-term studies, the Mayo Clinic study and the Framingham study sponsored by the National Institutes of Health, found little detectable relationship between diet cholesterol and serum cholesterol for people on a normal daily diet. This should not come as a great surprise, since cholesterol is not a foreign substance; most of it is synthesized by the body rather than derived from dietary sources. The human body will manufacture up to 1,800 mg cholesterol daily if none is consumed, and the amount the body produces drops as the amount ingested increases. Thus, on a normal diet, one's cholesterol level may be higher or lower depending on other factors such as exercise, smoking, genetics, and fiber in diet. Even more important when considering atherosclerosis is the fact that a diet low in cholesterol or containing cholesterol-lowering products, such as fiber and yogurt, results in only 10% to 15% reduction in the level of serum cholesterol. The serum cholesterol levels in Americans are 100% to 200% above those of the New Guinean high-landers, in whom atherosclerosis is rare. Therefore, the small 10% to 15% reduction in serum cholesterol associated with even the strictest diets does not make a major impact on the rate of atherosclerosis. The amount of cholesterol contained in average servings of various foods is listed in table 2–1.

Cholesterol, Homocysteine, Vitamin B₆, and Atherosclerosis

A current, hotly contested scientific debate involves the homocysteine theory and the role of vitamin B_6 in the prevention of atherosclerosis. Homocysteine, a very toxic sub-stance, is regularly produced from methionine, one of the amino acids that constitute all of the protein we eat. Since the body does not manufacture methionine, it must be obtained from dietary sources. Kilmer McCully, professor of pathology at Brown Univer-sity, is generally credited with suggesting that homocysteine is the cause of atherosclero-sis. He proposed in 1969 that too little vitamin B_6 would retard the conversion of homocysteine to cystathionine, lead to a buildup of homocysteine in the blood, and thus promote atherosclerosis. Implicit in this theory were several predictions and explana-tions:

1. If homocysteine is maintained in the blood of experimental animals, atheroscle-rosis should develop.
2. Humans and experimental animals eating diets deficient in vitamin B_6 should build up homocysteine in their blood.
3. People proven to have atherosclerosis, such as coronary patients, should show a tendency toward low vitamin B_6 in their blood.

Table 2–1 Cholesterol Levels in Average Servings of Food

Meat, Fish, Poultry, Eggs	
(average serving after cooking)	*Milligrams Cholesterol*
Liver (3 oz, 85 gm)	372
Egg (1 large, 50 gm)	252
Shrimp, canned, drained (3 oz, 85 gm)	128
Veal (3 oz, 85 gm)	86
Lamb (3 oz, 85 gm)	83
Beef (3 oz, 85 gm)	80
Pork (3 oz, 85 gm)	76
Chicken breast (½ breast, 80 gm)	63
Lobster (3 oz, 85 gm)	72
Clams, canned, drained (½ cup, 80 gm)	50
Chicken drumstick (1, 43 gm)	39
Oysters, canned (3 oz, 85 gm)	38
Fish, fillet (3 oz, 85 gm)	34–75

Dairy Foods	
(average serving)	*Milligrams Cholesterol*
Whole milk (8 oz, 244 gm)	34
Cheddar or Swiss cheese (1 oz, 28 gm)	28
Ice cream (½ cup, 67 gm)	27–49
American processed cheese (1 oz, 28 gm)	25
Low fat (2%) milk (8 oz, 246 gm)	22
Heavy whipping cream (1 tbsp, 15 gm)	20
Yogurt, plain or vanilla (1 cup, 227 gm)	17
Cream cheese (1 tbsp, 14 gm)	16
Cottage cheese (½ cup, 134 gm)	12–24
Butter (1 tsp, 5 gm)	12
Sour cream (1 tbsp, 12 gm)	8
Half-and-half (1 tbsp, 15 gm)	6
Cottage cheese, dry curd (½ cup, 100 gm)	6
Skim milk and Buttermilk (8 oz, 245 gm)	5

Desserts	
(average serving)	*Milligrams Cholesterol*
Ladyfingers (4, 44 gm)	157
Custard (½ cup, 133 gm)	139
Apple pie (⅛ of 9″ pie, 114 gm)	120
Custard pie (⅛ of 9″ pie, 114 gm)	120
Lemon meringue pie (⅛ of 9″ pie, 105 gm)	98
Bread pudding with raisins (½ cup, 133 gm)	95
Peach pie (⅛ of 9″ pie, 114 gm)	70
Pumpkin pie (⅛ of 9″ pie, 144 gm)	70
Yellow cake, from mix (1/16 of 9″ cake, 75 gm)	36
Chocolate cake, from mix (1/16 of 9″ cake, 69 gm)	33
Brownie, homemade (1, 20 gm)	17
Chocolate pudding, from mix (½ cup, 130 gm)	15
Rice pudding with raisins (½ cup, 133 gm)	15

In the last decade, each of these postulates has been confirmed, and the theory is gaining momentum, although a precise explanation of how homocysteine exerts its effects at the molecular level remains to be elucidated.

Vitamin B_6 is plentiful in fruits and vegetables, less plentiful in meats and dairy products. At a glance, it would seem unlikely that many people would be deficient in vitamin B_6. However, 80% to 90% of vitamin B_6 is lost in milling wheat to white flour, cooking vegetables inactivates 67% of their vitamin B_6, and cooking meat destroys 45% of the vitamin. Some studies have shown that most Americans eating normal diets do not have adequate levels of vitamin B_6. This is especially true in older Americans.

The homocysteine theory suggests that most Americans eat too much protein and not enough vitamin B_6. It appears that a new criterion for selecting foods is on the horizon, not based on cholesterol alone but on the relative B_6 and protein content (table 2–2). While 2 mg/day of vitamin B_6 is currently an adequate daily amount, many Americans

Table 2–2   Vitamin B_6 and Methionine Content of Some Foods

Food	B^a	M^b	B/M^c	Standard Portion (grams)
Apple	.03	4	7.5	150
Avocado	.42	19	22	123
Banana	.51	11	46	150
Beans, raw snap	.08	28	2.9	125 (1 cup)
Beef, raw round	.50	970	0.5	85 (3 oz)
Bread, white	.04	126	0.3	23 (1 slice)
Bread, whole wheat	.18	161	1.1	23 (1 slice)
Broccoli, raw	.19	54	3.6	150 (1 cup)
Butter	.003	21	0.1	7 (1 pat)
Carrots	.15	10	15	50
Cheese, cheddar	.07	653	0.1	17 (1 in. cube)
Chicken	.5	537	0.9	76 (½ breast)
Egg, hard-cooked	.11	392	0.3	50
Lettuce, head	.07	4	17	220 (4 in. head)
Milk, cow whole	.042	83	0.5	244 (1 cup)
Oranges	.06	2.7	22	210 (3 in. dia)
Peanut butter	.33	265	1.2	16 (1 tbsp)
Peas, raw	.18	44	4.1	160 (1 cup)
Potato, raw	.25	25	10	100
Spinach, raw	.28	54	5.2	180
Tomato, raw	.10	8	12.5	150
Yogurt, plain	.032	102	0.3	246 (1 cup)

[a]Vitamin B_6 (mg/100 gm).
[b]Methionine (mg/100 gm).
[c]Ratio of B_6 to methionine ($\times$ 1000).

consume less than that, and there is considerable evidence to suggest that this level is too low to safely cover the entire adult population. Clearly, groups prone to vitamin B_6 deficiency, such as pregnant and nursing mothers, women on a contraceptive pill, dieters (especially those on a high-protein regimen), and old people, should receive more than 2 mg/day. Present evidence suggests that 10 mg/day of vitamin B_6 would provide a more appropriate margin of safety. Such a level would require a vitamin supplement, as it is not easily found in our normal diet. Such levels are quite safe, because excessive vitamin B_6 is rapidly eliminated, and the toxic dose of the vitamin is more than 1,000 times greater than 10 mg/day.

Much remains to be learned about homocysteine. Conclusive proof of the theory awaits not only a molecular understanding of its action on the cells of blood vessels, but also conclusive results from large-scale clinical testing over several years. Still, with the cholesterol theory inadequate to explain all aspects of atherosclerosis, the homocysteine theory deserves serious consideration. It is suggested that a lower intake of protein and a higher amount of vitamin B_6 may be desirable. Indeed, even in following a low-cholesterol diet one would be helped, as a tendency toward lower protein intake would result.

Vitamin Controversies

A knowledge of vitamins is absolutely essential for those following a strenuous daily exercise program, since there may be a special need for vitamin supplements to achieve maximum benefit from exercise.

No human, indeed, no mammal, can be maintained on an exclusive diet of protein, carbohydrate, fat, and minerals. Additional factors present in natural foods are required in minute amounts (table 2–3). These organic substances, called vitamins, function as chemical regulators and are necessary for growth and the maintenance of life. There are 14 known vitamins divided into two basic groups: those soluble in fat (vitamins A, D, E, and K) and those soluble in water (vitamin C and the B-complex vitamins). Normally, a varied diet contains more than enough of these required vitamins. Since they do not contribute to body structure and are not a direct source of body energy, even the most active athlete needs little more of them than the sedentary individual. However, since the industrial revolution, urbanization, and sea travel, many people have not had access to a varied farm diet of recently harvested foodstuffs, thus causing vitamin-deficiencies. Sailors who spent months at sea without fruit or green vegetables developed scurvy from a lack of vitamin C; infants in crowded European slums, deprived of adequate sunlight, developed rickets from a deficiency of vitamin D; and, today, impoverished Southeast Asians, whose diets are restricted to polished rice, develop vitamin B deficiencies.

One man who has contributed much to our modern understanding of vitamin deficiency is Professor Victor Herbert. Professor Herbert states succinctly that "the sole unequivocal indication for vitamin therapy is vitamin deficiency" [9]. He discusses six ways in which vitamin deficiency develops: inadequate ingestion, absorption, or utilization; and increased destruction, excretion, or requirement. Of these six possible causes of vita-

Table 2–3 Recommended Daily Allowances of Vitamins (United States)

Vitamin	Infants and Children up to 4 Years	Children 4 Years to Adults
Vitamin A	2500 IU	5000 IU
Thiamine (B$_1$)	0.7 mg	1.5 mg
Riboflavin (B$_2$)	0.8 mg	1.7 mg
Vitamin B$_6$	0.7 mg	2 mg
Vitamin B$_{12}$	3 mg	6 mg
Folacin (B$_c$)	0.2 mg	0.4 mg
Biotin	0.15 mg	0.3 mg
Niacin	9 mg	20 mg
Pantothenic acid	5 mg	10 mg
Ascorbic acid (C)	40 mg	60 mg
Vitamin D	400 IU	400 IU
Vitamin E	10 IU	30 IU

min deficiency, inadequate ingestion is the only indication for dietary vitamin supplements.

The fat-soluble vitamins (A, D, E, and K) are stored in the liver and adipose tissue. Deficiencies develop only after months or years of inadequate intake, and excessive intake will cause abnormal accumulations and can produce toxic side effects. The water-soluble vitamins are not stored in the body and must be constantly replenished in the diet. Deficiencies can develop in weeks, and when excessive amounts are ingested, the excess is excreted in the urine, avoiding toxic accumulations.

Except during periods of extra nutrient demand such as pregnancy, lactation, or prolonged illness, the AMA does not recommend vitamin supplementation. Today, however, the use of multivitamin preparations is commonplace. Although this practice is not harmful as long as fat-soluble vitamins are not taken in excess, the essential foodstuffs can usually come from our diet and need not be found in any vitamin bottle. These essential nutrients, those that cannot be manufactured by the body, include water, sources of energy (primarily carbohydrates), nine amino-acid building blocks of proteins, one fatty acid, a number of mineral elements, and vitamins. Only a diet including a selection from a wide variety of foods will ensure adequate intake of essential nutrients.

Vitamins in Deficiency States

The AMA advises that the use of vitamin preparations as dietary supplements should be restricted to specific instances of deficiency; then, only the deficient vitamins in therapeutic amounts should be prescribed along with measures to correct any dietary inadequacies. Common medical conditions requiring vitamin therapy include the malabsorption syndromes (tropical sprue and celiac disease), where vitamins A, D, E, and K may be required. Therapeutic amounts of folic acid and/or B_{12} are needed in specific deficiency states, including pernicious anemia. Pathologic conditions of the intestines that require bowel resection or intestinal bypass will require vitamin therapy, the specific needs being dictated by the location of the bowel resection. In burn victims and patients with extensive wounds, vitamin C and the B vitamins are frequently prescribed.

Although a number of specific deficiency states do require vitamin therapy, to date no conclusive evidence has been found to indicate that multivitamin preparations or megavitamin dosages have ever helped a patient. In fact, critical research is needed to be certain that such practices are not harmful. The toxic effects of excessive intake of vitamins A, D, and folic acid are known, and the Food and Drug Administration restricts the amounts of these vitamins available over the counter. The question remains unanswered, however, regarding the possible harmful effects of prolonged megavitamin doses of any of the other vitamins.

The Vitamin C Controversy

No vitamin has a more historical past or controversial present than vitamin C. The value of this vitamin, which is present naturally in citrus fruits, was first recognized by James Lind, a physician in the eighteenth-century British Navy, who linked its deficiency with scurvy, but the specific protective agent in the lime was not identified as vitamin C until 1932.

Today, vitamin C is in the news again because the Nobel Prize-winning scientist Dr. Linus Pauling has proclaimed that large doses of vitamin C help the body withstand infection. Controversy rages, but no conclusive proof exists that vitamin C in megadoses protects against the common cold or any other infection.

While average nonexercising persons may not need to supplement their diets with vitamin C, it has been shown that persons who engage in high levels of physical stress or consume large quantities of alcohol deplete their stores of that vitamin. Smoking and even chewing tobacco, if the tobacco juice is swallowed, also lower vitamin-C levels. Charcoal-broiled beef contains cholesterol oxide, a powerful oxidizer that quickly depletes both vitamins C and E. Our bodies cannot manufacture vitamin C; it must be ingested. Thus it comes as no surprise that most athletes involved in endurance sports take supplemental vitamin C at the rate of 500 mg to 1 gm per day.

A recent poll of members of the American Medical Joggers Association preparing for the Boston Marathon revealed that over 90% of them took vitamin C as a supplement. While no scientific proof exists, many trainers and endurance athletes feel that supplemental vitamin C greatly reduces the incidence of muscle and tendon injuries. Vitamin C has also been implicated in the pathogenesis of atherosclerosis. A deficiency of vitamin C may allow the lining of arteries (the endothelium) to degenerate and form sites for arteriosclerotic deposits.

From a medical standpoint no harm is done, since excesses of vitamin C are promptly excreted in the urine. Indeed, for the vigorously exercising individual, 500 mg to 1 gm of vitamin C per day may well be beneficial. However, since ingestion of more than 4 gm per day has been associated with kidney stones, massive amounts are discouraged.

Caffeine, Alcohol, and Physical Exercise

There is considerable evidence to suggest that caffeine stimulates the sympathetic nervous system to mobilize free fatty acids. For endurance sports such as long-distance running, this affords the competitor a slight advantage. For other than endurance sports, it is of no value.

Moderate-to-heavy coffee-drinking was suggested to predispose to heart attack, but more recent studies show that coffee by itself is not harmful to the heart [24]. The earlier reports failed to account for the fact that many coffee-drinkers are also cigarette-smokers, a practice that does predispose to heart attack, emphysema, and cancer. When cigarette smoking was taken into account, no increased incidence of heart attack was found in coffee-drinkers.

Preliminary investigations have shown the rate of cancer of the pancreas to be two to three times higher in moderate-to-heavy coffee-drinkers [15]. The fact that no such correlation was found for tea suggests it is not caffeine that is the responsible agent. Since this was purely an epidemiologic study, investigators now are attempting to confirm the initial findings.

Also contrary to earlier investigations, scientists now believe that moderate alcohol consumption appears to protect the heart. One study, which covered a six-year period, reported that moderate beer-drinkers had only one-half the incidence of heart attack of total abstainers [24]. The mechanism appears to be a raising of the high-density-lipoprotein–cholesterol (HDL–C) fraction. Both endurance exercise and moderate alcohol consumption raise HDL–C levels [1, 4, 13, 14, 24], which are known to protect against coronary heart disease [10]. Furthermore, a report of marathon runners showed that those who drank moderately had an even higher HDL–C level than those who abstained [23]. This suggests that alcohol consumption is associated with an increase in HDL–C in excess of that resulting from vigorous exercise alone. The precise mechanism by which alcohol raises HDL–C levels is not known. One theory is that alcohol induces hepatic microsomal-enzyme activity [24], which increases the production of high-density lipoproteins.

Beer is now very popular as a replacement solution during long-distance runs. Indeed, beer has been credited with keeping the kidneys functioning during endurance exercise by blocking antidiuretic-hormone (ADH) secretion, thus preventing kidney stones and hematuria from bruising the bladder. It has a high potassium-to-sodium ratio (5:1), so that it is a safe sweat replacement, preventing hypokalemia. It also replaces silicon and raises the level of high-density lipoproteins. While there is no proof of improved performance from beer-drinkers, it does appear that some discomfort may be alleviated.

One caution concerning alcohol consumption concerns its high caloric content, seven calories per gram. Only fat, with nine calories per gram, has more (protein and carbohydrates contain only four calories per gram). Anyone dieting should be told of the high caloric content of alcohol and should avoid its use. Everyone should be aware that excessive alcohol intake may cause direct toxic damage to the liver and, in some cases, to the heart. This is true even with an adequate diet. The old belief that cirrhosis of the liver develops primarily in people who drink heavily and eat poorly is not true. Recent studies show that an average-sized person who drinks a half-bottle of 86-proof beverage per day for 25 years has a 50% chance of developing cirrhosis of the liver regardless of the diet [17]. Today in the United States, there are over 10 million alcoholics, and in urban areas cirrhosis of the liver is the third major cause of death between the ages of 25 and 65 years. Therefore, while moderate alcohol consumption, especially of beer, is certainly not harmful and may even protect the heart, heavy drinking is hazardous and poisons the brain, heart, and liver. Recent investigations have prompted a warning from the Surgeon General that cancer has been linked to heavy alcohol consumption.

The Importance of Dietary Fiber

The most significant food sources of fiber are unprocessed wheat bran, unrefined breakfast cereals, and whole wheat and rye flours. Breads and cereals made from whole-grain flours (wheat, rye, or oats) are highest in fiber, as are breakfast cereals with bran in the name. Additional sources include fresh and dried fruit, raw vegetables, and legumes. Those fruits with edible skin and/or seeds are highest in fiber. To obtain the highest fiber, the skin and pulp of the fruit should be eaten. It is not necessary to eat fruits and vegetables raw since cooking does not affect fiber content. It appears that wheat bran is the most effective in increasing fecal bulk. This has led to commercial wheat-bran products with recommendations to add six teaspoons daily to everything from soup to chiffon cake.

Why is fiber important in our diet? First let us review the hard data. Dietary fiber adds bulk. Because most sources of fiber are relatively low in calories, one will feel full on fewer calories than on a low-fiber diet. The increased bulk greatly facilitates transit time through the digestive tract. In one study, the transit time decreased from 48 hours to 12 hours when the same subjects switched from a low- to a high-fiber diet [2].

A high-fiber diet also produces stools that are soft, more bulky, more frequent (an average of one bowel movement every 19 hours), and contain twice as much carbohydrate, fat, and protein. Increases in dietary fiber, or roughage, increase fecal nutrient loss which translates into energy loss that could account for an eight to ten pound weight difference over a one-year period [2]. Thus, a diet high in fiber aids in weight control or reduction in two ways: it allows one to feel full with fewer calories consumed, and it affords a greater fecal loss of calories.

A high-fiber diet has been found to lower blood cholesterol and especially low-density-lipoprotein–cholesterol levels (LDL–C) [17]. While some investigators suggest that this is accomplished by impaired intestinal absorption of cholesterol and bile acids, reports are conflicting, and it seems most reasonable to conclude that the mechanism by which dietary fiber lowers cholesterol is unknown. The fact that it occurs, however, raises speculation that the amount of fiber in the diet may be a factor in the prevention of atherosclerosis.

The intake of crude fiber in the American diet has dropped by 28% since the turn of the century [11]. While the intake of fiber from vegetables has remained relatively constant, that from potatoes, fruit, cereals, and dried peas and beans has declined. Coincident with this reduction of dietary fiber has been an increase in a host of ailments, including coronary heart disease, cholesterol gallstones, diabetes, obesity, hiatal hernia, peptic ulcer, constipation, diverticulosis, hemorrhoids, varicose veins, and cancer of the colon. All of these have been linked to overconsumption of sucrose and highly milled starches and underconsumption of fibrous materials in the diet. While most of the postulates remain controversial and inconclusive and are based on epidemiologic relationships (that is, populations with high-fiber diets who have a low incidence of these problems), it is still interesting to recapitulate the physiologic explanation.

Fiber, by adding bulk to the feces, will eliminate constipation and render diverticulosis asymptomatic in over 70% of people. Since the stool is soft and one does not have to strain, the problem of hemorrhoids is lessened. Obesity can be combated by a high-fiber diet, and its control affords a reduction in adult-onset diabetes and problems of varicosities. The antiobesity and cholesterol-lowering effects of fiber are both cited to explain its beneficial effect on heart disease [19]. The cholesterol-lowering effects account for the alleviation of cholesterol gallstones.

The transit time of feces may be a factor in hiatus hernia, ulcer, and, most important, colon cancer. In the last fifty years, while fiber consumption has decreased 20% from fruits and vegetables and 50% from cereals and grains, the incidence of colon cancer has risen significantly. Although the idea is not proven, speculation exists that by decreasing the transit time through the colon threefold, the carcinogen or cancer-provoking agent, whether a virus or food-breakdown product, is exposed to the large bowel for a much shorter time. It therefore has a diminished opportunity to break down the natural resistance of the colon and produce cancer.

Whether more fiber prevents colon cancer or not, most Americans do need to increase the fiber content of their diets to achieve the known beneficial effects just discussed. While some may wish to sprinkle bran on various foods or substitute one-fifth bran for an equal part of flour in baked items, a significant increase in dietary fiber can be achieved by enjoying unprocessed cereals, a slice of whole-wheat bread, a nice salad, and some fresh or processed fruit regularly.

Nutrition for Endurance Sports

The primary dietary requirements for the endurance athlete are increased caloric intake and increased fluid consumption, each equal to their respective losses. The vitamin, mineral, and protein needs of most athletes are not very different from those of sedentary spectators. Energy is provided very inefficiently from protein, better from fats—which should be largely polyunsaturated, and best from carbohydrates. Food servings should be larger, particularly in carbohydrates such as cereals, grains, and the natural sugars found in fruit. Except for endurance sports, diet matters little to performance. To understand why increased carbohydrate intake is important to endurance performance, it is helpful to review the metabolism of exercise.

The Metabolism of Exercise. While fat and carbohydrate each contribute about 40% of the caloric content of the average American or European diet, the body stores fuel almost entirely (80% to 85%) in the form of fat (free-fatty-acid stores in adipose tissue). The remainder of our immediate fuel stores is glucose, stored in muscles and liver as glycogen. During the earliest phase of muscular activity (the first five to ten minutes), glucose stored in the muscles is the major fuel source. By consuming a diet high in carbohydrate for 48 to 72 hours prior to vigorous prolonged competition, a muscle glycogen supercompensation can be achieved [3]. This overloading of muscle glycogen is increased if the muscles are first exercised to the point of glycogen depletion (exhaustion). Only in those muscles exercised does this glycogen overstorage occur. This process, called carbohydrate loading, affords the exercising muscle a greater initial store of energy. Therefore, in the three or four days preceding endurance competition, the diet should be shifted to 75% to 90% carbohydrates to ensure muscle glycogen supercompensation.

As exercise continues, glucose is released from the liver, and muscle blood flow and glucose uptake rise seven to twenty times the resting level depending on the intensity of the exercise performed [20]. Initially, most of the glucose released from the liver is through glycogenolysis, the release of glucose already stored in the liver as glycogen. The glycogen stores in the liver are also increased by a diet high in carbohydrates. As duration and intensity of exercise increases, a greater amount of liver-glucose release occurs from the process of gluconeogenesis. Gluconeogenesis, the synthesis or manufacture of glucose from its substrate precursors (lactate, pyruvate, glycerol, and amino acids), increases from about 10% at rest to more than 40% of hepatic glucose release after four hours of exercise.

After forty minutes of exercise, blood-borne glucose is responsible for 70% to 90% of glucose metabolized [20]. However, in prolonged exercise between one and four hours, the blood-glucose level falls progressively, and the level of free fatty acids released from adipose tissue rises to become the major fuel source. A slight fall in blood glucose occurs because the hepatic glucose output fails to keep pace with the greatly augmented increase in muscle uptake and utilization of glucose. Thus, there is a triphasic sequence of fuel utilization in prolonged exercise. First, the muscle burns off glucose already stored in it; then glucose, primarily released from the liver, is taken from the bloodstream; and finally, the main fuel source of free fatty acids from the body's fat stores is used. Endurance exercise increases the body's ability to mobilize and metabolize free fatty acids.

After exercise ceases, blood flow to muscle decreases, but the uptake of glucose remains three to four times the resting level for nearly an hour. The full replenishment of muscle glycogen takes about 48 hours[3]. Liver-glucose replenishment, on the other hand, is complete in 24 hours. Insulin levels rise after exercise to facilitate this response. However, insulin levels decrease during exercise, yet muscle uptake of glucose is improved. This indicates that the muscle uptake of glucose during exercise does not require increased insulin. The exact mechanism by which exercising muscle can take glucose from the bloodstream and utilize it is not fully understood. Endurance training improves this process so that insulin sensitivity is increased, a lesser amount facilitating a greater muscle-glucose uptake.

The Ideal Precompetition Meal

The pre-exercise meal contributes little to the energy requirements of the impending event, since it requires up to 24 hours to restore liver glycogen and 48 hours to replenish muscle glycogen. The precompetition meal should minimize hunger, ensure hydration equal to expected fluid loss, provide for prompt emptying of the gastrointestinal tract, protect against nausea, and, to a degree, reflect individual food preferences.

Fluid losses depend on air temperature and on the intensity and duration of exercise. While fluid should be replaced during vigorous exercise, it should be realized that the intestinal tract absorbs water at about 60 ml per hour. If perspiring freely, one cannot keep up with the water loss simply by drinking fluids. For this reason, endurance athletes such as marathon runners, who know that they will lose 4 to 8 pounds of water during a race, spend the hours immediately before the race drinking fluids until their urine is clear. They actually start the competition with several extra pounds of water in their bodies that will be lost during the race. The vigorously exercising adult should also precede a workout by drinking fluids. Thirst is not immediately sensitive to serious body dehydration, so increased fluid consumption should be based on anticipated fluid losses.

Too much has been made of the fact that salt is lost in perspiration. Actually, well-conditioned athletes lose only trace amounts of salt in their sweat, and their kidneys become proficient at losing very little sodium in the urine. Habitual exercisers on well-rounded diets should not be concerned about salt needs. Salt is ubiquitous in processed foods and already overly plentiful in most diets. For most people, three daily meals easily replace the salt lost in up to 10 pounds of exercise-induced sweat; there is no need to reach for the salt shaker during the precompetition meal.

The precompetition meal should be light (approximately 500 calories), consist mainly of carbohydrates, and be consumed three to four hours before the event. Carbohydrates rapidly empty from the stomach and do not produce urinary diuresis. Taking sugar or honey for a quick energy lift one-half hour before an event actually impairs performance [3], because the rapid rise in blood glucose causes the release of extra insulin, which in turn impairs the release of liver glycogen and muscle utilization of free fatty acids. This places greater energy requirements on muscle glycogen and blood glucose and can result in hypoglycemia after the onset of exercise. Performance can be impaired by as much as 19% [3].

A heavy meal, especially one containing sizeable portions of fat and protein, consumed within two hours of competition also impairs performance. Thus, the traditional pregame steak dinner is not recommended as a nutritional preparation for vigorous exercise. Protein, a virtually useless source of immediate energy, compromises hydration by increasing urine. Fat delays emptying of the stomach and upper gastrointestinal tract, thereby impairing respiration and placing excessive stress on the circulation. This can also lead to nausea and emesis.

In the two hours preceding an event, it is best to eat no solid foods, but clear fluids of low caloric content may be consumed in limited amounts. Caffeine has been shown to mobilize free fatty acids and thus make more fat available for energy. For this reason, many endurance athletes will consume a caffeine drink (coffee, tea, cola) shortly before the event. Once exercise has started, the ingestion of sugar does not cause a rise in plasma insulin. Sugar taken during exercise tends to maintain blood-glucose levels and retard the breakdown of liver glycogen [5, 6]. It is not presently proven, however, that glucose taken during competition improves performance.

References

1. Belfrage, P., Berg, B., Hagerstrand, I., Nillson-Ehle, P., Tornqvist, H., and Wiebe, T. Alterations of lipid metabolism in healthy volunteers during long-time ethanol intake. *Eur. J. Clin. Invest.* 7:127–31, 1977.
2. Beyer, P. L. and Flynn, M. A. Effects of high- and low-fiber diets on human feces. *J.Am.Diet Assoc.* 72:271–276, 1978.
3. Buxbaum, R. and Micheli, L. J. *Sports for Life.* Boston: Beacon Press, 1979.
4. Castelli, W. P., Doyle, J. T., Gordon, T., et al. Alcohol and blood lipids: The Cooperative Lipoprotein Phenotyping Study. *Lancet* 2:153–155, 1977.
5. Costill, D. L. Sports nutrition: The role of carbohydrates. *Nutrition News* 41:1 & 4, 1978.
6. Costill, D. L., Bennett, A., Branam, G., and Eddy, D. Glucose ingestion at rest and during prolonged exercise. *J.Appl.Physiol.* 34:764–769, 1973.
7. DeWeese, V. A. No such thing as "localized" arteriosclerosis, say surgeons. *JAMA* 238:571, 1977.
8. Durnin, J. V. G. A. The influence of nutrition. *Can.Med.Assoc.J.* 96:715–720, 1967.
9. Fletch, A. P. The effect of weight reduction upon the blood pressure of obese hypertensives. *Q. J.Med.* 23:331–345, 1954.
10. Gordon, T., Castelli, W. P., Hjortland, M. C., Kannel, W. B., and Dawber, R. High density lipoprotein as a protective factor against coronary heart disease: The Framingham Study. *Am.J. Med.* 62:707–714, 1977.
11. Heller, H. P. and Hackler, L. R. Changes in the crude fiber content of the American diet. *Am.J. Clin.Nutr.* 31:1510–1514, 1978.
12. Henry, D. A., Bell, D. G., and Glithers, P. Plasma high-density lipoproteins. *N.Engl.J.Med.* 300:798, 1979.
13. Henze, K., Bucci, A., Signoretti, P., Menotti, A., and Ricci, G. Alcohol intake and coronary risk factors in a population group of Rome. *Nutr.Metab.* 21 (Suppl 1):157–159, 1977.
14. Hulley, S. B., Cohen, R., and Widdowson, G. Plasma high-density lipoprotein cholesterol level: Influence of risk factor intervention. *JAMA* 238:2269–2271, 1977.
15. MacMahon, B., Yen, S., Trichopoulos, D., Warren, K., and Nardi, G. Coffee and cancer of the pancreas. *N.Engl.J.Med.* 304:630–633, 1981.
16. Mann, G. V. The influence of obesity on health. *N.Engl.J.Med.* 291:178–185, 226–232, 1974. Reprinted by permission from the *New England Journal of Medicine.*
17. Lieber, C. S. Pathogenesis and early diagnosis of alcoholic liver injury. *N.Engl.J.Med.* 298:888–893, 1978.
18. Mayer, J. Food fads for athletes. *Atlantic Monthly,* 208:50–53, 1961.
19. Munzo, J. M. Effects of some cereal brans and textured vegetable protein on plasma lipids. *Am.J.Clin.Nutr.* 32:580–592, 1979.
20. Van Huss, W. D., Mikles, G., Jones, E. M., Montoye, H. J., Cederquist, D. C., and Smedley, L. Effect of milk consumption on endurance performance. *Res.Q.* 33:120–127, 1962.
21. Van Itallie, T. B. and Yang, M. U. Current concepts in nutrition diets and weight loss. *N.Engl. J.Med.* 297:1158–1161, 1977.

22. Willett, W., Hennekens, C. H., Siegel, A. J., Adner, M. M., and Castelli, W. P. Alcohol consumption and high-density lipoprotein cholesterol in marathon runners. *N.Engl.J.Med.* 303:1159–1161, 1980.
23. Wood, P. D., Haskell, W. L., Stern, M. P., Lewis, S., and Perry, C. Plasma lipoprotein distribution in male and female runners. *Ann.N.Y.Acad.Sci.* 301:748–762, 1977.
24. Yano, K., Rhoads, G. G., and Kagan, A. Coffee, alcohol, and risk of coronary heart disease among Japanese men living in Hawaii. *N.Engl.J.Med.* 297:405–409, 1977.

3 / Exercise and Life-Style Modification in Primary-Care Practice

Today, sports medicine involves not only the prevention and treatment of injuries but the promotion of health and fitness through aerobic exercise, appropriate life-style, and adequate nutrition. Newer subdivisions include cardiac rehabilitation, sports psychology, and biomechanics, in addition to the more basic sports physiology and nutrition. Those in sports medicine believe that the greatest potential for improving one's health is to be realized in what one does and does not do to oneself. Individual decisions about diet, exercise, and smoking are critical. A study at Massachusetts General Hospital showed that three out of five hospitalizations could have been avoided if people had taken better care of themselves [1]. While exercise alone is no panacea, the medical evidence is overwhelming that people who live sensibly and keep fit are healthier, feel better, are more productive, have lower absenteeism and better morale at work, and live longer.

Today, a new direction concentrating on positive health rather than curative treatment must be undertaken. Health depends less on medicine than on genetics, life-style, environment, and culture. Our government realizes that the most potent tool to limit health-care expenditures is to concentrate on keeping people healthy, rather than returning them to health after they have become ill. Table 3–1 lists some of the common diseases directly attributable to, or their severity and occurrence accelerated by, an inadequate life-style.

How do you alert the average person to the dangers of an inadequate life-style? A life-style analysis should be done at the initial visit, including documentation of age, sex, occupation, smoking history, diet pattern and quality, current or past regular exercise habits and types, known medical or surgical conditions, current or past regular medication (including over-the-counter drugs), known allergies, and significant family history. The complete history and physical examination, which allow not only a detailed analysis

---

Tables 3–1 to 3–6 and some of the written content of this chapter are reproduced with permission from Henry D. Childs, M.D. Exercise and lifestyle modification in family practice. In Robert C. Cantu, M.D. (Ed.). *Health Maintenance Through Physical Conditioning.* Littleton, Mass.: PSG Publishing Co. Inc., © 1981.

37

Table 3–1 Common Diseases Attributable to Poor Life-Style

Chronic depression and anxiety

Chronic fatigue and lethargy

Chronic obstructive pulmonary disease (COPD) and other smoking-related diseases

Coronary artery disease

Essential hypertension

Generalized atherosclerosis

Hyperlipidemias (especially low HDL, high LDL)

Marital, family, sexual maladjustments—eventual severe reactive depressions, alcoholism, drug dependency, suicide

Maturity-onset (noninsulin-dependent) diabetes

Obesity

Osteoporosis

Poor job performance due to mental and physical deconditioned status

Postretirement involution (decreased mental, physical, and social activity)

Stress-related symptoms (over 70% of presenting complaints in patients under 50 years of age in most primary-care practices include tension headaches and neckaches, back and chest pain, functional abdominal distress)

Symptomatic osteoarthritis (other arthritides?)

Unnecessary injuries or illnesses due to poor overall condition

of problems but time to do some teaching as well, is the ideal vehicle to inculcate needed life-style changes. A complete history and physical examination includes an occupational history and job-satisfaction report; present worries, symptoms, and problems; and past medical history, including operations, hospitalizations, significant injuries, past disabilities, allergies, medications, infectious illnesses, immunizations, foreign travel, military-service duty and locations, and special tests. A family medical history is also important.

Social history is of the utmost importance and contains type, location, and number of residences, marital and sexual satisfaction, concerns about children, family planning, hobbies, other interests and activities outside of the job, amount of sleep, diet quality and pattern in some detail, type and regularity of exercise, smoking history, alcohol pattern and amount, and drug use or abuse. A review of systems is taken, of course. Finally, a physical examination, basic blood and urine tests, and a resting ECG are taken.

Special testing may be indicated by the patient's age, sex, or any identified risk factors (table 3–2) such as fasting lipid profile, glucose tolerance test, and stress ECG. At the end of this comprehensive examination, it is important not only to delineate for the patient all the significant problems that have been uncovered, but also to assess the state of health (which means simply the presence or absence of organic or emotional disease) and the patient's physical condition. If a detailed exercise history has been taken, it is relatively easy to compare this with the known aerobic (2,000 kcal per week) standards. After such a dynamic analysis, the patient can be told where he or she stands with regard to a very good standard of preventive medicine, his or her physical condition, and general health.

Table 3–2   Risk Factors that May Indicate the Need for Special Testing

Family history of cardiac disease and/or hyperlipidemia

Family and/or personal history of heavy smoking or alcohol abuse

Overweight

Poor diet quality and pattern

Sedentary life-style

Hypertension

Prediabetic or established diabetic status

Hyperlipoproteinemia, and/or high triglycerides and total cholesterol, especially with high
   LDL and/or low HDL

Highly stressed personality (type A but? constructive vs. destructive stress)

Cardiopulmonary symptoms or signs

Abnormal hematologic, metabolic, or other blood or urine testing

Degree of motivation and ability to improve life-style

Life-Style Modification

Having gone through the history, examination, testing, and identifying the risk factors, laying the groundwork for a life-style change means first making sure the patient understands that the changes must be permanent (table 3–3). The short-term goals and short-term approach generally do not work. The many positive rewards experienced when a poor life-style is improved, especially with proper diet and aerobic exercise, should be emphasized, including improved energy and sense of well-being, better stress-coping, and automatic eventual control of excess body fat. Weight should be deemphasized and patients should not concentrate on it. The scale measures not only fat, but muscle, bone, and fluid as well. It is a common and tragic mistake to think that the minute the scale shows a weight gain, that gain is fat. Actually, a thin person following a good aerobic exercise program and eating properly may gain some weight but still will have lost excess body fat. The muscle-mass increase accounts for the added weight. This point must be stressed over and over again because most people are conditioned to think in terms only of weight loss.

    Other benefits of improved life-style are the apparent protection against coronary-artery disease measured by incidence of myocardial infarction, and better control of hyperglycemia, often without medication, as muscles are shown to have an increased sensitivity to insulin [3]. Systolic and diastolic hypertension control is improved, as is the quality of sleep. Job performance is improved and so is self-image.

    Aerobic exercise may be useful in reducing addictive behavior. Many people who

Table 3–3 Laying the Groundwork for Life-Style Change

Get across the idea of permanent changes in life-style, that is, acquiring new, regular, and lasting habits that are ultimately much more enjoyable. Shun the short-term goals.

Emphasize the many positive rewards commonly experienced when poor life-styles and risk factors are improved, especially with proper diet and enough aerobic exercise. These include:
Improved energy and sense of well-being
Better stress-coping (physical and mental)
Automatic eventual control of excess body fat
Apparent protection against coronary artery disease as measured by incidence of myocardial infarction
Better control of hyperglycemia, often without medication
Better control of systolic and diastolic hypertension, sometimes without medication
Better quality of sleep (more restful)
Better job performance
Significantly improved self-image and pride accompanying superior fitness, loss of obesity, cessation of smoking,
Importance of good example for one's children or youth groups and peers
Significant improvement in depression and anxiety, often reduction in need for medication
Improved energy for extracurricular activities
Significant reduction in long-term cost of medical care, as unnecessary illness is prevented or deferred
Greater longevity with good quality of life

Avoid scare tactics—the identified risk factors should be presented matter-of-factly, simply as items of important information to help an intelligent person make a commitment to a life-style change.

Understanding takes teaching, which takes time, but it begets willingness to make a commitment—after that, it is just organization.

have not been able to cut down on alcohol or quit smoking, or who have trouble with compulsive eating, find the ability after starting an aerobic-exercise program. Significant improvement in depression and anxiety is also seen. Some psychiatrists use aerobic exercise as the primary therapeutic tool to treat depression.

It is encouraging to see patients who formerly went home to collapse in front of the television set now energized and involved in various community tasks and activities. One can do a great deal not only at personal and family levels but also at the community level if he or she has the energy. Finally, there can be a significant reduction in the long-term cost of medical care as unnecessary illness is prevented or deferred. In one study [2], a group of patients with fit life-styles was compared with a group having more typical sedentary and unfit life-styles. Over a four-year period, there was a more than $4,000 difference in costs of hospital and office expenses between these two groups.

Finally, the question of greater longevity with good quality of life is raised. Too many people die too young from coronary-artery disease. If it is possible to protect against this—and there is good evidence to say we can—then we may indeed live longer and enjoy a better quality of life.

Motivation

I like to discuss the aforementioned subjects with my patients because they emphasize the positive rather than use scare tactics. An intelligent person apprised of the benefits that can result from a life-style change can do three very important things: (1) understand the need for change; (2) make a commitment to a life-style change; and (3) organize and schedule the change. Such terms as self-discipline and willpower should be avoided; they are sometimes used as an excuse not to change.

Table 3–4 shows some points to focus on when discussing a life-style change. Cigarette smoking is an extremely dangerous problem. The risks are not only pulmonary (cancer, emphysema), but cardiovascular. It can be useful to point out to parents that their

Table 3–4   Selecting Options for a Life-Style Change

Stop smoking.

Shun special calorie-counting or otherwise restricted diets; teach proper quality and pattern of eating (solid breakfast, light lunch, and moderate supper).

Emphasize the enormous variety, with good quality, that is available within the above pattern —the many high-fiber cereals with whole and cracked grains, fruits, lean meats, juices, milk, fresh vegetables, and large salads, particularly as a main course at supper.

Do not focus on weight. Excess fat always disappears if a proper and permanent diet quality and pattern are accompanied by solid levels of aerobic exercise.

Explain aerobic exercise in practical terms—steady activity generating 75% to 80% age-adjusted maximal heart rate for progressively longer periods as good condition is achieved; new standard of 2,000 kcal/week approximately equals three hours at this heart rate.

Help patient pick whatever truly aerobic exercise form seems most enjoyable but also most practical and safe. Jogging is the least expensive and most efficient for many, but other options include swimming, cross-country skiing, bicycling, snowshoeing, rowing, ice skating, roller skating, roller skiing, fast walking, walk-jogging, or nonstop squash, racquetball, or handball.

behavior influences that of their children. If they smoke there is a greater chance that their children will become smokers. Children of smokers also have a higher incidence of upper-respiratory infections and allergies.

Avoiding calorie counting or restricted diets is very important, unless restrictions are needed for medical purposes. The quality and pattern of eating is enormously important. The short-term solution of the special diet should be avoided. If persons can be taught to eat a solid breakfast of high quality, a light lunch, and a moderate supper, they will be able to perform better mentally and physically. Emphasize eating large salads at dinner because it is the problem meal in our society—much too large and full of too many things that have the metabolism struggling all night—thus making breakfast a much more difficult proposition. Having patients (particularly breakfast-skippers) eat only salads for dinner, at least for a while, greatly reduces calories while providing excellent nutrition. Eating a good breakfast then becomes easier as one is hungrier by morning. Again, the emphasis should not be on weight. With proper diet and exercise, excess body fat will disappear. How long this takes will depend on how much exercise a person is able to do.

Society at large is only beginning to be aware of what aerobic exercise really is and, unfortunately, there are misunderstandings. There are many fairly trim people with big muscles whom the public regards as being in superb condition. Although they may be isometrically in excellent condition, the cardiovascular system may not have been well trained. It is not uncommon to find some of these people in their forties and fifties dead on arrival in the emergency room or staring in bewilderment at the coronary-care-unit ceiling after a heart attack. Aerobic exercise, where the heart rate gets up to 70% to 80% of age-adjusted maximal rates for progressively longer periods as good condition improves, is more important to stress and should be recommended.

There are many aerobic pursuits. Any activity that is steady and causes a relatively high heart rate qualifies. While cross-country skiing, roller skating, and running rank at the top of the list in energy expenditure, the list is very long. The next chapter focuses on writing an exercise prescription that takes into account particular likes, physical liabilities, and time constraints.

The best way to make all of these life-style changes is to try to do them simultaneously (table 3–5). People will very often say, "Let's see, this sounds like a lot. I would rather quit smoking and wait on the other things, or maybe I'll do some exercise but I'm not so sure about the diet or the smoking." If a person is going to commit himself to a life-style change, these activities support each other.

Safety should be emphasized. The patient must understand that a gradual progression is essential in any aerobic-exercise program, particularly in jogging, which has the highest injury rate. The patient must understand proper warm-up, especially stretching exercises, which are important for preventing injury. Patients, especially runners, should be advised to do distance first, rather than worrying about pace. Too many people spend too much time thinking about what they did the day before or what their neighbors are doing. Patients must understand that this is their own individual program, and it is much more important to arrive at good distances safely and enjoyably than it is to go too hard, too fast, and get hurt. A proper cooling-off period must also be emphasized.

Table 3–5   How to Help Your Patient Implement Life-Style Changes

Urge that all necessary changes be begun and continued simultaneously—they support each other.

Emphasize the absolute necessity for regularity—organization and scheduling (not self-discipline or willpower—these terms are used as cop-outs).

Stress the importance of proper warm-up (especially stretching exercises), gradual progression of pace (this is endurance conditioning, and learning to do distance/time first and faster paces later is important), and proper cooling-off.

Outline the teaching function of follow-up visits to ensure safe and effective progress, and insist on them. Point out the patient's investment of time and money in self.

Require a well-maintained exercise record to assess regularity, degree, and rate of progress, and whether the patient is pushing too hard or fast.

Reinforce progress (the means are simple, but life-style change itself is tough for many), and try to be nonjudgmental about failures. Locate the obstacle to progress if possible and try to help the patient find a way around it.

Set a good personal example. Patients are impressed if their own doctor is a jogger or vigorous regular aerobic exerciser of any type.

Graduate your successful patient from regular follow-up (assuming it is not needed for other medical problems) when you have ascertained that he or she is self-sustaining at a good aerobic level (2,000 kcal/week) and enjoying it, without overuse symptoms or other exercise-related problems. Then help keep the patient self-sustaining by as-needed visits if illness or injury intervenes, or annual examinations by mutual agreement.

Reinforcement

The teaching function is essential if a person is going to achieve a life-style change successfully. People must come back for follow-up visits. You cannot launch a boat, slide it down the way, break a bottle of champagne over it, say good-bye, good luck, see you in a year; the boat still has to be steered. Many people, because of conditioning, see doctors only when sick and do not come back for follow-up. The original motivation and excitement dwindle, interruptions occur, and the life-style change gets nowhere. Follow-up is essential.

Keeping a well-maintained exercise record is very important in the training stages. The instructor needs to know exactly what is going on to avoid an overuse problem. The record should include a daily account of the type, duration, and intensity of primary exercise. Any warm-up or cooling-off exercises as well as duration and type of any nonrecreational exercise, such as mowing the lawn, shoveling snow, and vacuuming the house, should also be listed.

Reinforcing progress is vital, as is praising anything that is a step in the right direction, even if it is not up to the standards that have originally been outlined. Change can be discouraging at first, and follow-up visits serve as reinforcement. Being nonjudgmental about failures is also important because many people who are trying to achieve and are not having good luck feel guilty. It is best to find out what the problem is and try to work around the obstacle.

A personal example is important. The physician, nurse, physical therapist—anyone working with patients—should do some aerobics with regularity. It improves teaching effectiveness to practice what you preach. Many patients ask in a somewhat challenging manner if I run or exercise. I would feel very uncomfortable if I could not answer positively.

References

1. Kotulak, R. Doctors try scare tactics to save patients' lives. *Chicago Tribune*, 30 April 1976, p. 6.
2. Keeping fit holds medical bills down, says Purdue study. *Medical World News*, 25 December 1978, p. 16.
3. Soman, V. R. et al. Increased insulin sensitivity and insulin binding to monocytes after physical training. *N.Engl.J.Med.* 301:1200–1204, 1979.

4 / Writing a Precise Aerobic Exercise Prescription

Before prescribing an exercise program, a specialized exercise history and physical examination should be carried out. The details of this examination are discussed in chapter two. Additional desirable laboratory studies include a blood-lipid profile, resting blood pressure, and a resting 12-lead electrocardiogram (ECG). An exercise 12-lead ECG is recommended for those over 40 years or over 30 years if there is a family history of heart disease. While not infallible, the stress test is still the best way to detect latent arrythmias and signs of heart strain. If cardiac irregularities appear, the exercise program must be greatly modified to avoid the risk of heart attack. As the stress ECG improves, the level of physical conditioning can be advanced. The maximal heart rate (the rate of exercise that leaves one totally out of breath) and associated blood pressure are also recorded.

It is helpful, although not essential, to record the maximum oxygen uptake. This test permits an objective comparison of the patient's present level of fitness with age-related tables. It gives an accurate indication of his or her present level of fitness and performance capability. Moreover, by retaking the examination at regular intervals after beginning an exercise program, it is possible to document the rate of physical improvement. Obviously, such a test is also of immense usefulness to coaches and competitive athletes planning training programs.

While a test of maximal oxygen consumption (VO_2 max.) is the most precise measurement of one's fitness, several practical considerations render this test undesirable for all but the superbly conditioned athlete. First, since the goal of this test is exhaustion, one must consider whether the subject quit short of exhaustion (because of low tolerance to physical discomfort, lack of motivation, or even fear of a coronary). Because of these drawbacks, submaximal oxygen-consumption testing is the test most used to determine fitness. It is based on the fact that oxygen consumption and heart rate increase in a straight line in response to increased physical effort. Thus, this test involves physical effort, usually running on a treadmill or riding a bicycle ergometer, which brings the heart rate up to 50% and 75% of one's age-computed maximal level as read from tables. Maximal oxygen consumption is also measured at these two points, and the VO_2 max can be computed from these figures. There is also a simplification of the submaximal test that uses tables which relate heart rate and oxygen consumption. Here heart rate is plotted against workload to obtain a predicted VO_2 max from a table of average equivalents that is accurate within a range of 10%. This test eliminates the need to collect and analyze expired air, making it practical in an office setting.

Although not essential, the complete fitness examination should include an assessment of body composition, that is, lean body mass versus body fat. The only precise method of determining body fat is the immersion technique, which is unavailable except in certain exercise laboratories. However, an adequate alternative technique involves measuring body fat at four sites: behind the triceps muscle (back of the upper arm), over the biceps muscle, at the inferior angle of the scapula, and at the suprailiac (vertical skin fold on the crest of the hip at the midaxillary line) (figure 4–1). A caliper is used to measure the skin-fold thickness in each area in millimeters, and the total millimeters are calculated. This is the fat index. Table 4–1 computes percent of body fat ($\pm 5\%$) from the fat index. Table 4–2 shows suggested percents at various ages. With exercise, a 20% to 25% reduction in skin-fold fat measurements, even without loss in total body weight, can be anticipated. If dieting is used in conjunction with exercise, a much greater reduction of body fat will occur.

Since muscle weighs more than fat, it is possible to sustain a given weight during an exercise program and still lose considerable body fat. This is especially true for the already lean person. Underweight persons may even experience a slight weight gain as muscle is added. This principle applies to the conditioning of the cardiovascular-pulmonary system.

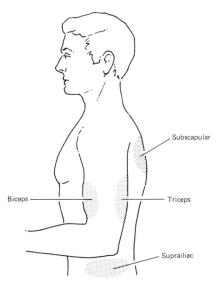

Figure 4–1   Four sites to measure body fat for assessment of body composition.

Table 4–1 Fat content, as a percentage of body-weight, for a range of values for the sum of *four* skinfolds (biceps, triceps, subscapular and suprailiac) of men and women of different ages.

Skinfolds mm	Males (age in years)				Females (age in years)			
	17–29	30–39	40–49	50+	16–29	30–39	40–49	50+
15	4.8	—	—	—	10.5	—	—	—
20	8.1	12.2	12.2	12.6	14.1	17.0	19.8	21.4
25	10.5	14.2	15.0	15.6	16.8	19.4	22.2	24.0
30	12.9	16.2	17.7	18.6	19.5	21.8	24.5	26.6
35	14.7	17.7	19.6	20.8	21.5	23.7	26.4	28.5
40	16.4	19.2	21.4	22.0	28.4	25.5	28.2	30.3
45	17.7	20.4	23.0	24.7	25.0	26.9	29.6	31.9
50	19.0	21.5	24.6	26.5	26.5	28.2	31.0	33.4
55	20.1	22.5	25.9	27.9	27.8	29.4	32.1	34.6
60	21.2	23.5	27.1	29.2	29.1	30.6	33.2	35.7
65	22.2	24.3	28.2	30.4	30.2	31.6	34.1	36.7
70	23.1	25.1	29.3	31.6	31.2	32.5	35.0	37.7
75	24.0	25.9	30.3	32.7	32.2	33.4	35.9	38.7
80	24.8	26.6	31.2	33.8	35.1	34.3	36.7	39.6
85	25.8	27.2	32.1	34.8	34.0	35.1	37.5	40.4
90	26.2	27.8	33.0	35.8	34.8	35.8	38.3	41.2
95	26.9	28.4	33.7	36.6	35.6	36.5	39.0	41.9
100	27.6	29.0	34.4	37.4	36.4	37.2	39.7	42.6
105	28.2	29.6	35.1	38.2	37.1	37.9	40.4	43.3
110	28.8	30.1	35.8	39.0	37.8	38.6	41.0	43.9
115	29.4	30.6	36.4	39.7	38.4	39.1	41.5	44.5
120	30.0	31.1	37.0	40.4	39.0	39.6	42.0	45.1
125	30.5	31.5	37.6	41.1	39.6	40.1	42.5	45.7
130	31.0	31.9	38.2	41.8	40.2	40.6	43.0	46.2
135	31.5	32.3	38.7	42.4	40.8	41.1	43.5	46.7
140	32.0	32.7	39.2	43.0	41.3	41.6	44.0	47.2
145	32.5	33.1	39.7	43.6	41.8	42.1	44.5	47.7
150	32.9	33.5	40.2	44.1	42.3	42.6	45.0	48.2
155	33.3	33.9	40.7	44.6	42.8	43.1	45.4	48.7
160	33.7	34.3	41.2	45.1	43.3	43.6	45.8	49.2
165	34.1	34.6	41.6	45.6	43.7	44.0	46.2	49.6
170	34.5	34.8	42.0	46.1	44.1	44.4	46.6	50.0

Finally, to increase the efficiency of the heart and lungs, it is essential to perform continuous rhythmic exercises long enough to stress the cardiovascular-pulmonary system. Brisk walking, jogging, bicycling, or cross-country skiing, for example, should be maintained until the subject begins to perspire and the pulse rate rises above 130 beats

Table 4–2 Suggested Percentage of Body Fat not to be Exceeded

	Age			
	17 to 29	*30 to 39*	*40 to 49*	*50+*
Men	12%	20%	22%	25%
Women	23%	27%	30%	34%

per minute for several minutes. Within ten minutes after exertion, the pulse rate should return to normal and the patient should not feel fatigued.

Components of an Exercise Program

There are four elements of a fitness prescription: type, frequency, duration, and intensity of exercise prescribed. Each exercise session should also have three parts: a warm-up period, an endurance phase, and a cooling-off period. This is analogous to the racehorse warming up, running the race, and returning to the paddock to be cooled off by walking.

The *warm-up* phase should be for at least five minutes and include rhythmic slow stretching movements of the trunk and limb muscles. This increases blood flow and stretches the postural muscles, preparing the body for sustained activity. This first stage is critical for the middle-aged person who has not exercised in several years. To ignore the warm-up is to risk muscle-pulls or more severe injuries. Table 4–3 lists 14 warm-up exercises, and the patient may choose any combination for the five-minute warm-up period. The exercises should vary on different days to avoid monotony.

The *endurance* phase should last fifteen to thirty minutes. During this period, the cardiovascular system is stressed to increase aerobic capacity. To achieve maximal cardiovascular improvement, the patients should exercise vigorously enough during the endur-

Table 4–3 Warm-up Exercises

Back flattener	*Sitting bend*
Single-knee raise	*Deep-knee bend*
Single-knee hug	*Posture check*
Double-knee hug	*Bend and stretch*
Single-leg raise	*Wall push-up*
Partial sit-up	*Hop 3 minutes*
Advanced sit-up	*Divers stance*

ance phase to be breathing at approximately 70% of aerobic capacity. For most people, this means increasing the pulse rate to 120 to 140 beats per minute. Table 4–4 depicts the target zone heart rate for various ages. Practically speaking, the target zone translates into a pace where one is breathing hard but not falling into greater oxygen debt (gasping for air). As aerobic capacity increases, one will also have to increase the duration and intensity of the endurance phase in order to maintain the same 70% effort.

Dr. Kenneth Cooper successfully presents a readily understood method of quantifying exercise in his best-selling books on aerobics. Dr. Cooper has definite ideas about the essential elements needed to achieve total physical fitness. He summarized his research in two basic principles: (1) if one exercises 20 to 30 minutes per day, it must be vigorous enough to sustain a heart rate of 140 beats per minute; (2) if the exercise is not that vigorous, it must be sustained for a longer period to be equally beneficial. Table 4–5 cites some common fitness activities and their caloric expenditures.

After five or six months of regular physical activity, the patient will be nearing an optimal training level after which aerobic capacity gains tend to plateau. One will progress further only by sharply increasing the intensity and duration of workouts. Practically speaking, except for those persons competing in endurance sports, there is no physiological or psychological benefit in exercising beyond three to four times per week in the endurance phase. This permits adequate recovery between fitness sessions and prevents soreness and tiredness.

Table 4–4 Recommended Exercise Target Heart Rates for Achieving Maximal Aerobic-Training Effect

Age (Years)	Exercise Heart Rate (beats per minute)
20	138 to 158
25	137 to 156
30	135 to 154
35	134 to 153
40	132 to 151
45	131 to 150
50	129 to 147
55	127 to 146
60	126 to 144
65	125 to 142
70	123 to 141
75	122 to 139
80	120 to 138
85	119 to 136

Table 4–5   Endurance Exercises

	KCal/hour
Cross-country skiing	1,000
Roller skiing	1,000
Running (10 mph)	900
Scull rowing (racing)	800
Wrestling	800
Gymnastics	700
Cycling (20 mph)	650
Fencing, handball, racquetball, squash	600
Mountain climbing	600
Swimming (5 mph)	600
Vigorous digging or shoveling (snow, sand,)	600
Boxing	500
Basketball	500
Waterskiing	500
Tennis (singles)	450
Carrying over 50 lbs weight	400
Hockey	400
Ice skating	400
Walking up a steep hill	400
Chopping or sawing wood	400
Football (American)	360
Downhill skiing	350
Roller skating	350
Table tennis	350

The *cooling-off* phase is too often omitted in exercise. While the endurance phase significantly raises body temperature, increases heart rate and blood pressure, and builds up lactic acid and other waste products in the muscles, the cooling-off phase allows the bodily functions to gradually return to normal. Also, it helps to eliminate waste products from the muscles, minimizing the chance of stiffness and soreness the next day. The cooling-off phase should last at least five minutes and can last longer if desired. It should include gross body movements that emphasize range of motion of the joints. Calisthenics are ideal for this final step in the exercise program. Any three cooling-off exercises from table 4–6 should be done for five minutes.

Practically any vigorous physical activity can be used in the endurance phase provided it is performed long enough and with sufficient intensity. For example, a weekend ski trip or a vigorous tennis match can count for one of the required workouts, or one can substitute hard physical labor (shoveling snow or sawing wood) for one of the endurance periods. The exercises should be performed at least three times a week, although working out daily may be desirable for some persons.

Table 4–6 Cooling-Off Exercises

Walking 5 minutes	Wing stretches
Alternate walk-jog 3 minutes	Single-leg raise and knee hug
Rotate head	Straight arm and leg stretch
Body bender	Heel-toe walk
Wall press	Heel-toe beam walk
Arm circles	Knee push-up
Half-knee bend	Side-leg raise

Determining Level of Fitness

Because the exercise prescription for a fit athlete will differ drastically from that for a middle-aged adult who has not regularly exercised for years, the level of fitness must be determined. While the exercise stress test can be used to determine fitness level, the walk test and the program shown in appendix 4-A are especially useful for middle-aged and senior patients beginning a fitness program.

The intent of the walk test is to determine how many minutes, up to ten, the patient can walk briskly on a flat surface without experiencing undue shortness of breath or discomfort. If the patient can do this for only three or fewer minutes, he or she is at Level 3. If three minutes can easily be exceeded, but walking for ten minutes is uncomfortable, he or she is at Level 2. If the patient can easily walk ten minutes, then he or she may be at Level 1. To determine if the patient is at Level 1, an additional test that consists of walking and jogging should be used. The patient should alternately walk 50 steps and jog 50 steps for a total of six minutes. The patient should be walking at a rate of at least 120 steps per minute and jogging at a rate of 144 steps per minute. If he or she stops before six minutes have elapsed, the patient is at Level 2. If the six-minute test can be completed easily, he or she is at Level 1. Those patients who can complete twelve minutes can move beyond Level 1 to any of the endurance exercises.

The exercises for each level should be carried out in the sequence given, as both a warm-up and cooling-off period are built into each series. The cooling-off period has recently received much attention in the Olympic Games. It has been shown that the cooling-off phase allows muscles to be drained of lactic acids—the products of aerobic metabolism—and is the best way to prepare the body for strenuous activity the next day. If possible the patient should keep a record of the exercises performed, how many repetitions were done, and how much time was required. Many find that doing the exercises to music makes them more enjoyable. Others find that watching television or listening to the radio while exercising relieves boredom. The exercises can be done alone or with family or friends. Clothing should be loose, comfortable, and stretchable rather than restrictive. Shoes should have no heels and nonskid soles. Exercises that cause frank pain that does not disappear in 48 hours should be discontinued.

Instructions for Level 3 (Table 4–7)

The patient should attempt to complete the entire exercise sequence without rest periods of more than two minutes. If necessary, however, a longer rest period may be taken. An indication of improvement in the level of fitness will be the patient's ability to comfortably complete the sequence in a decreasing amount of time. A patient should never be allowed to execute an exercise in a jerky manner to improve speed. All exercises should be done as smoothly as possible.

For the first week, only the fewest repetitions or shortest duration of time shown for each exercise should be prescribed. If after one week this level still requires a strenuous effort, the patient should not increase the duration or repetitions. Only when the patient feels comfortable with an exercise where a range of repetitions is given, should the number be increased by one additional repetition per week. When the maximum number of repetitions indicated for each exercise can be carried out without resting, the patient is ready to move on to Level 2.

Instructions for Level 2 (Table 4–8)

For the Level 2 exercise program, the patient should proceed in a manner similar to Level 3. He or she should start at the fewest number of repetitions and gradually advance one repetition at a time until the highest continuous number of repetitions of each exercise is reached. When this can be accomplished without straining or undue fatigue, the patient is ready to advance to Level 1.

Instructions for Level 1 (Table 4–9)

Again, starting with the fewest repetitions and gradually increasing to the maximum number without rest periods should be the goal at this exercise level. When the patient

Table 4–7   Level 3 Exercise Program

Walk 2 minutes
Bend and stretch: 2 repetitions increasing to 10
Rotate head: 2 repetitions each way increasing to 10
Body bender: 2 repetitions increasing to 5
Back flattener: 2 repetitions increasing to 5
Wall press: 2 repetitions increasing to 5
Arm circles: 5 repetitions each way
Wing stretcher: 2 repetitions increasing to 5
Single-knee raise: 3 repetitions increasing to 10
Straight arm and leg stretch: 2 repetitions increasing to 5
Heel-toe walk
Side-leg raise: 2 repetitions increasing to 5
Partial sit-up; 2 repetitions increasing to 10
Alternate walk-jog: 1 to 3 minutes
Walk: 1 to 3 minutes

Table 4–8 Level 2 Exercise Program

Walk 3 minutes
Bend and stretch: 10 repetitions
Rotate head: 10 repetitions each way
Body bender: 5 repetitions increasing to 10
Back flattener: 5 repetitions increasing to 10
Wall press: 5 repetitions
Arm circles: 5 repetitions increasing to 10
Half-knee bend: 5 repetitions increasing to 10
Wing stretcher: 5 repetitions increasing to 10
Single-knee hug: 3 repetitions increasing to 10
Single-leg raise: 3 repetitions increasing to 10
Straight arm and leg stretch: 5 repetitions
Heel-toe beam walk:
Knee push-up: 2 repetitions increasing to 10
Side-leg raise: 2 repetitions increasing to 10
Advanced sit-up: 2 repetitions increasing to 10
Sitting bend: 2 repetitions increasing to 5
Deep-knee bend: 2 repetitions increasing to 5
Alternate walk-jog: 3 to 6 minutes
Walk: 1 to 3 minutes

Table 4–9 Level 1 Exercise Program

Alternate walk 50 steps and jog 50 steps for 3 minutes
Bend and stretch: 10 repetitions
Rotate head: 10 repetitions each way
Body bender: 10 repetitions
Back flattener with legs extended: 10 repetitions
Wall press: 5 repetitions
Posture check: 5 repetitions
Arm circles: 10 repetitions each way increasing to 15
Half-knee bend: 10 repetitions increasing to 20
Wing stretcher: 10 repetitions increasing to 20
Wall push-up: 10 repetitions
Double-knee hug: 3 repetitions increasing to 10
Single-leg raise and knee hug: 3 repetitions increasing to 10
Straight arm and leg stretch: 5 repetitions
Heel-toe beam walk:
Hop: 5 repetitions on each foot
Knee push-up: 5 repetitions increasing to 10
Side-leg raise: 10 repetitions
Advanced modified sit-up: 2 repetitions increasing to 10
Sitting bend: 5 repetitions increasing to 10
Diver's stance: hold 10 seconds
Deep-knee bends: 5 repetitions increasing to 10
Alternate walk-jog: 5 minutes
Walk: 3 minutes

can perform the maximum number without rest periods, he or she can either continue to increase the number of repetitions and speed of their execution or advance to other more vigorous exercises and sports.

After attaining Level 1 status, it is time to liberalize and vary the exercise program to make it more stimulating and enjoyable. Certain basic concepts are stressed. For example, the program should include exercises that promote flexibility, coordination, agility, balance, muscular strength, and endurance. Muscles, if not used, grow soft and atrophy. The natural slow decline of muscular strength and endurance can be retarded only by keeping the muscles toned through regular exercise. Also, the balance and equilibrium mechanisms of the body can be kept fit only through use; accelerated degeneration occurs with disuse. The tissue surrounding joints increases in thickness and loses elasticity with advancing years. This process, as is true in arthritis, is greatly retarded by a daily exercise program that moves the joints through the full range of motion. Exercise will keep one's joints flexible, muscles supple and springy, and heart feeling young.

It is suggested that an exercise prescription include the following:

Warm-up: Select any three exercises from table 4–3. Start with three repetitions and gradually increase to ten.

Endurance: Execute any one or two activities from the maximal section in table 4–5 for 30 minutes at a pulse rate of 120 to 140 beats per minute, or at an intensity that induces forced deep breathing. Nearly equal benefit can be obtained from 60 minutes of activity from the moderate section.

Cooling-off: Select any three exercises from table 4–6. Start with three repetitions and gradually increase to ten.

As the tables suggest, the great advantage of this fitness program is that the patient can tailor it to personal choices. Practically any vigorous physical activity can be used in the endurance phase, provided it is performed long enough and with sufficient intensity. For example, a weekend ski trip or a vigorous tennis match can count for one of the required workouts, hard physical labor such as shoveling snow or sawing wood can substitute for one of the endurance periods. If the patient enjoys sports, then 30 minutes of maximal exercise sports such as running, cycling, cross-country skiing, or swimming, or 60 minutes of moderate sports activity, such as tennis or skiing, can substitute for one of the endurance periods.

For the Super Achiever

Some patients may wish to push beyond the physical-fitness program outlined above and enter competitive middle-aged athletics. Interest in competitive sports seems to go in cycles. Today, jogging and long-distance running are very popular. Not long ago, golf was popular, then tennis. One important point should be made concerning the risks of competing in sports instead of following a personal-fitness program. Competition should be avoided if the primary objective is physical fitness only, since competition will invariably bring on a stress-related injury resulting in an enforced layoff. The injury rate for the competitive athlete is almost 100%. For some, however, the stimulus of competition makes otherwise tedious exercise more tolerable. Training that is not directed toward a specific objective is difficult to maintain. Also, there is a special joy in competing, whether against an opponent in tennis or against the clock in long-distance running. In distance races, so many people usually enter that, except for three or four in each class, most are running against their previous best time. By retaining the common sense of never extending oneself too far in competition, rewards will overshadow any minor injuries. However, participation in one sport should not be a replacement for a total exercise program.

Suggested Readings

Cantu, R. C. *Toward Fitness: Guided Exercise for Those with Health Problems.* New York: Human Sciences Press, 1980.

Cooper, K. H. *Aerobics.* New York: M. Evans & Co., Inc., 1968.

Cooper, K. H. *The New Aerobics.* New York: Bantam, 1970.

Cooper, K. H. *The Aerobics Way.* New York: M. Evans & Co., Inc., 1977.

Wilmore, J. H. and Behnke, A. R. An anthropometric estimation of body density and lean body weight in young men. *J.AppliedPhysiol.* 27:25–31, 1969.

Yuhasz, M. S. The Effects of Sports Training on Body Fat in Man with Prediction of Optimal Body Weight. Unpublished doctoral thesis, Urbana, Ill.: Univ. of Illinois, 1962.

Appendix 4A
Exercises

(1) Walk (3 minutes)

Objective: An excellent warm-up exercise to loosen muscles for the ensuing exercises.

Basic Exercise: Stand erect and be well balanced on the balls of the feet. Walk rapidly on a level surface.

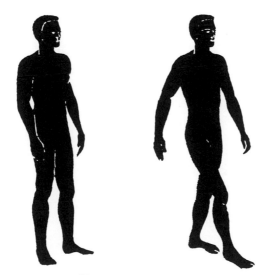

Figure A–1   Walk.

Adapted from Robert C. Cantu, *Toward Fitness: Guided Exercise for Those with Health Problems.* New York: Human Sciences Press, 1980.

(2) Alternate Walk-Jog (3 minutes)

Objective: Warm-up exercises for more advanced exercises; good for legs and circulation.

Basic Exercise: Stand erect with arms flexed and forearms roughly parallel to the floor. Walk 50 steps, then break into a slow run (jog) for 50 steps. When jogging, stride easily, landing on the heels and rolling to push off on the toes. This heel-toe movement is in contrast to a fast run where one lands on the balls of the feet. Arms should swing freely from the shoulders in opposition to the legs. Breathing should be deep, but never labored to the point of gasping.

Figure A–2   Alternate Walk-Jog.

(3) Bend and Stretch

Objective: Loosen and stretch the back, hamstring, and calf leg muscles.

Basic Exercise: Stand erect with feet a shoulder-width apart.

A. Slowly bend forward at the waist and touch the fingers of outstretched arms to toes, bending knees to whatever degree is necessary. The maximal effort is achieved when the knees can remain locked.

B. Return slowly and smoothly to the starting position.

(4) Rotate Head

Objective: Loosen and relax muscles of the neck and firm up the throat and chin line.

Basic Exercise: Stand erect with feet a shoulder-width apart and hands on hips. In a smooth motion slowly rotate head in a full circle from left to right; then from right to left.

(5) Body Bender

Objective: Stretch arm, trunk, and leg muscles.

Basic Exercise: Stand erect with feet a shoulder-width apart and hands extended overhead with fingertips touching as in a praying-hand posture.

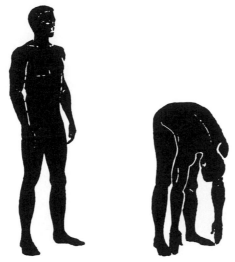

Figure A–3 Bend and Stretch.

Figure A–4 Rotate Head.

A. Bend at the waist slowly sideward to the left as far as possible, keeping hands together and arms extended straight.

B. Return to starting position.

C. Repeat same movements to the right.

(6) Back Flattener

Objective: Strengthen gluteal (buttock) and abdominal muscles and flatten the low back.

Figure A–5   Body Bender.

Figure A–6   Back Flattener.

Basic Exercise: Lie on back on padded floor with knees well bent. Relax with arms above head. A small pillow may be placed under the head if desired. Squeeze buttocks together as if trying to hold a piece of paper between them. At the same time, suck in and tighten the abdomen muscles. The back should be flat against the floor. This is the *flat-back position.* Hold this position for a count of ten (10 seconds), relax, and then repeat the exercise three times. Gradually increase to 20 repetitions.

Advanced Modifications

Buttock Raise: After the basic exercise has been done for a week or more, additional flattening can be achieved by doing the exercise with the buttocks slightly raised (1 to 2 inches) off the floor at the time the buttocks are squeezed and abdomen tensed. Hold for the count of ten, relax, and repeat.

Legs Extended: After several weeks of the basic exercise, gradually do the exercise with the knees less bent, until the exercise can be done with legs straight out. The buttock raise need not be combined with this modification.

(7) Wall Press

Objective: Promote good body alignment and posture while strengthening abdominal muscles.

Basic Exercise: Stand erect with head and neck in a neutral position, back against the wall, and heels three inches away from the wall. Suck in stomach and press low back flat against the wall. Hold this position for six seconds, relax, and return to the starting position. Low back should continually be in contact with the wall and head and neck should not extend backward.

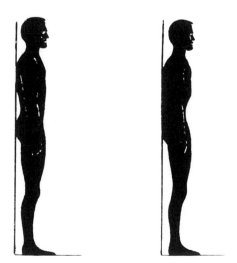

Figure A–7   Wall Press.

(8) Posture Check

Objective: Stand and walk correctly.

Basic Exercise: Stand with back to the wall pressing heels, buttocks, shoulders, and head against wall. There should not be any space between low back and the wall; if one does feel space, the back is too arched and not flat. Move feet forward bending knees so that back slides a few inches down the wall. Now again squeeze buttocks and tighten abdominal muscles flattening lower back against the wall. While holding this position, walk feet back so you slide up the wall. Now, standing straight, walk away from the wall and around the room. Return to the wall and back up to it to be certain the proper posture has been maintained.

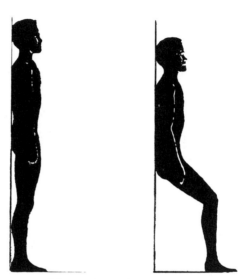

Figure A–8   Posture Check.

(9) Arm Circles

Objective: Strengthen the muscles of the shoulder while keeping the joint flexible.

Basic Exercise: Stand erect with arms outstretched sideward at shoulder height, palms up. While keeping head erect, make small backward circular movements with hands. Now with palms down, carry out the circular movements in a forward position.

(10) Half-Knee Bend

Objective: Strengthen and stretch quadriceps (upper front thigh) muscles while improving balance.

Basic Exercise: Stand erect with hands on hips. While extending arms forward, palms down, bend knees halfway. Keep heels on the floor, pause and return to the starting position.

(11) Wing Stretcher

Objective: Strengthen the muscles of the upper back and shoulders while stretching the chest muscles and promoting good posture.

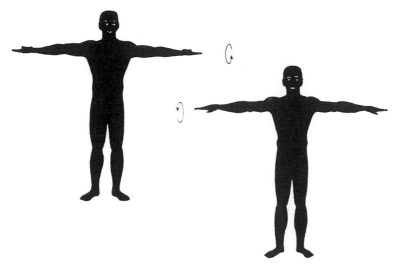

Figure A–9   Arm Circles.

Figure A–10   Half-Knee Bend.

Basic Exercise: While standing erect, bend arms in front of chest with elbows at shoulder height and extended fingertips touching. Count 1, 2, 3; on each count pull elbows backward as far as possible while keeping arms at shoulder height and then returning to the starting position. On count 4 swing arms outward and sideward, shoulder height, palms up and return to the starting position.

Figure A–11 Wing Stretcher.

(12) Wall Push-up

Objective: Strengthen arm, shoulder, and upper-back muscles while stretching chest and posterior thigh muscles.

Basic Exercise: Stand erect squarely facing the wall with feet six inches apart and arms extended straight in front with palms on the wall lightly bearing weight. Slowly bend elbows and lower body towards the wall turning head to the side until the cheek almost touches the wall. Then slowly push away from the wall extending elbows while returning to the initial position. Repeat slowly, turning head to the opposite side.

Figure A–12 Wall Push-up.

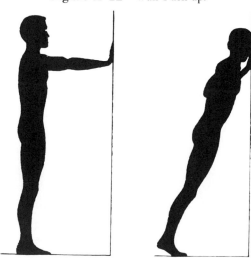

(13) Single-Knee Raise

Objective: Stretch low back, hip flexor, and hamstring (posterior thigh) muscles.

Basic Exercise: Lie on back on a padded floor with arms above head and knees bent. Tighten buttocks and abdominal muscles. Raise one knee over chest toward chin as far as possible, hold for ten seconds, then return to starting position and relax a few seconds before repeating with the opposite leg. Start with three repetitions of each knee, gradually advancing to ten.

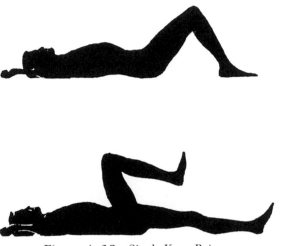

Figure A–13   Single-Knee Raise.

(14) Single-Knee Hug

Objective: Same as single-knee raise.

Basic Exercise: The single-knee hug is essentially the same exercise as the single-knee raise except the hands are not placed above the head, but around the knee to be raised. The arms are used to pull (raise) the knee higher, which produces greater stretching of the low back and hamstrings. The same ten-second hold, number of repetitions, and advanced modification pertain as with the single-knee raise.

(15) Double-Knee Hug

Objective: Stretch low back and hamstring muscles, strengthen abdominal and hip-flexing muscles.

Basic Exercise: Lie on back on a covered floor with knees bent, arms at side, and pillow under head if desired. Tighten buttocks and abdominal muscles so that low back is flat against the floor. Grasp both knees with hands and raise them slowly over chest as far as possible. Hold ten seconds, return to starting position, relax a few seconds, then repeat. Start with three repetitions and gradually build to ten.

Advanced Modification: After a month or more of the basic exercise, at-

Figure A–14   Single-Knee Hug.

Figure A–15   Double-Knee Hug.

tempt the double-knee hug starting with both legs extended straight. Tense buttocks and abdomen and then, taking care to keep the back flat, bend both knees, grasp knees with hands and raise over chest, hold ten seconds, and return to starting position to relax before repeating. The low back tends to arch when lifting and lowering the knee. If this cannot be done with the back against the floor, the patient is not yet ready for this modification and the basic knees-bent position should be resumed. This extended leg starting position strengthens both the hip flexing and abdominal muscles.

(16) Single-Leg Raise

Objective: Stretch low back and hamstring muscles, strengthen abdominal and hip-flexing muscles.

Basic Exercise: Lie on back on a covered floor with one knee bent and one leg straight, arms at side and a pillow under head if desired. Tighten buttocks and abdominal muscles, then slowly raise the straight leg, keeping the leg straight and the back flat. Raise the leg as far as comfortably possible, then slowly lower the leg to the floor, keeping it straight and the back flat. Relax a few seconds and then repeat with the other leg. Start with three repetitions of each leg and gradually increase to ten.

Advanced Modification: After a month or more, attempt the single-leg raise starting with both legs extended straight. Tense buttocks and low back, and with back flat and legs out straight, raise one leg up as far as possible. As the leg is raised, the back may not remain flat. Check by using hands to see if back lifts from the floor when the leg is lifted and lowered. If it does, resume the basic exercise with one knee bent.

Figure A–16　Single-Leg Raise.

(17) Single-Leg Raise and Knee Hug

Objective: Strengthen low back and abdominal muscles while increasing flexibility of hip and knee joints.

Basic Exercise: Raise extended left leg 12 inches off the floor, slowly bend knee and move it toward chest as far as possible using abdominal, hip, and leg muscles. Place both hands around knee and pull it slowly toward chest as far as possible. Slowly extend leg to the position 12 inches off the floor, then return to the starting position. Repeat two to five times with each leg. Do the number desired with the left leg, then repeat with the right leg.

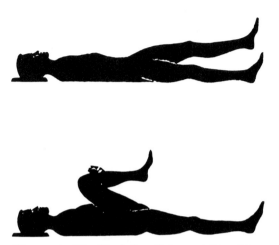

Figure A–17   Single-Leg Raise and Knee Hug.

(18) Straight Arm and Leg Stretch

Objective: Strengthen abdominal muscles while stretching the muscles of the arms.

Basic Exercise: Lie on back, legs extended, feet together, arms at side, buttocks and abdomen tensed so back is flat against the floor. Slowly move arms and legs outward along the floor as far as possible, hold a moment, and slowly return to the starting position. Repetitions as indicated for each level.

(19) Heel-Toe Walk

Objective: Improve balance and posture.

Basic Exercise: Stand erect with abdomen and buttocks tensed, with left foot along a straight line and hands held out from body to aid in balance. Walk ten steps along the straight line by placing the right foot directly in front of the left with the right heel touching the left great toe, then alternate feet placing the left in front of the right, heel to toe. When ten such steps in a straight line have been taken, stop. Return to the starting position by walking backward along the same line, alternately placing one foot behind the other, toe to heel.

(20) Heel-Toe Beam Walk

Objective: Improve balance and posture.

Basic Exercise: Level 2 will walk ten steps on a 2-inch-high by 6-inch-wide board placed flat on the floor; Level 1 will use a 2-inch-high by 4-inch-wide board placed flat on the floor. Walk ten steps along the board by placing the right foot directly in front of the left with the right heel touching the left great toe, then alternate feet, placing the left foot in front of the right, heel to toe. When ten such steps have been taken, stop. Return to the starting position

Figure A–18 Straight Arm and Leg Stretch.

Figure A–19 Heel-Toe Walk.

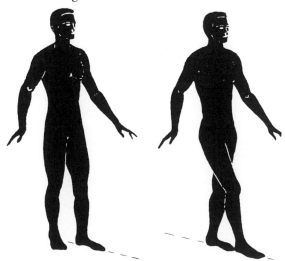

by walking backward along the same board alternately placing one foot behind the other, toe to heel.

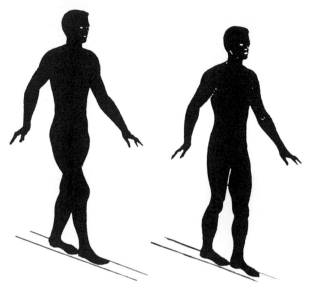

Figure A–20   Heel-Toe Beam Walk.

(21) Hop

Objective: Improve balance, strengthen the extensor muscles of the leg and foot, and increase circulation.

Basic Exercise: Stand erect, low back flat, with weight on right foot, left leg bent at the knee, and left foot several inches off the floor. Hold arms slightly out from body to aid in balance. Hop five times on right foot and five times on left foot.

(22) Knee Push-Up

Objective: Strengthen the muscles of arms, shoulders, and trunk.

Basic Exercise: Lie on the floor with face down, legs together, knees bent with feet off the floor and hands palm down flat on the floor under shoulders. Slowly push upper body off the floor extending arms fully and keeping low back flat so body is in a straight line from head to knees. Slowly return to starting position and repeat.

(23) Side-Leg Raise

Objective: Improve the flexibility of the hip joint and strengthen the lateral muscles of the trunk and hip.

Basic Exercise: Lie on the floor on the right side with head resting on right arm and both legs extended together. Lift extended left leg sideways (upward) off the right leg as far as possible. Stop, then return to the starting position and repeat. After the proper number of repetitions are done with the left leg, roll over on left side and repeat the exercise with right leg.

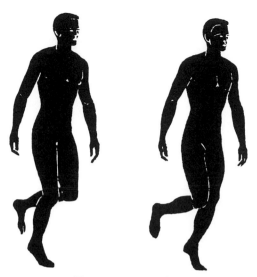

Figure A–21   Hop.

Figure A–22   Knee Push-Up.

(24) Partial Sit-Up

    Objective: Strengthen low back and abdominal muscles.

    Basic Exercise: Lie on back on a covered floor with knees well bent. Squeeze buttocks and tighten abdominal muscles. With low back on the floor, slowly raise head, neck, and shoulders as arms extend to knees. Keep low back flat on the floor. Hold this position ten seconds, return to starting position,

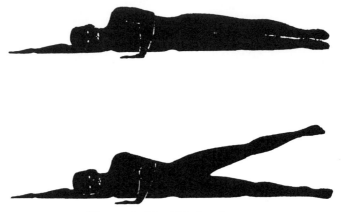

Figure A–23   Side-Leg Raise.

rest a few seconds, and repeat. Start with three repetitions and progress to
at least ten.

Advanced Modification: Lift head and shoulders farther from the floor.
Back will now lift off the floor. Keep knees bent. In the beginning it may help
to place feet under a heavy chair or some other restraint. Once abdominal muscles are strong enough, this should not be necessary and should not be done,
since this action actually allows the legs to help the abdomen in allowing you
to raise. The motion should be a gentle smooth curling and uncurling. Never
jerk to achieve greater height or an additional repetition and never strain or
exert beyond reasonable comfort. Start with three repetitions and progress to
at least ten.

Figure A–24   Partial Sit-Up.

(25) *Advanced Sit-Up*

    Objective: Maximally strengthen low back and abdominal muscles.

    Basic Exercise: Lie on back on a covered floor with knees well bent. Squeeze buttocks and tighten abdominal muscles. Start with arms folded over waist and lift head, shoulders and back smoothly until arms are touching knees. Hold ten seconds, return to the starting position, relax a few seconds, and repeat. Start with three repetitions and progress to at least ten.

Figure A–25   Advanced Sit-Up.

(26) Advanced Modified Sit-Up

    Objective: Maximally strengthen low back and abdominal muscles.

    Basic Exercise: Progress gradually until ten of the basic advanced sit-ups can be easily and comfortably executed. Then try folding the arms in front of the face instead of the waist. Curl up to knees, hold ten seconds, return to the starting position, relax a few seconds, and repeat. Start with three repetitions. When this modified version can be accomplished ten times, attempt a sit-up with hands clasped behind head. When this version can also be done ten times, attempt the maximal version of a sit-up. This involves lying on the back on a padded inclined surface (a tilt board with the foot end elevated). Knees should be bent as always, then with hands clasped behind neck slowly and carefully execute the sit-up, hold ten seconds, slowly uncurl to the starting position, relax, and repeat. This last version is clearly optional. The more inclined the board, the greater strength and effort will be required.

Figure A–26   Advanced Modified Sit-Up.

(27) *Sitting Bend*

    Objective: Strengthen low back while stretching low back and hamstring muscles.

    Basic Exercise: Sit on a hard chair, feet flat on the floor, knees not more than 12 inches apart, arms folded loosely in lap. Squeeze buttocks and tighten abdominal muscles so that back goes flat against the chair. Bend over, letting head go between knees with hands reaching for the floor. Bend as far as is comfortable, hold for a count of five, then slowly pull body back to the flat-back-sitting starting position. Relax a few seconds, then repeat three times, gradually increasing to ten repetitions.

Figure A–27   Sitting Bend.

(28) Divers Stance

Objective: Improve balance and posture while strengthening extensor muscles of legs and feet.

Basic Exercise: Stand erect with buttocks and abdomen tensed, feet slightly apart, and arms at sides. Lift up on toes while extending arms upward and forward so they are extended, palms down at shoulder height parallel to the floor. Hold this position for ten seconds, return to the starting position and repeat.

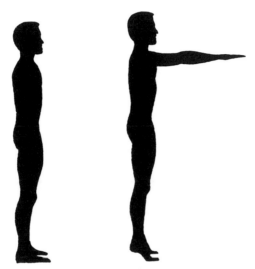

Figure A–28 Divers Stance.

(29) Deep-Knee Bend

Objective: Strengthen hamstring and quadriceps muscles.

Caution: Do not begin this exercise until a good back flattener can be done. Most should not attempt this exercise until a month into the exercise program. Discontinue the exercise if there is considerable lasting discomfort in knees or hips.

Basic Exercise: Stand behind a sofa, desk, heavy chair or similar structure, holding onto it for balance. Squeeze and tighten buttocks and abdomen. Slowly bend knees and with a flat-back squat down as far as is reasonably comfortable, stop, then stand up using only legs and not arms. Relax for a second or two; repeat three times and gradually build up to ten repetitions.

(30) Alternate Walk-Jog

Objective: Strengthen leg muscles while mildly stimulating the cardiovascular system.

Basic Exercise:

Level 1: Gradually increase to walk 100 steps then jog 100 steps alternately for five minutes.

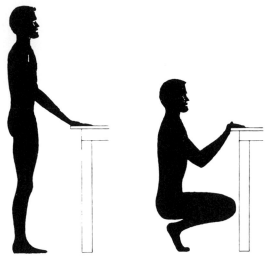

Figure A–29 Deep Knee Bend.

Level 2: Walk 50 steps then jog 25 steps alternately for three to six minutes.

Level 3: Walk 50 steps then jog 10 steps alternately for one to three minutes.

(31) Walk

Objective: To slowly reduce the physical exercise as pulse, respiration, and blood pressure return to normal.

II / Special Sports-Medicine Considerations

5 / Sports Injuries in Young Athletes

Young athletes are not merely small adults. They incur different types of acute sports injuries because they have immature bones and ligaments that can easily be overstressed. They present the following unique problems that must be recognized:

1. The normal growth and development of children varies enormously in stages of development at any one time. Figure 5–1 shows the range of normal growth. The average weight of an 11-year-old boy is 78 pounds; however, this weight may vary from 50 pounds to 108 pounds in a child this age and still be within the normal range. The maturation of the nervous system resulting in coordination of large-muscle groups may also vary for a given age. Finally, the maturity factor must be considered. A 14-year-old boy may exhibit very little pubertal change or may be fully developed. Since muscle power, coordination, and oxygen consumption develop rapidly with the hormonal changes of puberty, especially in boys, the prepubertal athlete has a significant disadvantage when competing with the postpubertal athlete, even if both are the same size. All of these factors have obvious implications in contact or collision sports. Coaches, trainers, and team physicians must keep this in mind when selecting and matching teams for competition in contact sports. Fortunately for the pre-high-school athlete, collision injuries are usually minor because they occur at a slow speed. This is no longer the case by high-school age, however, and as a result, the number and severity of collision injuries increase, with the lighter, smaller, less physically mature athlete being the major recipient.

2. All athletes are impatient about the restrictions that an injury may impose. Young athletes lacking judgment and experience are the least likely to follow recommended limitations of activity, even when the limitations are essential for the proper diagnosis and healing of injuries. Therefore, it is prudent to maintain an extremely close follow-up regimen for the injured young athlete and to anticipate impatient behavior.

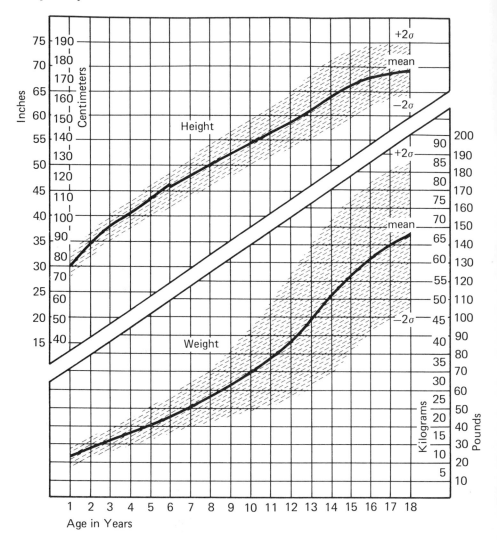

Figure 5–1 Normal physical growth ranges in children (supine length to 6 years, standing height from 6 to 18 years).

3. Open epiphyses, immature apophyses, and flexible ligamentous structures result in musculoskeletal injuries unique to the young athlete, and require prompt orthopedic evaluation and treatment:

Epiphyseal Injury. Bones lengthen primarily by growth in the cartilage of the epiphyseal plate [14]. Once growth has occurred in the cartilage matrix by interstitial expansion, the cartilage degenerates and is replaced by new bone in the metaphysis. This new bone is weaker and has a thinner cortex. Thus, the growing bone of the young athlete has an inherent area of weakness due to the very processes of growth itself. The epiphyseal plate has less resistance to both sheer and tensile forces than adjacent bone, while the thin cortex of the metaphysis has less resistance to compressive forces. While most epiphyseal-plate fractures heal without sequelae, all should be handled by an orthopedic surgeon, because injury of either the vascular supply to the cells or the cells themselves may result in permanent growth arrest with deformity. Twelve to thirteen years of age is the peak incidence for epiphyseal fracture. The distal radial epiphysis is the most commonly injured [13]. Epiphyseal-plate fractures are recognized on x-ray. The torus fracture or compressive fracture of the metaphysis appears as a bulge at the end of a long bone. Because of the proximity to joints, epiphyseal-plate fractures may be passed off as sprains. The key to proper recognition is that tenderness is maximal over the metaphysis, not within the joint or collateral ligaments. While rarely resulting in deformity, they do require external protection to prevent further injury.

Epiphyseal-plate injuries can also occur in the young athlete because the ligaments are stronger than the epiphyses. In joints where a ligament attaches to the epiphysis, injuries that would normally result in a ligamentous injury in the adult often result in epiphyseal fractures in the young athlete. The knee, ankle, and elbow are especially prone to this injury, and orthopedic evaluation is necessary.

Apophyseal Injury. The apophyseal centers are eminences, tubercles, or other protruberances on bones where major muscle tendons are inserted. They have separate areas of growth, and enlarge as the tendons increase in size. The growth occurs much the same as in the epiphyseal plate. Thus, they represent another area of weakness. The apophyses can become partially or completely separated from the bone when large-muscle forces are suddenly applied. In the adult hamstring muscle, ruptures occur with hyperflexion of the hip combined with an extended knee. In the skeletally immature young athlete, the ischial apophysis may be avulsed instead. Other apophyses that may incur a similar injury are in the pelvis, proximal femur, iliac crest, lesser trochanter, and greater trochanter. Apophyseal injury, if not recognized and not treated, may result in significant physical impairment [6, 7, 10].

Ligament and Tendon Injuries. Because the ligaments and tendons of a young athlete are more flexible than those of an adult, strains are less common. They do occur, however. In a young athlete, it is not uncommon to see microtears of a tendon with resulting hemorrhage, involving the patellar tendon where it attaches to either the inferior pole of the patella (Sinding-Larson syndrome) or to the tibial tubercle (Osgood-Schlatter's disease), or where the Achilles tendon attaches to the apophysis of the calcaneus (Sever's disease). Most of these syndromes respond to varying periods of rest.

4. Young athletes may have unrecognized congenital conditions that place them at increased risk for athletic injury. Defects such as unicameral bone cysts, fibrous dysplasia, and nonossifying fibromas, may occur during ossification, weakening the bone. Therefore, whenever a young athlete incurs a fracture with minimal trauma, the lesion should be suspected.

5. Young athletes often lack the motivation to work diligently to thoroughly condition their bodies for endurance, strength, and acclimatization to heat. Thus, the coach, trainer, or team physician must make sure that the young athlete is properly conditioned, not only to achieve maximal performance, but to sustain minimal risk of injury as well.

6. Young athletes are frequently indifferent about the fitting, adjustment, and care of their protective equipment. In contact and collision sports especially, protective equipment is designed to prevent injury. It will fail to function if not properly fitted and may directly cause injury. Since it is vital to their health and success, young athletes must be educated in proper equipment fitting, maintenance, and usage. Full equipment must always be worn in contact and collision sports, in practice or in a game. Any equipment used in practice should be mandatory in a game. If a knee pad or extra hip padding is used in a game, it must be used in practice. Coaches, trainers, and team physicians must constantly check that full protective equipment and any necessary special equipment is always worn during games and practice alike. Failure to do so will eventually lead to needless injury.

7. The young athlete frequently lacks the supervision and advice of a qualified athletic trainer. These duties are usually assumed by a coach or parent, or by a physician who may be available only by telephone. Many worrisome problems could be alleviated if certified athletic trainers were available to oversee the health of the young athlete.

Risk Factors

The primary factor in the incidence of injuries in young athletes is the inherent violence of the sport itself. The injury rate in football and wrestling is far greater than it is in tennis and swimming [3]. The American Academy of Pediatrics found injuries occurring in young athletes most often in football, wrestling, gymnastics, basketball, ice hockey, and lacrosse [2, 15]. However, surveys show that the incidence of injuries in unsupervised play activities such as bicycling, skateboarding, or skating, to be much higher than in supervised football or soccer [1,4,5]. Even football, the sport with the highest rate of injury, most serious injuries, fractures, knee injuries, and hospitalizations, is far safer per hour of exposure than riding in a car or in the school bus [15].

A second risk factor is the age, size, and maturity of the young athlete. As size and age increase, speed and violence of collision and contact is greater. The high-school athlete is at higher risk of injury for a given sport than the junior-high and grade-school athlete. While more boys are injured than girls as a result of the sports selected, sex is not a factor in injury rates for sports with equal participation. Furthermore, in the prepubertal age group, sex is not a factor in determining injury predisposition or even performance [14].

The risk of injury to specific body parts is highest for the head, fingers, knees, and ankles [15]. The low back is especially prone to injury in gymnastics. The risk of permanent injury is low, about 1% of all injuries, with the knee being the most vulnerable part of the body [15].

Injury Prevention

Avoidance of injury in young athletes starts with a comprehensive sports health examination. A sport's history must elucidate potential problems that might rule out the sport in question, while assessing the athlete's fitness and maturation level. All accidents, injuries, illnesses, or operations that may conceivably affect an athlete's performance in a given sport must be examined. Treatable conditions should be discovered, and a plan of treatment implemented. While a complete physical examination for each sport is not necessary, the sport's health history should be mandatory for each sport. Table 5–1 pro-

Table 5–1   Health-History Assessment Suggested for Sports Physical Examination

To be completed by parent or student before student participation in each competitive sport

I. Complete physical examination within the last two years _____
   date _____
   name of physician _____
   positive findings   none _____ yes _____
   if *yes*, list _____

	No	Yes
II. Do you have now or have you had		
1) loss of eye, lung, kidney, ovary, or testis	___	___
2) loss of vision or hearing	___	___
3) a seizure, convulsion, or epileptic attack	___	___
4) a suggestion that you have a brain wave test (EEG, electroencephalogram)	___	___
5) loss of consciousness	___	___
if *yes*, check one		
a. knocked out ___		
b. passed out, blacked out, fainted ___		
Were you hospitalized?		
6) a concussion	___	___
if *yes*,		
a. how many times? ___		
b. how long before complete recovery? ___		
c. how many games missed after concussion?		
7) a skull fracture	___	___
8) a spine fracture (neck or back)	___	___
9) an x-ray of neck or spine	___	___
10) an injury-producing weakness or numbness of arms or legs	___	___
11) a pinched nerve	___	___
12) heat exhaustion	___	___
13) diabetes, congenital heart disease, rheumatic heart disease, or other serious illness in the past year	___	___
14) are you currently taking any medicines or drugs?	___	___
if *yes*,		
a. What medication and dose _____		
b. Why? _____		

III. Since last examination have you had any injury to:

	none	yes
head	_____	_____
eyes	_____	_____
neck	_____	_____
chest	_____	_____
back	_____	_____
abdomen	_____	_____
arms, legs	_____	_____
kidneys	_____	_____
genitals	_____	_____

if *yes,* please have a physician complete this section of the form in regard to the injury.

nature of injury _____

any disability   none _____ yes _____

if yes, what _____

comment or recommendation   none _____ yes _____

if *yes,* what _____

date of examination _____

signature of physician _____

IV. Physical fitness test:

You must be able to successfully complete the following test before you can engage in any competitive sport.

	Boy		Girl	
1) mile (walk, run) in 8 min.			mile (walk, run) in 10 min.	
2) sit-ups				
age 10 to 12	35		age 10 and over	20
age 13 to 14	55			
age 15 and over	60			
3) 50-yard dash				
age 10 to 12	8.5 s		age 10 and over	9.0 s
age 13 to 15	7.6 s			
age 15 and over	7.0 s			

I agree to the above conditions in order to engage in _____

    Name of Sport

        Signature of Student _____

Upon completion of the above, I give permission for _____

to compete in _____ Signature of Parent _____

            Date _____

vides an example of a health-history form modified from the American Academy of Pediatrics. Barring injury or illness, the athlete's physical examination may be done annually by a primary-care physician or pediatrician, and supplemented with periodic health-history appraisals for each sport. Any injury or illness would, of course, require medical clearance with respect to that problem before resumption of participation.

A second major factor in injury prevention is education in the proper way to play the sport and wear the equipment. A recent study reported that nearly one-third of all sports injuries in the young are avoidable [15]. Young athletes must be taught the proper fitting, use, and maintenance of their equipment. They must realize that improperly fitted or used equipment can cause injury. Since most injuries occur in practice [11], full use of equipment is mandatory for practice.

The most glaring misuse of equipment is the use of a football helmet to spear or butt-block. Now declared illegal when detected, these practices were responsible for a rash of cervical-spine fracture dislocations and quadriplegias, especially in high-school football in the mid-1970s.

While recognizing that it is impossible to conduct all youth sports activities under optimal conditions, the Committee on Pediatric Aspects of Physical Fitness, Recreation, and Sports [2] has suggested that the following be implemented whenever possible:

1. Medical care should always be readily available. If not on-site, a physician or athletic trainer should be within close proximity.

2. Prior to the first practice session, preparation for the care of injuries should be planned and implemented. Medical and other emergency materials must be available.

3. The physician and/or athletic trainer must have sole authority to make decisions regarding management of medical care and return to play after injury.

4. Management of injuries must never be based on expediency, but on sound medical judgment and practice. Concessions must never be made.

5. While tradition normally excludes the physician from the playing field until summoned, this practice should not apply when young athletes are involved. If potentially permanent injuries are to be avoided, immediate care and prompt diagnosis are essential. Before the athlete is transported from the playing field, the physician should speak to the injured athlete and, if necessary, to other players and officials to learn how the injury was incurred.

Special Physical Considerations

The young student-athlete must be viewed differently than the professional whose livelihood depends on his or her performance. Certain conditions, therefore, must be considered to alter or exclude participation in a given sport. For example, the absence of a paired internal organ (i.e., kidney or testis) or one eye should eliminate participation in collision or contact sports (boxing, football, ice hockey, lacrosse, or rugby). This would not prevent participation in other noncontact noncollision sports such as baseball, golf, tennis, running, or swimming. For the young athlete with one eye, sports with a high liklihood of face injury (racquet sports) should be avoided, in addition to contact/collision sports.

Two grade-II concussions or one grade-III concussion should eliminate the return to competition during a season. The young athlete must be asymptomatic at maximal exertion before returning to competition after a concussion. Concussions are more fully discussed in chapter 9.

Following febrile illness (i.e., virus, otitis media, bronchitis, or sinusitis), it is recommended that the young athlete be afebrile for 48 hours before resuming strenuous athletic activity. With mononucleosis, the recovery will be much longer; no contact is to be allowed until the spleen has returned to normal size.

Disability under control is no contraindication for any sport. The same is true for the idiopathic seizure-disorder youth under good control—no seizures for over one year on medication. Most asthmatic persons, unless exercise induces an attack, can participate in all sports. Endurance sports are contraindicated in the severe exercise-induced-asthma athletes. By the age of ten, almost all congenital heart conditions that would preclude sports participation have been diagnosed. There are many young athletes who have heart murmurs without heart disease. It has been estimated that 30% to 50% of all children will at one time or another have a heart murmur [11]. Most of these innocent murmurs are of short duration, always systolic, and may be present or absent from time to time in the same child. While the pediatric cardiologist makes the final recommendation, there is no reason to restrict the athletic activity of a child with an innocent heart murmur.

Psychological Considerations for the Young Athlete

The psychological needs of young athletes are the same as for older athletes, but to a greater degree. Young people require positive input and approval at frequent intervals, and competitive athletes need even more. Yet, what we often find in organized youth sports programs are adults who act like children when children do not play like adults. Some adults, when given a whistle, baseball cap, and jersey with the word coach printed on it, forget that young athletes require frequent praise and need to be treated respectfully. Instead, these adults consider that because they are athletes themselves, discipline, criticism, and intimidation of their players are acceptable behavior. The young athlete criticized in public by his coach learns nothing of positive value.

From the work of Orlick [12], Martens [9], and the Michigan Youth Sports Study [8], one learns the primary negative reasons that young athletes quit a sport. They include:

1. *Not Getting to Play.* While it may seem harsh to cut a young athlete from a team, it is far more cruel to allow him to expend exhausting amounts of time and energy in practice and then not participate in games. Surveys have shown that young athletes value playing more than winning. More than 90% of the young athletes questioned said they would rather play on a losing team than ride the bench of a winning team.

2. *Mismatching.* The physical maturation of the young athlete, especially in the 10-to-16-year age range, varies widely. Two boys the same age may differ up to 60 months in skeletal age. When young athletes are significantly mismatched, the smaller, skeletally immature youth finds no enjoyment in constantly being defeated and physically abused by a much larger opponent.

3. *Negative Reinforcement.* While negative reinforcement and criticism may temporarily motivate young athletes to try harder, constant criticism over time discourages them. As with adults, the young athlete must learn new techniques and skills. This pro-

cess will occur at varying rates. No one wishes to be made to feel inadequate during this period, and all desire to have progress acknowledged. The coach, rather than pointing out what a young athlete is doing wrong, should instruct in the proper way to execute the activity.

4. *Overorganization.* Practices can become so over-regimented that the young athlete is deprived of the most powerful incentive for sport, *fun.* When a sport ceases to be fun, young athletes will likely turn their attention elsewhere.

5. *Psychological Stress.* High levels of stress can also eliminate fun from sports in young athletes. This is especially true when they perceive that more is being demanded of them, whether by parents, coaches, peers, or themselves, than is realistically attainable.

6. *Failure.* Constantly losing, especially when reminded of failures by coaches, parents, or peers, also eradicates fun from sports for the young athlete. We all wish to feel successful and worthy. Repeated failure creates anxiety, lessens motivation, and reduces performance and feelings of self-esteem.

While the psychological needs of the young athlete are not unique, each youngster is unique as a person. He or she varies in physical and psychological maturity, response to criticism, perception of what is stressful, and goals derived from sports. These differences play an important role in determining readiness for participation, degree of involvement, and enjoyment perceived from sport. Because of these variables, no specific best age can be given for all young athletes to begin sports competition. Some guidelines are available for youths who mature at a normal rate: 6 years of age for noncontact sports (swimming, tennis, track and field); 8 years of age for contact sports (basketball, soccer, and wrestling); 10 years of age for collision sports (ice hockey, lacrosse, and football) [4]. Perhaps the best indication of when a youth is ready to compete is when he or she, without adult influence, spontaneously expresses a desire to participate in a given sport. The initial intensity of competition should be low, increasing with skill and interest. If matched for size and maturity, most young athletes will find sports exhilarating, challenging, safe, and enjoyable.

By employing the information in this chapter in our medical practices and ongoing educational programs for coaches and parents, we can aid the young athlete in knowing the joy of sport and the benefits of a physically active life.

References

1. Chambers, R. B. Orthopedic injuries in athletes (ages 6 to 17). Comparison of injuries occurring in six sports. *Am. J. Sports Med.* 7:195–197, 1979.
2. Flynn, T. G., et al. Committee on pediatric aspects of physical fitness, recreation, and sports. Injuries to young athletes. *Physician Sportsmed.* 9:107–110, 1981.
3. Garrick, J. G. and Requa, R. K. Injuries in high school sports. *Pediatrics* 61:465–469, 1978.
4. Godshall, R. W. Junior league football: Risks vs. benefits. *Am. J. Sports Med.* 3:139–144, 1975.
5. Goldberg, B., Whitman, P. A., Gleim, G. W., et al. Children's sports injuries: Are they avoid-

able? *Physician Sportsmed.* 7:93–101, 1979.

6. Hamsa, W. R. Epiphyseal injuries about the hip joint. *Clin. Orthop.* 10:119–124, 1972.
7. Howard, F. M. and Phia, R. J. Fractures of the apophyses in adolescent athletes. *JAMA* 192:150–152, 1965.
8. Joint legislative study on youth sports programs. Lansing, Mich., 1978.
9. Martens, R. The uniqueness of the young athlete: Psychological considerations. *Am. J. Sports Med.* 8:382–385, 1980.
10. Milgram, J. E. Muscle ruptures and avulsions with particular reference to the lower extremities. *Am. Acad. Orthop. Surg. Inst. Course Lect.* 10:223–243, 1953.
11. Murray, J. J. Pediatric sportsmedicine. In P. Vinger and E. Hoerner (Eds.). *Sports Injuries, the Unthwarted Epidemic.* Littleton, Mass.: PSG, 1980.
12. Orlick, T. D. The athletic dropout—a high price for inefficiency. *CAHPER J.* 41:21–27, 1974.
13. Peterson, C. A. and Peterson, H. A. Analysis of the incidence of injuries to the epiphyseal growth plate. *J. Trauma* 12:275–281, 1972.
14. Wilkins, K. E. The uniqueness of the young athlete: Musculoskeletal injuries. *Am. J. Sports Med.* 8:377–385, 1980.
15. Zarieznyj, B., Shattuck, L. J. M., Mast, T. A., Robertson, R. V., and D'Elia, G. Sports related injuries in school-aged children. *Am. J. Sports Med.* 8:318–324, 1980.

Suggested Reading

Albinson, J. G. and Andrew, G. M. (Eds). *The Child in Sport and Physical Activity.* Baltimore: University Park Press, 1976.

Albohm, M. How injuries occur in girls' sports. *Physician Sportsmed.* 4:46–49, 1976.

Allman, F. L., Jr. Prevention and recognition of athletic injuries. *J. Med. Assoc. GA* 66:599–604, 1977.

AMA Committee on the Medical Aspects of Sports. The team physician. *J. Sch. Health* 37:497, 1967.

AMA Committee on the Medical Aspects of Sports. *Medical Evaluation of the Athlete.* Chicago: American Medical Association, 1977.

AMA Committee on the Medical Aspects of Sports. *Standard Nomenclature of Athletic Injuries.* Chicago: American Medical Association. 1966.

Blyth, C. S. and Mueller, F. O. *An Epidemiologic Study of High School Football Injuries in North Carolina—1968–1972.* Final Report. Washington, D. C.: U. S. Consumer Product Safety Commission, 1974.

Booker, J. Football Injuries in High School Athletes. Thesis. Salt Lake City: University of Utah, 1975.

Clark, D. M. Some medical aspects of precollege sports for boys. In American Medical Association. *Proceedings of Sixth National Conference on Medical Aspects of Sports, November 29, 1964.* Chicago: American Medical Association, 1965. Pp. 24–30.

Clarke, K. S. The national athletic injury/illness reporting system (NAIRS). In C. A. Morehouse (Ed). *Sports Safety II.* Proceedings of the Second National Sports Safety Conference. Washington, D. C.: The American Alliance for Health, Physical Education, and Recreation, 1977. Pp. 41–56.

Clarke, K. S. Calcualted risk of sports fatalities. *JAMA* 197:894–896, 1966.

Collins, H. R. and Evarts, C. M. Injuries to the adolescent athlete. *Postgrad. Med.* 49:72–78, 1971.

DeStefano, V. J. Athletic injuries. *J. Sch. Health* 47:234, 1977.

Fox, E. L. and Mathews, D. K. *Interval Training: Conditioning for Sports and Physical Fitness.* Philadelphia: W. B. Saunders, 1974.

AMA Committee on the Medical Aspects of Sports. *Fundamentals of Athletic Training.* Chicago: American Medical Association and the National Athletic Trainers Association, 1971.

AMA Committee on the Medical Aspects of Sports. *Fundamentals of Athletic Training.* Chicago: American Medical Association, 1975.

Gallagher, J. R., Heald, F. P., and Garell, D. C. *Medical Care of the Adolescent.* (3rd ed.) New York: Appleton-Century-Crofts, 1975.

Harata, I, Jr. *The Doctor and the Athlete.* (2nd ed.). Philadelphia: J. B. Lippincott, 1974.

Hincamp, J. F. High school athletic injuries. *Illinois Med. J.* 148:127, 1975.

Johnson, W. R. and Buskirk, E. R. (Eds.). *Science and Medicine of Exercise and Sports.* (2nd ed.). New York: Harper and Row, 1973.

Klafs, C. E. and Arnheim, D. D. *Modern Principles of Athletic Training: The Science of Sports Injury Prevention and Management.* (4th ed.). St. Louis: C. V. Mosby, 1977.

Mathews, D. K. and Fox, E. L. *Physiological Basis of Physical Education and Athletics.* (2nd ed.). Philadelphia: W. B. Saunders, 1976.

O'Donoghue, D. H. *Treatment of Injuries to Athletes.* Philadelphia: W. B. Saunders, 1976.

Robey, J. M., Blyth, C. S., and Mueller, F. O. Athletic injuries: Application of epidemiologic methods. *JAMA* 217:184–189, 1971.

Smith, N. J. *Food for Sport.* Palo Alto, Calif.: Bull Publishing Co., 1976.

Tanner, J. M. *Growth at Adolescence.* (2nd ed.). Philadelphia: J. B. Lippincott, 1962.

Zoller, G. W. Hazards in school sports. *Physician Sportsmed.* 1:69–71, 1973.

6 / Women and Sports

Roseanna Hemenway Means, M.D. and Arthur J. Siegel, M.D.

Within the relatively new field of sports medicine, little attention has been paid to the unique problems of women athletes. Mandatory inclusion in all sports from the Title IX legislation of 1974 has seen a doubling in the number of women athletes participating in structured athletic programs at the high-school and college levels. An historic obstacle has been the traditional belief that women are too fragile and physically incapable of handling the physical demands of prolonged strenuous exercise. Once excluded from the Olympic Games entirely, women have won the right to participate in certain events, such as the marathon, for the first time in the forthcoming competitions of 1984. World records for women in track and field clearly establish similar patterns of improvement as those for men. The ability of women to approach men's records, as in the marathon, clearly establishes the physiologic capacities of women to undertake such demanding events.

Figures from the President's Council on Fitness and Sport indicate that up to 15 million women in the United States engage in regular physical exercise, ranging from keep-fit activities to serious professional participation. Women athletes differ from men in anatomy and physiology, with particular respect to endocrine-reproductive function. This creates a unique set of considerations for the primary-care physician treating the woman athlete in office practice.

This chapter covers three major areas relative to treating the female athlete: (1) special medical considerations, as in heat-stress susceptibility and risk of iron deficiency, (2) musculoskeletal injury susceptibility, and (3) effects of exercise on menstrual and reproductive function.

Medical Considerations

Statistically, women differ from men in body composition. Women in general have less muscle mass than men, muscle comprising roughly 23% of total body weight compared to 40% in men. Women tend to have more body fat, 22% to 25% of ideal body weight, compared to 14% to 18% in men. Some exercise physiologists have speculated that this edge in percent of body fat might mean that women have a greater capacity for endurance training and performance.

Difference in body composition notwithstanding, all evidence points to identical patterns of physiologic adaptation for endurance training in women and men with respect to cardiovascular and musculoskeletal responses. Women athletes are as capable of achieving progressive increases in VO_2 max. as men, although muscular changes with progressive training in elite women athletes have been less well studied than in men.

Adaptation of the athlete to environmental stresses, such as heat, cold, or altitude, depends on specific physiologic responses, which may be different in women. The capacity to dissipate body heat generated during prolonged strenuous exercise depends on internal and environmental factors. The capacity for heat acclimatization, as judged by changes in sweat rate in acclimatized men versus women, shows similar patterns. After acclimatization, women's heart rates and rectal temperatures in hot and humid conditions at rest and after activity are the same as those of men [20]. Lower sweat rates in women are required to maintain comparable body temperatures, suggesting an improved efficiency in heat-released mechanisms. An increased risk for heat exhaustion might be hypothesized in women during the second half of the menstrual cycle from elevations in basal body temperature due to progesterone effects. Wells studied the heat responses of women at different stages in their menstrual cycles in hot-dry and neutral environments. There was no difference in sweat rates or evaporative heat loss in a variety of conditions for these different physiologic stages [19].

Drinkwater studied heat adaptation in women marathon runners and showed a relationship between physical fitness as measured by VO_2 max. and resistance to heat injury [4]. Women runners with higher VO_2 max. (49 mL/kg/min vs. 39 mL/kg/min) had lower heart rates, lower skin and rectal temperatures, and quicker onset of sweating compared to less-conditioned individuals. These findings are similar to patterns in men, and confirm a resistance to heat-stress injury from physical conditioning. A high level of physical fitness, however, does not protect an athlete from heat exhaustion or potentially fatal heat stroke, which may accompany overexertion in a given level of training. Considerations for women are almost identical to those in men for heat-intolerance susceptibility. Similar studies in women during cold exposure and physiologic adaptation at altitudes show similar patterns as in men under the same environmental stresses.

In summary, women are as equally susceptible to environmental stress as men during prolonged exercise, but equally capable of physiologic adaptation. Acclimatization to hot weather is facilitated by underlying fitness capacity, but still requires seven to ten days for optimal adaptation. Competitive athletes and recreational runners alike, men or women, must respect the limitations of internal (adaptive) and external (climatic) stresses. Copious consumption of fluids, especially water, during prolonged exercise is the best preventive medicine. Guidelines for prevention of heat injury as outlined by the American College of Sports Medicine should be considered, whether racing or out for a recreational jog [17].

Hematologic Effects of Exercise in Women: Iron Status and Anemia

Obligatory iron loss through menstruation creates a potential risk for iron depletion and, if mild or subclinical, secondary anemia. Studies in apparently normal, healthy young women of college age document the depletion of total body iron stores—by examination of stained bone-marrow aspirates—in up to 25% of subjects [14]. Rates of iron deficiency among apparently healthy college athletes may be somewhat higher, as reported in one blood study [12].

Confusion is likely to rise between true iron-deficiency anemia and the so-called pseudoanemia of endurance training. Systematic observations have documented a drop in hemoglobin, hematocrit, and red-blood-cell count with onset of a nine-week training program in previously sedentary college women [13]. Values may fall to low-normal or within abnormal ranges during progressive training, with a return to baseline upon resumption of sedentary status. Such effects also occur in men athletes and constitute a hemodilution due to increased plasma volume. Studies of red cell mass in athletic pseudoanemia show normal or high values with low hemoglobin parameters from an expanded plasma volume. Specific measurement of body iron stores, or its reflection in normal values for serum iron and iron-binding capacity or ferritin levels, establishes this dilutional cause of a low hemoglobin concentration.

The diagnosis of true iron-deficiency anemia in men or women requires specific measurement of serum iron and iron-binding capacity, or serum ferritin. Low values for serum iron with a reciprocally increased serum iron-binding capacity or a low serum ferritin indicate depletion of total body iron stores and the need for specific supplementation. Studies indicate that iron supplementation in nondeficient athletes yields no benefit [1], while treatment of iron deficiency is clearly beneficial. Iron supplementation should consist of 300 mg ferrous sulphate, given twice daily for approximately six months. Remeasurement of the serum iron and iron-binding capacity should be undertaken to establish a ratio greater than 20% to 25%. Insufficient supplementation for too brief a time may result in incomplete response to treatment. Women athletes are at risk for developing iron-deficiency anemia. Low hemoglobin values should be investigated with measurement of serum iron and total iron-binding capacity. A ratio of less than 15% is diagnostic of iron deficiency, whereas 15% to 20% saturation is borderline. Iron supplementation is advisable in both ranges. Treatment should be twice daily for a minimum of six months with subsequent testing to ensure an adequate clinical response.

Cardiovascular Risk

While the incidence of coronary heart disease is low in women compared to men, diseases of the circulatory system account for roughly two-thirds of all deaths among women in the United States. The incidence of mild myocardial infarction or death from coronary heart disease in premenopausal women is below 1 in 10,000 per year. A large number of cardiovascular deaths occur in women after age 75, but cardiovascular deaths also account for one-third of all deaths from age 65 to 74. Death rates from cardiovascular disease in women are 40% lower than in men for persons between 35 and 64 years of age, and relative mortality for women falls to 25% of male levels for ages 35 to 44[7].

Nevertheless, cardiovascular disease rates may be on the increase in women, perhaps related to increased rates of smoking. Risk factors for coronary heart disease in women include the standard triad of hypertension, hypercholesterolemia, and cigarette smoking, as well as a possible influence from oral-contraceptive use. Rates for coronary heart disease in women under 45 years of age have not increased in the United States despite oral-contraceptive use corrected for cigarette smoking. Framingham data from other studies indicate an increase in coronary disease in postmenopausal women, with a risk profile similar to that observed in men. Regular exercise produces a beneficial effect on such a risk profile, including changes in lipids and body composition. Advice to women to exercise and give up smoking may be mutually reinforcing and beneficial.

Musculoskeletal Injury Susceptibility

Musculoskeletal injuries are a common complication of sports participation, not only in high-impact activities, but also in jogging. Injury rates from jogging are estimated at up to 54% in men and women, as measured by symptoms severe enough to require at least temporary discontinuation [5]. These rates are positively related to increased intensity, frequency, and duration of exercise. Increased body weight may be an additional predisposing factor for injury, although leaner athletes tend to exercise more intensively, which enhances their susceptibility to injury.

Women are vulnerable to the same musculoskeletal problems that occur in men but may carry a predilection for certain injuries based on the female anatomy as well. The wider pelvis may, in fact, place extra stress on the knees, resulting in a propensity to increased patellar syndromes (figure 6–1) [9]. Extra caution is necessary during the initial weeks of a training program, at which time the athlete is at highest risk. Flexibility and muscle-strengthening exercises, as well as warm-up calisthenics, may ease the musculoskeletal stress during this high-risk period. Instruction in proper running mechanics and initial light-to-moderate exercise intensity help to avoid overuse syndromes. Lowered training frequency (less than three sessions per weekend), and a shorter duration of workouts (less than 30 minutes per session) may protect against injury and subsequent drop out from training. Proper equipment such as appropriate footwear, avoidance of unidirectional running on hard or uneven surfaces, and attention to external training factors may favorably influence injury rates. Prevention is always easier than cure.

The treatment of musculoskeletal injury in women is similar to that in men. The intensity of symptoms is usually a guide to the need for workup, including a search for tendon disruption and/or stress fractures. After evaluation, recommendations might range from complete rest to selective training with a cycle ergometer to maintain cardiovascular fitness during musculoskeletal repair. Physical therapy, such as ultrasound treatments or whirlpool, and anti-inflammatory medication may be useful for nonsurgically treated cases or after surgical intervention. Stretching exercises and a slow return to training are resumed as symptoms and resolution of injury permit. Modification of equipment, such as orthotic appliances, may be useful, particularly for overcompensatory foot prona-

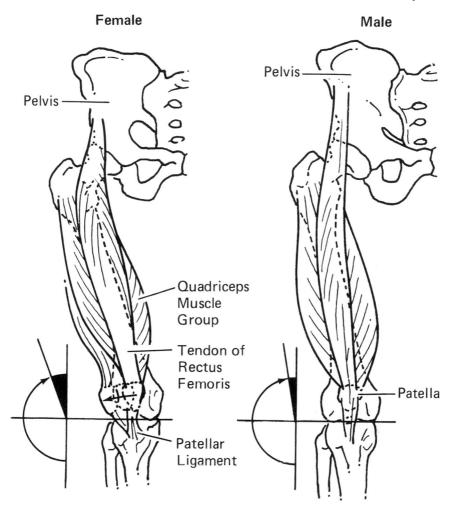

Figure 6–1   Why runner's knee is more prevalent in women. Because of their wider pelvis, women have a more-acute angle between the axis of the patellar ligament and the quadriceps mechanism, and the contraction of the quadriceps tends to pull the patella laterally (arrow). As a result, women have an increased incidence of lateral displacement of the patella, which can result in chondromalasia (runner's knee). Adapted from Haycock, C.E. Sports-related problems in women. *Consultant,* July 1981, page 243.

tion leading to recurrent knee symptoms. Orthotics can redistribute body weight during foot plant into a more neutral and injury-free position.

Given the diversity of sports activities, few generalities can be made regarding specific injuries. Table 6–1 summarizes the findings of several studies comparing injury rates in men and women athletes.

Women seem to suffer more sprains and strains than any other injury. Sprains and

Table 6–1   Common Athletic Injuries According to Sex

Women	*Men*
Tibial stress syndrome (runners)	Achilles peritendinitis (runners)
Lower-extremity injuries (cross-country skiers)	Patellofemoral pain syndrome (runners)
Recurrent patellar subluxation	Knee injuries in general (runners)
Tibial and femoral stress fractures and overuse injuries (all sports)	Overexertion injuries in fit middle-aged men (all sports)
Stress-related injuries such as sprains, strains, and heat illness (all sports)	Iliotibial friction band syndrome

strains account for one-third of the injuries to field hockey players, one-quarter of the injuries to gymnasts, and 42.5% of the injuries reported in nine varsity intercollegiate sports. Basketball, gymnastics, volleyball, and field hockey account for the majority of college sports injuries in women. Studies of injury rates during running are relatively new, with the current popularity of the sport and the growth of collegiate women's cross-country teams. Contrary to a long-held belief, injuries to the breast are the least-common injury in women's sports.

Anatomic and physiologic differences between men and women explain the different patterns of injury. Women are less muscular and have more body fat; they have less experience in athletics before participation in strenuous exercise; they have valgus knees; they lack preseason conditioning; and they have greater mobility (more-elastic connective tissue, smaller tendons, and less hindering—and stabilizing—muscle mass).

Recommendations for reducing injury rates in college athletes include preseason conditioning, the presence of coaches and trainers educated in sports injuries, and development of protective devices. Women should be encouraged to have a complete physical examination before participating in a sport, noting evidence of old injury, weakened muscle groups, and degree of fitness for the intended sport. It is also important that equipment manufacturers design their products for the anatomic and physiologic differences between men and women. Use of protective devices has decreased the rate of injury in sports, but has also caused new injuries to occur because of lack of specifically adaptive designs.

As a final point of clarification, many women's magazines are concerned with the development of cutaneous laxity on the face or breasts as a consequence of regular sports participation. There is no evidence that regular exercise is damaging to subcutaneous connective tissue or that premature wrinkling will be a delayed consequence of an active lifestyle. In fact, much anecdotal evidence from woman athletes points to the contrary!

Summary

Ample evidence exists that women can undergo the stress of endurance training as well as power or weight training with an injury susceptibility profile similar to that of men.

Women undertaking strength training in competitive track and field events such as discus or shot put may develop strength increases equal to that of men without disproportionate increases in muscle size. Studies in master women distance runners with a mean age of 43.8 years show that regular running can maintain a VO_2 max. substantially higher (by more than 25%) than age-matched, sedentary normal women.

The mean body fat in ten master women long-distance runners was 18.3%, which is approximately 40% of the value for a control group of age-matched sedentary women [18]. The benefits of such body composition characteristics related to cardiovascular risk are persuasive.

Effects of Exercise on the Menstrual Cycle

The women's sports movement has focused special attention on the relationship between sports activity and endocrine-reproductive function. The literature is full of apparent contradictory data, as the variable influences of physical training, nutrition, and stress of competition are difficult to separate. In addition, there is a need to separate out complex questions such as the relationship of physical activity to delay in onset of puberty, its effect on menstrual periodicity, and the subsequent influence of such activity on future fertility.

The impact of female hormones is perhaps nowhere more dramatically illustrated than in the different performances of gold-medal gymnast Nadia Comaneci in the 1976 Olympics at Montreal and in the World Individual Gymnastics Championships in 1979. A difference of four inches in height and 20 pounds in weight converted the fast, streamlined, prepubertal adolescent into a more powerful performer with an altered repertoire of skills. The impact of such hormonal change at menarche on body habitus and physical capacity are clearer than the impact of sport on ovulation and fertility potential. While women as athletes may welcome reduced frequency of menses as a convenience during training and competition, large studies of female athletes are necessary to answer questions on these basic underlying relationships.

Exercise and Puberty:

In 1974, Frisch and McArthur proposed that a critical weight to height ratio was necessary to initiate or sustain menses [6]. They proposed that a critical level of percent body fat was necessary for neuroendocrine activation of the ovulatory cycle. Multiple studies have shown that menarche coincides with a body-fat content of 17% to 20% of total body weight. Observations based on voluntary weight loss among normal, healthy women, as well as in athletes in a variety of sports, point to the validity of this concept [15,16]. Whether intense physical training to suppress the acquisition of adipose tissue can, in fact, produce a delay in menarche has also been studied. A 9-month delay of puberty below the national average of 12.8 years was found in 400 female swimmers. A two-year study is underway to compare training intensity with age at menarche, using a high-intensity and medium-intensity training group and age-matched but sedentary controls.

Body-fat composition and time of puberty can be compared to determine the importance of body-fat percentages on age of menarche. The impact of apparent delay in puberty from physical training has an undetermined effect on body weight as long bones continue to grow through the completion of menarche. It is possible that delay in puberty through physical training might result in incremental height as a secondary effect. Data on body composition with precise height and weight measurements in a sufficient sample size will establish if delay of puberty causes alteration of body habitus.

Once menarche has occurred, many questions remain about the influence of training intensity and body composition on temporary cessation of menses and future reproductive potential. Exercise, nutrition, and physical and psychological stress can affect the hypothalamic-pituitary-gonadal axis. Multiple forces may exist as athletic training, peer pressure, food aversion, and academic stress influence rates of weight loss in committed young athletes.

Distance runners have, perhaps, been the most systematically studied in terms of the relationship of body composition to endocrine-hormonal fluctuations. Dale and Wilhite studied gonadotrophin levels in lean (less than 17% body fat) amenorrheic runners and found that gonadotrophins were in the low-normal range, without cyclic variation [2]. Estrogen levels in such anovulatory women are generally low compared to sedentary, ovulatory control subjects. This profile resembles the hypothalamic-induced hypogonadotrophism seen with rapid weight loss or in anorectic illness. Recent studies show that nonathletic women may experience interruption of their menstrual cycles with a weight loss of 10% to 15% of total body weight, which corresponds to roughly one-third of total body-fat stores. The ratio of lean body weight to total fat stores may be a crucial factor in the cessation of cycles.

Middle-distance women runners may experience interruption of menses during vigorous training because of a change in body composition, even in the absence of substantial absolute weight loss. Frisch and McArthur are currently investigating college-age women endurance athletes to correlate medical and reproductive histories with anthropomorphic measurements through training cycles. Diaries of nutritional intake, energy expenditure in training, and menstrual activity will help to clarify these relationships [20].

A spectrum may in fact exist from mild to more-marked suppression of pituitary-ovarian function with increasing doses of exercise. Mild alteration in body composition may interfere with precise midcycle gonadotrophin release and result in anovulatory cycles. Irregular menstrual flow may persist in this situation. The next level of interference would be marked by sustained gonadotrophin suppression with lower levels of circulating estrogen from a reduced degree of gonadal stimulation. Oligomenorrhea may result, but withdrawal bleeding would still occur after administration of exogenous progestins such as Provera. More profound or prolonged pituitary suppression would lead to peripheral estrogen depletion and insufficiently primed endometrium to produce withdrawal bleeding after progestational agents. Pituitary gonadotrophin-releasing factors would still result in elevations of serum LH and FSH, which would establish normal pituitary function.

The management of secondary amenorrhea should include a differential diagnosis, avoiding unnecessary testing in the presence of a sports-related explanation for reduced menstruation [11].

Interest has also focused on the relationship between menstruation and competitive performance in women athletes. Gynecologic surveys generally report reduced levels of premenstrual tension and dismenorrhea among active women compared to nonathletic counterparts. In addition to reduced menstrual difficulties, active women appear at a reduced risk for unusual menstrual conditions such as toxic-shock syndrome.

Gynecologic surveys performed among elite women athletes after the Montreal Olympic Games show that gold medalists performed during all phases of the menstrual cycle, indicating that menstruation does not preclude world-class performance.

Athletics and Fertility

Previous discussion has established that changes in body composition and fatness may delay menarche and result in reduced menstruation or secondary amenorrhea in subsequent years. The relationships of these effects to subsequent fertility or reproductive capacity are uncertain and under current investigation. Ongoing studies document the safety of endurance and strenuous sports for women during established pregnancy. Observation during physical training in pregnancy shows that women are capable of sustaining endurance capacity with regular exercise through even the third trimester. Careful documentation of fetal heart rates indicates no adverse effect on the placental circulation from such exercise [3]. There is concern that exercise during pregnancy can cause a placental-steal syndrome, where a shunting of blood might occur from the placental-fetal circulation to exercising muscle. Recent reports from Ruhling indicate, however, that conditioned regular exercise is safe pending more extensive prospective observations [10]. Investigations into labor and delivery likewise show that running in the advanced stages of pregnancy is complication-free and that "double-runners" may participate in competitive races without hazard [8] The current data indicate that healthy women athletes may continue to enjoy their sports participation during pregnancy [10]. Some caution has been expressed for potentially hazardous sports such as scuba diving where accidental hypoxemia may carry a risk to both fetus and mother. Medical complications of pregnancy should be treated in the customary obstetric fashion, and specific complications such as placenta previa and preclampsia would modify exercise recommendations.

References

1. Cooter, G. R. and Mowbray, K. W. Effects of iron supplementation and activity on serum iron depletion and hemoglobin levels in female athletes. *Res.Q.* 49:114, 1978.
2. Dale, G. and Wilhite, A. Menstrual dysfunction in distance runners. *Obstet. Gynecol.* 54:47, 1979.
3. Dressendorfer, R. H. and Goodlin, R. C. Fetal heart rate response to maternal exercise testing. *Physician Sportsmed.* 8(11):90, 1980.
4. Drinkwater, B. L., Kupprat, I. C., Denton, J. E., and Horvath, S. M. Heat tolerance of female distance runners. *Ann. N. Y. Acad. Sci.* 301:777, 1977.
5. Franklin, B. A., Lussier, L., and Buskirk, E. R. Injury rates in women joggers. *Physician Sportsmed.* 7(3):105, 1979.

6. Frisch, R. and McArthur, J. W. Menstrual cycles: Fatness as a determinant of minimum weight for height necessary for their maintenance or onset. *Science* 185:949, 1974.
7. Gordon, T. Cardiovascular risk factors in women. *Practical Cardiology* 5(7):137, 1979.
8. Hage, P. Exercise and pregnancy compatible, MD says. *Physician Sportsmed* 9(5):22, 1981.
9. Haycock, C. E. Sports-related problems of women. *Consultant,* July, 1981.
10. Korcok, M. Pregnant jogger: What a record! *JAMA* 246(3), 1981.
11. McArthur, J. W., Bullen, B. A., Beitins, I. Z., Pagano, M., Badger, T. M., and Klibanski, A. Hypothalamic amenorrhea in runners of normal body composition. *Endocr. Res. Commun.* 7(1):13, 1980.
12. Pate, R. R., Maguire, M., and Van Wyk, J. Dietary iron supplementation in women athletes. *Physician Sportsmed,* 7(9):81, 1979.
13. Puhl, J. L. and Runyan, W. S. Hematological variations during aerobic training of college women. *Res. Q.* 51(3):533, 1980.
14. Scott, D. E. and Pritchard, J. A. Iron deficiency in healthy young college women. *JAMA* 199(12):147, 1967.
15. Shangold, M. Sports and menstrual function. *Physician Sportsmed,* 8(8):66, 1980.
16. Shangold, M., Freeman, R., Thysen, B., and Gatz, M. The relationship between long-distance running, plasma progesterone and luteal phase length. *Fertil. Steril.* 31(2):130, 1979.
17. Statement of the American College of Sports Medicine. Prevention of heat injuries during distance running. *J. Sports. Med.* 16:345, 1976.
18. Vaccaro, P., Morris, A. F., and Clarke, D. H. Physiological characteristics of master female distance runners. *Physician Sportsmed,* 9(7):105, 1981.
19. Wells, C. L. Sexual differences in heat stress response. *Physician Sportsmed,* 5(9):78, 1977.
20. Wyndham, C. H., Morrison, J. F., and Williams, C. G. Heat reactions of male and female caucasians. *J. Appl. Physiol.* 20:357, 1965.

Suggested Reading

Bolton, M. G. Scuba diving and fetal well-being: A survey of 208 women. *Undersea. Biomed. Res.* 7(3):183, 1980.

Clement, D. B., Taunton, J. E., Smart, G. W., and McNicol, K. L. A survey of overuse running injuries. *Physician Sportsmed.* 9(5):47, 1981.

Cox, J. S. and Lenz, H. W. Women in sports—the Naval Academy experience. *Am. J. Sports Med.* 7(6):355, 1979.

Dill, D. B., Soholt, L. F., McLean, D. C., Drost, T. F., and Loughran, M. T. Capacity of young males and females for running in desert heat. *Med. Sci. Sports* 9(3):137, 1977.

Double runners. *The Boston Globe.* 9 May 1981. P.6.

Dressendorfer, R. H. Physical training during pregnancy and lactation. *Physician Sportsmed.* 6(2):74, 1978.

Dunn, Kathleen. Toxic shock victims had less exercise, study says. *Physician Sportsmed,* 9(6):21, 1981.

Frisch, R., Wyshak, G., and Vincent, L. Delayed menarche and amenorrhea in ballet dancers. *N. Engl. J. Med.* 303(1):17, 1980.

Gillette, J. When and where women are injured in sports. *Physician Sportsmed.* 3(5):61, 1975.

Graham, G. P., and Bruce, P. J. Survey of intercollegiate athletic injuries to women. *Res.Q.* 48(1):217, 1977.

Graham, R. L., Grimes, D. L., and Gambrell, R. D. Amenorrhea secondary to voluntary weight loss. *South. Med. J.* 72(10):1259, 1979.

Gunby, P. What does exercise mean for the menstrual cycle? *JAMA* 243(17):1699, 1980.

Haycock, C. E. The female athlete—Past and present. *JAMA* 31(9):350, 1976.

Haycock, C. E. and Gillette, J. V. Susceptibility of women athletes to injury. *JAMA* 236(2):163, 1976.

Kowal, D. M. Nature and causes of injuries in women resulting from an endurance training program. *Am. J. Sports Med.* 8(4):265, 1980.

Malina, R. M., Spirduso, W. W., Tate, C., and Baylor, A. M. Age at menarche and selected menstrual characteristics in athletes at different competitive levels and in different sports. *Med. Sci. Sports* 10(3):218, 1978.

Noakes, T. D. National Conference of Sports Medicine, Johannesburg, October 22–25, 1977. *S. Afr. Med. J.* 53(18):723, 1978.

Orava, S. Iliotibial tract friction syndrome in athletes—an uncommon exertion syndrome on the lateral side of the knee. *Br. J. Sports Med.* 12(2):69, 1978A.

Orava, S. Overexertion injuries in keep-fit athletes. *Scand. J. Rehabil. Med.* 10:187, 1978B.

O'Shea, J. P., and Wegner, J. Power weight training and the female athlete. *Physician Sportsmed.* 9(6):109, 1981.

Pate, R. R., Maguire, M., and Van Wyk, J. Dietary iron supplementation in women athletes. *Physician Sportsmed.* 7(9), 1979.

Powers, J. A. Characteristic features of injuries in the knee in women. *Clin. Orthop. Rel. Res.* (143):120, 1979.

Ritter, M. A., Gioe, T. J., and Albohm, M. Sport-related injuries in women. *J. Am. Coll. Health Assoc.* 28(5):267, 1980.

Rose, C. P. Injuries in women's field hockey: A four-year study. *Physician Sportsmed,* 9(3):97, 1981.

Smith, N. J. Academic and sports pressures may cause excessive weight loss. *Physician Sportsmed,* 9(5):17, 1981.

Snook, G. A. Injuries in women's gymnastics. *Am. J. Sports Med.* 7(4):242, 1979.

Ullyot, J. *Women's Running.* Calif., World Publications Mountain View, 1976.

Webb, J. L., Millan, D. L., and Stolz, C. J. Gynecological survey of American female athletes competing at the Montreal Olympic Games. *J. Sports Med.* 19:405, 1979.

Zaharieva, E. Survey of sportswomen at the Tokyo Olympics. *J. Sports Med. Phys. Fitness* 5:215, 1965.

7/Medical Conditions Arising During Sport

Arthur J. Siegel, M.D.

A colleague recently related the following case:

> A cachectic middle-aged man was found unresponsive with a blood pressure of 80/
> 40, a pulse rate of 36 beats per minute, and a respiratory rate of 8. Lung fields
> were clear. The heart was enlarged with an anterior systolic lift, a panapical
> systolic murmur, and an S–3 gallop. Neck veins were flat, and there was no edema.
> Laboratory data included a hematocrit value of 34%, a urinalysis positive for
> protein, and hemoglobin with hyaline casts in the sediment. The creatinine level
> was at the upper limits of normal with elevations of serum LDH, SGOT, and CPK
> up to three times normal. Chest x-ray showed cardiomegaly without congestive
> heart failure. The EKG showed a first degree AV block with voltage criteria for
> LVH and anterior ST segment changes consistent with early repolarization or
> ischemia [13].

This case might lead to an exciting differential diagnosis from acute nephritis to
bacterial endocarditis or even Reye's syndrome. The correct diagnosis is, however, a
sleeping marathon runner! This not-so-exaggerated case illustrates the number of so-
called abnormalities that may arise both on physical examination and in laboratory
screening tests in endurance athletes. The primary-care physician must bring a knowledge of the variants in normal findings, both clinically and in the laboratory, to the evaluation of athletes when seen as patients. A number of pseudosyndromes have been
recognized, from the athletic heart to a pseudonephritis and pseudoanemia in athletes.
These are examples of abnormal laboratory findings without evidence of underlying organ
malfunction.

Such pseudosyndromes must be differentiated from a range of medical complications
that may arise during strenuous prolonged exercise, especially to exhaustion. A major
example is acute renal failure, rarely seen in marathon runners after competition [51].
Abnormalities in the urinary sediment are characteristic of the volume depletion accom-

panying such activities, while prolonged untreated volume depletion in association with other metabolic stress may lead to renal tubular injury. The physician who is aware of the potential risks of dehydration can be ready to respond to such situations with appropriate treatment. Exercise-induced anaphylaxis is another example of a potentially life-threatening condition that may arise specifically related to exercise, and which may be successfully treated with specific therapy [47]. This chapter will look at the various apparent and real conditions seen in trained athletes and, increasingly, among recreational athletes as well.

Cardiovascular Considerations

It has long been appreciated that endurance training can lead to changes in virtually every measurable cardiovascular parameter. Electrocardiographic changes include a variety of rhythm and conduction disturbances, as well as depolarization changes characteristic, in other clinical settings, of various diseases [9]. The heart as studied by echocardiography shows changes in both chamber size and myocardial mass, which vary with type of training [40]. Endurance-trained athletes tend to have dilated chambers, with a minor degree of increase in left-ventricular-wall thickness resembling the volume-overload pattern seen in valvular regurgitation. In contrast, isometric or strength training induces a greater increase in wall thickness and total myocardial mass without chamber dilation, after the pattern seen in valvular aortic stenosis. Work hypertrophy, as documented by these studies, is associated with supernormal left-ventricular performance during exercise, and like the arrhythmias which may coexist it is usually benign in nature. It is generally felt that asymptomatic athletes with documented myocardial hypertrophy and abnormal electrocardiograms do not require provocative or invasive cardiovascular testing prior to training or competition. In the absence of chest pain or syncope, bradyarrhythmias, or even low grades of heart block and ventricular irritability, need not be pursued as they would in symptomatic patients with suspected heart conditions.

The sole caveat is the rare occurrence of sudden cardiac death in young athletes during sport. Recent intensive medical examinations have documented that hidden cardiac disorders often underlie such events. Maron and coworkers at the National Heart, Lung, and Blood Institute have studied hearts from athletes ranging in age from 14 to 30 years and documented cardiovascular abnormalities possibly responsible for sudden death in 20 of 23 cases [31]. Hypertrophic cardiomyopathy was present in 14 cases, where sudden decrements in cardiac output associated with volume depletion and perhaps arrhythmias might have been responsible for cardiovascular collapse. Standard-screening physical examinations given to prospective athletes would not be sufficient to detect these disorders, and such features might, in fact, be relatively common were extensive testing to be undertaken. Current costs would be approximately $150 to evaluate each athlete. A recent symposium by the American Heart Association on the cardiovascular risks of sport concluded that health screening of prospective athletes should include a search for a family history of sudden death and a personal history of syncope [2]. A physical examination should screen for blood pressure and unusual murmurs that might indicate the need for specific testing. Abnormalities on echocardiography suggestive of asymmetric hypertrophic cardiomyopathy might contraindicate strenuous competitive sports participation, if associated either with symptoms or with a family history of sudden or premature death.

The cardiovascular conditions seen in sudden death in young athletes differ from the predominant findings of coronary heart disease in exercise-related sudden death in patients over 40 years of age. Studies of cardiovascular deaths while running show that while coronary heart disease is the predominant underlying cause, extensive pretesting with stress electrocardiography would be unlikely to identify potential victims of such events [53]. Studies by Waller and Roberts document extensive coronary atherosclerosis in victims of sudden cardiac death, even in long-distance runners, showing that such activity does not guarantee against development or progression of significant coronary disease [54]. Emphasis has been placed on the potential value of exercise testing to screen for potential complications and to clear asymptomatic individuals for strenuous exercise programs. Such studies show that while exercise testing is a predictor of heart-disease risk and sudden death in some populations, its value as a screening clearance for individuals is suspect [7]. A reasonable strategy is to advise progressive incremental exercise for the asymptomatic low-risk individual, including men in their mid-40s, without electrocardiography or other screening tests. [21].

A rationale for exercise testing may, however, apply to exercise clearance for individuals at high risk of underlying coronary heart disease. This would include especially men with a family history of heart disease, or a personal history of hypertension, hypercholesterolemia, or cigarette smoking. These risk factors create a prior risk for underlying coronary disease and increase the likelihood that stress electrocardiography will test for the possibility of clinically significant, but silent, coronary obstruction. Such high-risk individuals may undergo symptom-limited maximal exercise testing with great safety [35].

An extensive amount of literature exists on the value of exercise training for patients with established coronary heart disease including angina pectoris or prior myocardial infarction. Reviews by Wenger conclude that exercise rehabilitation is a valuable adjunct to restoring a patient to an active and full life-style [55]. Exercise testing soon after uncomplicated myocardial infarction may assist in prescribing exercise levels that are safe and can be used as a guideline for specific exercise rehabilitation [10]. This can help patients return to their previous levels of functioning, including employment, recreation, and restoration of sexual activity [1].

An active life-style, including moderate amounts of dynamic exercise, has been shown to promote cardiovascular fitness and to be associated with a reduced profile for development of coronary heart disease [10]. Discussion of how much exercise is enough to realize such benefits indicates that regular, sustained, repetitive activity for 20 to 30 minutes three to four times a week is sufficient for maintaining fitness [39]. Extreme degrees of physical exertion, such as in long-distance running and marathon competition, may carry risks for the heart without evidence of additional protective benefit [36]. A life-style with a balanced approach to exercise, diet, and even alcohol should be the goal when advising and counseling patients on exercise patterns that may facilitate and preserve health. Debate continues in scientific circles on the exercise-heart and diet-heart hypotheses, which means that correlations of diet and exercise patterns on alteration of risk are still under dissection in the epidemiologist's microscope. Prudent recommendations to patients, however, may be made on the strength of available evidence and its translation into sensible guidelines.

Environmental Hazards of Sport

Heat, cold, and altitude present special problems in the maintenance of body homeostasis during exercise. These problems apply to the well-conditioned athlete and novice alike. A clinical spectrum exists in heat injury, from heat exhaustion with rectal temperatures of less than 40°C to heat stroke with body temperatures above 41°C and potentially fatal outcome. Physicians who are involved in warm-weather road races should be familiar with the clinical syndromes of heat injury and develop a plan for identification and immediate management. As the best medicine is prevention, the physician must play a leading role in educating runners to maintain adequate hydration and monitor level of effort, avoiding what is, no doubt, the runner's worst enemy. Heat injury, in fact, involves climatic variables such as ambient temperature, humidity, and sunshine, but also depends on the perceived level of exertion for the runner's state of conditioning. A properly educated runner can avoid heat injury by adhering to relatively straightforward guidelines.

The metabolic heat produced in one mile of running can raise body temperature more than 3°F, were it not for the body's mechanism for dissipating this excess heat. Air temperature and movement, relative humidity, and solar radiation are factors that affect the rate at which heat can be dissipated. Figure 7–1 shows the relationship between ambient temperature and relative humidity, in which the danger zone for heat injury occurs at lower temperatures as the humidity rises. As humidity rises, the amount of sweat that can evaporate and dissipate heat decreases. Sweating is increasingly less efficient as humidity rises so that higher temperatures become more hazardous. Simple measures, such as adequate fluid intake before hot-weather runs, can reduce hypovolemia. Wearing light, loose clothing and running in shade rather than full sun also protect against the rate of heat increase. Acclimatization is also an important factor as the rate of sweating increases and the sodium content decreases with conditioning in warm weather [25]. Studies of military recruits show that three to four weeks of physical training are required for optimal hot-weather adaptation to occur.

Exertional heat injury is perhaps more common in relatively inexperienced runners, as has been reported in the United States and Australia during mass-participation races [22, 51]. The novice runner is less likely to use cooling water sprays, keep up with fluid replacement, and be able to accurately monitor exertion level. Even world-class runners are not exempt from heat stress, as illustrated by the collapse of Alberto Salazar in the Falmouth road race in 1979. He was taken to a local hospital with a temperature over 41°C.

The dominant symptom in heat exhaustion is fatigue with abdominal cramps and mild nausea, usually followed by dizziness and confusion [25]. The runner may then have

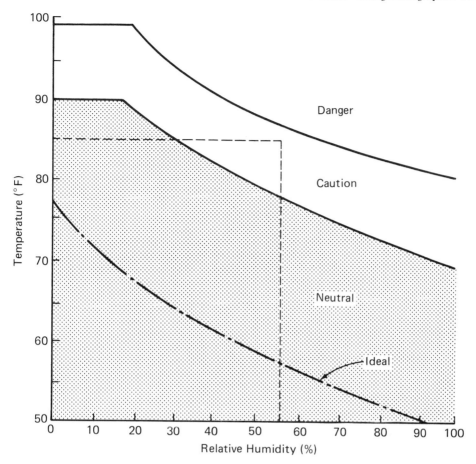

Figure 7–1 Relationship between ambient temperature and relative humidity. Determine temperature and humidity and plug the values into the graph. The point where the two lines intersect indicates the relative risk of heat injury under those conditions. The curves assume that one is acclimated to hot weather running, is running for about an hour, and is protected from solar radiation or running early or late in the day or on an overcast day. The example shown is for an 85°F day with 55% relative humidity. The intercept falls in the caution zone, indicating it is safe to run but care must be taken to avoid serious dehydration. The dashed curve indicates ideal conditions for running.

chills with vasoconstriction, although active sweating may continue. The associated problem of hypovolemia leads to an excessive pulse with an orthostatic drop in blood pressure. Runners who perceive these changes during training or in a race should drop out for fluids and to cool off. Continued exercise after the occurrence of volume depletion and hyperthermia will lead to further confusion and disorientation, followed by circulatory collapse.

The best treatment of heat injury is immediate rapid cooling performed on-site and without delay. In an Australian study, the mean time it took to cool patients who had rectal temperatures equal to or greater than 41.5°C was 37 minutes [51]. No runners experienced the severe sequelae of heat stroke with this rapid-cooling approach. If treatment is delayed, major medical complications including fulminant rhabdomyolysis, acute renal failure requiring dialysis, hepatic necrosis, and disseminated intervascular coagulation can infrequently occur [28, 50].

Educating runners about heat acclimatization, prehydration, and control of exercise intensity during training and racing should result in less-frequent heat injury. Emergency care when such complications do arise should prevent the fatalities that still occur from the medical consequences of severe exertional heat stroke. Physicians should encourage heat-injury precautions including races to be run at cooler times of the day and cancelled when wet-bulb temperatures exceed 28.0° C. Drinking 10 to 12 ounces of cold fluids, either diluted commercial drinks or fruit juice diluted with 2 to 3 parts of cold water, is recommended to replenish fluid and potassium losses. One should not wait to be thirsty since 2 to 4 pounds of fluid loss is required before thirst is noticed. Warm fluids should not be consumed since they are absorbed more slowly than cold fluids. Commercial drinks are high in sugar and may cause abdominal cramps if not diluted. Salt tablets and potassium supplements are not needed. One should acclimatize gradually, starting at 50% maximal effort and increasing 5% to 10% daily. Cotton socks to absorb sweat and white nonporous clothing to reflect the sun's rays are also recommended.

Cold-weather running presents much less threat, although significant complications may arise [15, 23]. Prolonged strenuous exertion with insufficient heat dissipation from over-dressing may lead to volume depletion and hyperthermia despite cold-weather conditions. A more common danger is fatigue, followed by a decrease in work effort with resultant fall in body temperature due to environmental losses below normal. Wind speed affects the wind-chill factor, which lowers the effective ambient temperature on body homeostasis. Critical chill temperatures can result with hypothermia and cardiac arrhythmia or arrest [57]. Figure 7–2 shows wind-chill-factor assessment.

Mild-to-moderate hypothermia should be treated with rapid warming, while advanced hypothermia (below 32°C) may require advanced life-support measures. Cold-induced bronchospasm or asthma, which result from insufficient hydration of airway during the humidification process, are complications of exercise in cold weather [34]. Frostbite of the airway or lungs does not, in fact, occur, although significant breathing discomfort may be encountered by runners or skiers. Warming the inspired air with a mask and using bronchodilating drugs such as Terabutaline or sodium chromalin by inhalation before exercise will alleviate this reaction [19]. Noses and earlobes should also be protected from the cold during prolonged exercise, as vasoconstriction may provide insufficient blood flow to maintain the tissues free of injury [26].

Genitourinary Abnormalities during Sport

A wide range of genitourinary conditions related to physical exertion may be encountered by the physician in both men and women. Participants in body-contact sports such as

---

WIND CHILL

Source: National Oceanic and Atmospheric Administration

A very strong wind combined with a temperature slightly below freezing can have the same chilling effect as a temperature nearly 50°F lower in a calm atmosphere. Arctic explorers and military experts have developed what is called the "wind-chill factor," which shows the combined effects of wind and temperature as equivalent calm-air temperatures. In effect, the index describes the cooling power of the air on exposed flesh. The wind-chill table here shows this cooling power for various combinations of wind and temperature, and will help you gauge how much protection you really need.

Directions: 1) Find actual (calm) air temperature across top of table. 2) Determine wind speed and follow across to correct calm-air temperature. Number given is equivalent temperature. For example, a 10° temperature with a 20 mph wind equals the equivalent of −24 degrees.

Equivalent Temperatures (F°)

Windspeed (Miles per hour) / Calm	35	30	25	20	15	10	5	0	−5	−10	−15	−20	−25	−30	−35	−40	−45
5	33	27	21	16	12	7	1	−6	−11	−15	−20	−26	−31	−35	−41	−47	−54
10	21	16	9	2	−2	−9	−15	−22	−27	−31	−38	−45	−52	−58	−64	−70	−77
15	16	11	1	−6	−11	−18	−25	−33	−40	−45	−51	−60	−65	−70	−78	−85	−90
20	12	3	−4	−9	−17	−24	−32	−40	−46	−52	−60	−68	−76	−81	−88	−96	−103
25	7	0	−7	−15	−22	−29	−37	−45	−52	−58	−67	−75	−83	−89	−96	−104	−112
30	5	−2	−11	−18	−26	−33	−41	−49	−56	−63	−70	−78	−87	−94	−101	−109	−117
35	3	−4	−13	−20	−27	−35	−43	−52	−60	−67	−72	−83	−90	−98	−105	−113	−123
40	1	−4	−15	−22	−29	−36	−45	−54	−62	−69	−76	−87	−94	−101	−107	−116	−128
45	1	−6	−17	−24	−31	−38	−46	−54	−63	−70	−78	−87	−94	−101	−108	−118	−128
50	0	−7	−17	−24	−31	−38	−47	−56	−63	−70	−79	−88	−96	−103	−110	−120	−128

(Zones labeled within table: VERY COLD, BITTER COLD, EXTREME COLD)

Figure 7–2 Wind-chill-factor assessment. Adapted from Burfoot, A. Winter running. *Runners World,* 1979, p. 79.

boxing, wrestling, and football may experience flank pain and gross hematuria related to traumatic injury [14, 45]. Such cases should be worked up for perinephric hematoma and other complications, with a systematic medical evaluation and intravenous pyelography. In contrast, abnormalities in urinary sediment, including proteinuria, hematuria, and, more rarely, formed elements, may occur in asymptomatic runners and endurance athletes after prolonged strenuous exertion [18, 19, 48]. Awareness of the full spectrum of abnormal findings will enable the physician to make rational and appropriate clinical decisions when evaluating these patients.

The occurrence of exercise-related urinary abnormalities has been extensively reviewed in the literature and in medical-specialty books, with the term "athletic pseudonephritis" applied to abnormal sediments [13]. Severe volume depletion and dehydration can, indeed, lead to proteinuria and hematuria with the presence of formed elements such as proteinaceous casts. A prospective study of 50 male physician marathon runners showed that microscopic hematuria occurred in 18% in initial postrace urinalyses, but cleared within 24 to 48 hours [48]. Exercise-related hematuria appears to be a frequent and self-limited benign condition that does not warrant extensive invasive work-up. Gross hematuria occurred in only 1 of 50 subjects, but it is also a known complication of nontraumatic sports such as running. Work-up of a series of patients with so-called 10,000-meter hematuria identified bladder trauma as the cause of this hematuria [4, 29]. As concomitant bladder or renal pathology cannot be summarily excluded after gross hematuria related to exercise, a case might be made for intravenous pyelography and panendoscopy to exclude specific causes [5].

Positive Hemastix reaction without detectable blood on microscopic analysis of urine is suggestive of myoglobinuria following strenuous exercise. This reaction may be quite common, if not universal, in marathon runners after peak efforts, resulting from transient rhabdomyolysis during such extended physical exertion [49]. Elevations of serum creatine kinase up to 30 times normal have been noted in marathon runners without perceived urinary symptoms or evidence of injury. Other studies have shown transitory decrements in creatinine clearance following marathon competition, which may be prerenal or related to volume depletion rather than due to tubular injury [8]. While exertional rhabdomyolysis is common, acute renal failure is extremely rare [29]. It has been reported in patients with sickle cell trait who are at increased risk of renal tubular necrosis following rhabdomyolysis, which may then proceed to other complications as in reported cases of disseminated intravascular clotting [45].

Heat stress, prolonged strenuous exercise, muscle injury, and urinary abnormalities are thus interrelated. It is crucial for physicians to identify runners with acute hypovolemia occurring in heat-stress injury in order to institute rapid rehydration to prevent attendant renal injury. Cases of acute renal failure following severe dehydration in marathon runners have been reported, although such injury is theoretically preventable [5]. There is no evidence that permanent or progressive renal injury results from prolonged strenuous training as in long-distance runners. Acute rises in serum creatinine levels are reported, but are readily reversible with rest and rehydration [38]. Progressive renal damage from recurrent low-grade rhabdomyolysis and myoglobinuria is a theoretical possibility but has thus far not been demonstrated. Again, prevention is the best treatment, and runners should be encouraged to take fluids liberally during and immediately after strenuous physical effort. The marathon runner, for example, should not leave the finish line (figuratively) until he or she has urinated.

Exercise-Induced Asthma and Anaphylaxis

Exercise-induced asthma is a relatively common, readily diagnosable and treatable form of reversible bronchospasm [20, 33]. It occurs with high frequency in individuals with an allergic or asthmatic background in whom exercise provokes or increases symptoms. Bronchospasm also occurs in subjects who do not have a clinical history of overt asthma, in whom symptoms may be unappreciated or subclinical until the additional work of breathing during exercise is imposed. The frequency with which such reactions are detected depends upon the sensitivity of measurements used, as well as on the type of exercise.

The typical course of symptoms is a slow onset of bronchospasm during the warm-up phase, reaching a peak six to eight minutes after the exercise phase begins. Symptoms often stabilize or subside if exercise is continued, as some asthmatics can exercise through their attacks after some initial difficulty. The postexercise rebound is well described, as difficulty may return or intensify after cessation of activity. Figure 7–3 shows the typical pattern of observed pulmonary function parameters with relationship to time in healthy subjects and those with exercise-induced asthma [20]. The four parameters of lung function shown reflect the impairment during and after exertion. Simple spirometry with measure of the timed or one-second vital capacity is adequate to confirm suspected clinical cases in most instances.

Figure 7–3 Comparison of typical spirometric measurements following exercise in healthy subjects and in patients with exercise-induced asthma. FVC, forced vital capacity; FEV$_1$, forced expired volume in one second; PEFR, peak expiratory flow rate; MMEFR, midmaximal expiratory flow rate. Adapted from Gerhard, H. and Schachter, E.N. Exercise-induced asthma. *Postgraduate Medicine*, March 1980, p. 93.

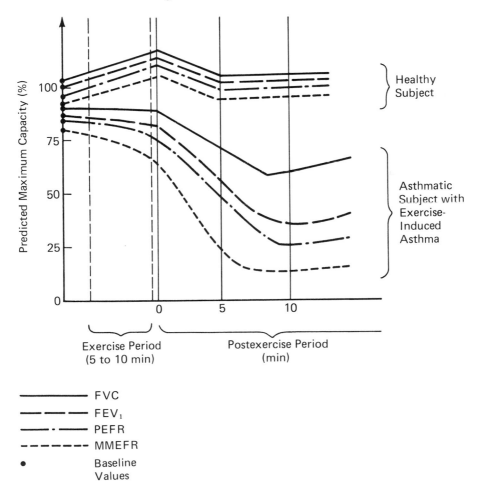

Exercise-induced asthma represents bronchial smooth-muscle constriction as the final common pathway in a way identical to the allergin-triggered asthmatic response. Recent investigations, however, reveal that exercise-induced asthma is not triggered by an allergic response, but by reactions of large and small airways to changes in humidity during cold-air breathing [33]. McFadden and others have shown that the magnitude of the bronchoconstrictive response to a fixed exercise task or to a fixed level of ventilation depends on the temperature and/or water content of the inspired air. Lower air temperatures and humidity favor the obstructive response, which does not occur in susceptible subjects when inspired air is fully saturated with water at body temperature. Airway cooling from heat loss during high ventilatory work is the specific precipitant. These findings explain why corticosteroids are ineffective in treating exercise-induced asthma, whereas warming of inspired air through a face mask can be proportionately more effective.

A wide range of treatments is available for patients with exercise-induced asthma, including airway warming as a preventive measure, and specific pharmacologic agents used in the treatment of traditional asthma. These agents can be used in addition to physical measures as preexercise doses to minimize bronchoconstriction. A warm-up period is often useful in minimizing the reaction, but timing of a bronchodilator, such as chromalin, with peak exercise efforts is essential. Sympathomimetics are disallowed in some competitive situations, so that alternatives such as chromalin sodium must be used. Physicians must be aware of these special stipulations as well as the range of treatments available to the recreational athlete.

Persons susceptible to exercise-induced asthma should be encouraged to participate in sports and exercise that may have a beneficial effect on general physical conditioning and preservation of lung function. The adequately-informed primary-care physician can enhance the capability of patients to lead full and active lives despite the need for specific treatment.

Exercise-Induced Anaphylaxis

Individuals with a background of allergic reactions such as childhood eczema, seasonal rhinitis, or even asthma are prone to a second exercise-related reaction that begins with diffuse itching and may result in generalized hives or urticaria. Such symptoms may occur after years or decades of being allergy-free, and may be limited to minor discomfort. The reaction can, however, progress to generalized angioedema, including facial swelling and laryngeal spasm, with potential upper airways compromised. This reaction was reported in a group of young athletes after a variety of sports and may be unpredictable in occurrence and severity for any individual [46]. Some authors have suggested that exposure to a specific allergin such as shellfish, to which the individual is subclinically susceptible, may then combine with exercise to trigger the reaction in a way similar to cold-induced urticaria [32]. Susceptibility is not related to training or expertise, as exercise-induced anaphylaxis has been reported in national champions and in world record holders [47]. Management can entail preventive measures such as administration of mild antihistamines or perhaps sodium chromalin prior to exercise. Such pretreatment may be necessary for individuals only at times of peak risk, as the urticarial response may occur only seasonally when allergic predisposition is heightened. Avoiding specific foods, as in the case of a shellfish-allergic patient, prior to exercise may control or eliminate the response.

The pathogenesis of exercise-induced anaphylaxis is identical to immunologic-mediated anaphylaxis even though the trigger is physical rather than allergenic. Effector mast cells fire to release histamine, the slow-reacting substance of anaphylaxis, bradykinins, and other mediators, which then cause the angioedema. Facial swelling is an indication for specific emergency measures, such as subcutaneous administration of aqueous epinephrine 1:1,000, 0.1 mL to 0.3 mL along with placement of an IV for fluid administration. Hypotension may develop from generalized vascular permeability, which may require stabilization with fluids and vasopressive drugs. Dopamine (400 mg) and D5W (500 mL), given intravenously at an appropriate rate, may sustain blood pressure in the face of circulatory collapse. While potentially life-threatening, exercise-induced anaphylaxis has not yet resulted in a reported fatality. Patients with this reaction, as well as individuals with known bee-sting sensitivity (hymenoptera), should have epinephrine available for administration if severe allergic manifestations develop. Vascular collapse and cardiac arrest after generalized urticaria have been reported and may represent a variation of this phenomenon [24].

The Psychology of Exercise

The impact of exercise on an individual's total health and well-being can be profound. Regular exercise may alter body composition, physical capacity, and psychological make-up. Much has been written about the positive and negative aspects of regular endurance training such as jogging or running. While there is little consensus on specific effects, the physician must be aware of the way in which exercise affects a patient's life and what ego-supportive or ego-disruptive effects may result.

The relationship of psychology to underlying psychopharmacology is in its infancy in biomedical investigation. Plasma catecholamines rise in stress as they do in exercise, but may have different end-organ effects [11]. The role of the sympathetic nervous system in the development of heart disease [41, 42], and its relationship to specific personality types [12], has been actively studied, but conclusions remain uncertain. Regular exercise may indeed be a prescription for the relief of depression and anxiety [6], although its value in treating more profound psychological disorders is limited. The idea that a hard-driving, type-A personality, such as the stereotypical business executive, can begin regular exercise as an antidote to a high risk for heart disease is speculative at best. Negative addiction is possible, such as turning exercise into a new obsession or disrupting work and family ties. Such negative addiction has been described [37], including the increased rate of marital disruption in overcommitted runners [3]. Recent studies from Stanford University deal with the type-A/type-B personality hypothesis and the effect of regular exercise on the psychological stability of exercise participants. Measurement of increases of high-density lipoprotein cholesterol are obviously more quantitative than the assessment of behavioral and mental changes, such as marital satisfaction or one's capacity as a sexual partner. Sensational headlines, such as "Have Marathon Runners Found the Way to the Good Life?" [27] suggest that running increases one's sexual capacity and enhances the pleasure of partners! The studies by Andres point out that the consequences may be quite to the contrary. Exercise may or may not be able to affect preexisting coronary-prone behavior or alter personality or function in a basic way. Exercise may, in fact, become a new modality through which old ways of interacting are channeled. Patients may seek advice from physicians regarding significant problems or life crises, and the relationship of exercise to the precipitation or solution of such problems should be appreciated. Prescription of exercise to relieve depression is adjunctive at best, and only for those individuals who are so inclined. It is certainly no substitute for full and open patient-physician communication.

Miscellaneous Sports-Related Problems

A number of medical complications of endurance sports remain to be discussed, although their scope may be less than those heretofore presented. Perhaps the major undiscussed risk is the susceptibility of the athlete to drugs of uncertain safety. The controversial substance dimethyl sulfoxide (DMSO) shows how the use of a substance by well-known athletes and/or their trainers can cause widespread use among recreational athletes. This substance is topically applied to pulled muscles, sprained ankles, or other injured parts of the body. DMSO is a solvent, for which there is no quality control in its manufacture. The absorption of DMSO through the skin has not been proven safe by standards of the Food and Drug Administration. The substance is nevertheless widely available, its sale is legal, and its use is spreading, especially in the Pacific Northwest [52]. The use of an untested substance in young athletes with the potential for prolonged exposure is unknown. Reports of renal injury linked with DMSO have begun to surface [58]. Local reaction from painted substances are reported, as in contact allergy to ethyl butyl tiouria in athletic shoes [43]. Such contact dermatitis is less dangerous than profound systemic effects such as aplastic anemia associated with rubber cement painted on by a runner to avoid blisters [44]. It is the prime responsibility of the physician to provide responsible guidance to athletes of all ages in the avoidance of such unproven substances.

Physicians should also be alert to the misdiagnosis of conditions masquerading as sports-related problems in runners or other athletes. Gastrointestinal dysfunction, for example, is common in runners who may have loose or watery movements during strenuous exercise. This may relate to heightened parasympathetic tone, and such reactions may, in fact, be diminished by pretreatment with parasympatholytic drugs such as Donnatal. Bloody diarrhea, however, is an example of a symptom that should not be attributed to exercise alone and warrants a careful workup for inflammatory-bowel disease or focal gastrointestinal pathology [17].

This is in contrast to hematuria during prolonged strenuous exercise, which occurs with higher frequency and may not require invasive testing if rapid spontaneous resolution occurs. Deep venous thrombosis that masquerades as intramuscular hematoma or other leg injury has been reported in runners, but must be separately identified and evaluated [30]. The effects of drugs on blood fibrinolytic activity is of unknown significance and clinical importance at this time [57]. Marathon training should clearly not be advanced as a treatment of deep venous thrombophlebitis. Informed judgment and clinical common sense should be the physician's goal in assessing complaints of patients who also may be runners.

References

1. Alpert, J. S. What do you tell your patients about sexual activity after MI? *J. Cardiovasc. Med.* February, 1981:154.
2. American Heart Association. The athlete: Risks of injury and sudden death: Preventive and therapeutic considerations. New York, December 4–6, 1980.
3. Andrews, V. Do marriage and mileage mix? *The Runner.* September, 1980:51–54.
4. Blacklock, N. S. Bladder trauma in the long distance runner. 10,000 metres hematuria. *Br. J. Urol.* 49:129–132, 1977.
5. Editorial: The hematuria of the long-distance runner. *Brit. Med. J.* 2 (6183): 159, 1979.
6. Brown, R. S., Ramirez, D. E., and Taub, J. M. The prescription of exercise for depression. *Physician Sportsmed.* 6(12):35–56.
7. Bruce, R. and DeRouen, T. Exercise testing as a predictor of heart disease and sudden death. *Hosp. Pract.* 13:69–75, 1978.
8. Bunch, T. W. Blood test abnormalities in runners. *Mayo Clin. Proc.* 55:113–117, 1980.
9. Cantwell, J. D. Cardiovascular rhythms of runners. *Physician Sportsmed.* 9(3):69, 1981.
10. Cooper, K. H., et al. Physical fitness levels vs. selected coronary risk factors: A cross-sectional study. *JAMA* 236 (2):166, 1976.
11. Dimsdale, J. E. and Moss, J. Plasma catecholamines in stress and exercise. *JAMA* 243(4):340–342, 1980.
12. Doyle, J. T. Type A–type B personality concepts and cardiovascular risks. *Practical Cardiology* 5(8):27–31, 1979.
13. Dresser, T. Abnormal medical findings in normal athletes. American Medical Joggers Association Symposium. Boston, Mass. 1981.
14. Elliott, R. S., Shafer, R. B. and Gibas, M. A. Demonstration of myoglobinemia in football players. *Arch. Phys. Med. Rehabil.* 48:229–232, 1967.
15. Chilled to the core. Editorial. *Emergency Medicine.* January 15, 1979: 173–175.
16. Fein, S. A., Klein, N. A., and Frishman, W. H. Exercise testing soon after uncomplicated myocardial infarction. *JAMA* 245 (8):1863, 1981.
17. Fogoros, R. N. "Runner's trots," gastrointestinal disturbances in runners. *JAMA* 243:17, 1980.
18. Furie, B. and Penn, A. S. Pigmenturia from conga drumming. *Ann. Intern. Med.* 80:727–729, 1974.
19. Gardner, K. D., Jr. Athletic pseudonephritis alteration of urine sediment by athletic competition. *JAMA* 161:613, 1956.
20. Gerhard, H. and Schacter, E. N. Exercise-induced asthma. *Postgrad. Med.* 67(3):91–93, 1980.
21. Graboys, T. B. The economics of screening joggers. *N. Engl. J. Med.* 303:395, 1980
22. Hanson, P. G. and Zimmerman, S. W. Exertional heatstroke in novice runners. *JAMA* 242(2):154–157, 1979.
23. Hershkowitz, M. Penile frostbite, an unforeseen hazard of jogging. *N. Engl. J. Med.* 296:179, 1977.
24. Howland, M. A., Flomenbaum, N., Lewin, N., Silverman, R. *Case Studies in Cardiac Emergencies.* New York: T. McBrian Communications, Inc. 1981.
25. Knochel, J. P. Environmental heat illness. *Arch. Intern. Med.* 133:841–864, 1974.

26. Knochel, J. P., Dotin, L. N., and Hamburger, R. J. Heat stress, exercise, and muscle injury: Effects of urate metabolism and renal function. *Ann. Intern. Med.* 81:321–328, 1974.

27. Knox, R. A. Have marathoners found the way to the good life? *The Boston Globe,* 19 April 1981.

28. Koppes, G. M., Daly, J. J., Coltman, C. A., and Butkus, D. E. Exertion-induced rhabdomyolysis with acute renal failure and disseminated intravascular coagulation in sickle cell trait. *Am. J. Med.* 63:313–317, 1977.

29. Llach, F., et al. The pathophysiology of altered calcium metabolism in rhabdomyolysis-induced acute renal failure. *N. Engl. J. Med. 305*(3):117, 1981.

30. Mackie, J. W. and Webster, J. A. Deep vein thrombosis in marathon runners. *Physician Sportsmed. 9*(5):91–98, 1981.

31. Maron, B. J., Roberts, W. C., McAllister, H. A., et al. Sudden death in young athletes. *Circulation* 62:218, 1980.

32. Maulitz, R. M., Pratt, D. S., and Schocket, A. L. Exercise-induced anaphylactic reaction to shellfish. *J. Allergy Clin. Immunol. 63*(6):433–434, 1979.

33. McFadden, E. R., Jr. Exercise-induced asthma. *Am. J. Med. 68:*4, 1980.

34. McFadden, E. R. and Ingram, R. H. Exercise-induced asthma. *Seminars in Med. of the Beth Israel Hosp., Boston. 301*(14):763–769, 1979.

35. Meller, J. and Ross, R. Noninvasive clinic. The risks of exercise stress testing. *Practical Cardiology 6*(1):91, 1980.

36. Milvy, P. and Siegel, A. J. Physical activity levels and altered mortality from coronary heart disease with an emphasis on marathon running: A critical review. *Cardiovasc. Rev. and Reports* 2(3):233, 1981.

37. Morgan, W.P. Negative addiction in runners. *Physician Sportsmed.* 7(2):57–70, 1979.

38. Neviackas, J. A. and Bauer, J. H. Renal function abnormalities induced by marathon running. *South. Med. J.* In press.

39. Pollock, M. L. How much exercise is enough? *Physician Sportsmed.* 6(6):49, 1978.

40. Raskoff, W. J., Goldman, S., and Cohn, K. The "athletic heart." *JAMA* 236(2):158, 1976.

41. Reder, R. F. and Rosen, M. R. The role of the sympathetic nervous system in sudden cardiac death. *Drug Therapy (Hosp.)* 7:43–55, 1978.

42. Reich, P. et al. Acute psychological disturbances preceding life-threatening ventricular arrythmias. *JAMA* 246(3):233, 1981.

43. Roberts, J. L. and Hanifin, J. M. Athletic shoe dermatitis. Contact allergy to ethyl butyl thiourea. *JAMA* 241(3):275–276, 1979.

44. Roodman, G. D., Reese, E. P., Jr. and Cardamone, J. M. Aplastic anemia associated with rubber cement used by a marathon runner. *Arch. Intern. Med.* 140:703, 1980.

45. Russell, S. M. and Lewis, A. Karate myoglobinuria. *N. Engl. J. Med.* 293(18):941, 1975.

46. Sheffer, A. L. and Austen, K. F. New exercise-induced anaphylactic syndrome identified. *Modern Medicine,* 1:96, 1981.

47. Siegel, A. J. Exercise-induced anaphylaxis. *Physician Sportsmed.* 8(1):55–64, 1980.

48. Siegel, A. J., Hennekens, C. H., Solomon, H. S., and Von Boeckel, B. Exercise-related hematuria. Findings in a group of marathon runners. *JAMA,* 241(4):391–392, 1979.

49. Siegel, A. J., Silverman, L. M., and Lopez, R. E. Creatinine kinase elevations in marathon runners: Relationship to training and competition. *Yale J. Biol. Med.* 53:275–279, 1980.

50. Stewart, P. J. and Posen, G. A. Case report: Acute renal failure following a marathon. *Physician Sportsmed.* 8(4):61, 1980.

51. Sutton, J. R. Heatstroke from running. *JAMA* 243(19):1896, 1980.

52. Effects of drug DMSO debated. *The New York Times.* 26 April, 1981. P.10.

53. Thompson, R. D., Stern, M. P., Williams, P., et al. Death during jogging or running. *JAMA* 242:1265, 1979.
54. Waller, B. F. and Roberts, W. C. Sudden death while running in conditioned runners aged 40 years or over. *Am. J. Cardiol.* 45:1292, 1980.
55. Wenger, N. Rehabilitation after myocardial infarction. *JAMA* 242(26):2879, 1979.
56. White, J. D. Cardiac arrest in hypothermia. *JAMA* 244(20):2262, 1980.
57. Williams, R. S., Logue, E. E., Lewis, J. L., et al. Physical conditioning augments the fibrinolytic response to venous occlusion in healthy adults. *N. Engl. J. Med.* 302:987–991, 1980.
58. Yellowlees, P., Greenfield, C., and McIntyre, N. Safety of intravenous DMSO challenged. *Modern Medicine*, 4:121, 1981.

8 / The Sports-Medicine Bag of the Primary-Care Team-Physician

While each team-physician's medicine bag will be unique, this chapter can serve as a foundation for physicians who are starting out in sports coverage.

Long before the team physician arrives at the football game or hockey match, a plan of emergency medical treatment (defined in writing with a procedural manual and appropriate support systems with phone numbers) should be established. Preferably, the physician should also have received training in cardiopulmonary resuscitation (CPR), emergency care and transportation, analysis of injury and accident etiology, effectiveness of early care, and principles of follow-up medical treatment. While such information can be gleaned from books and special courses, the team physician should consider participating in the local and national chapters of the American College of Sports Medicine to keep abreast of current thinking.

Many physicians feel that a plastic fishing-tackle box with sturdy sliding drawers and a large deep bottom that can accommodate bulky solutions such as intravenous preparations makes an ideal sports-medicine "bag." The contents can be divided into three categories: (1) medication to treat the acute phase of injury (table 8–1), (2) equipment and drugs for cardiopulmonary resuscitation (table 8–2), and (3) a means to summon an ambulance immediately.

The items in table 8–1 will vary depending on a number of factors and should serve only as a comprehensive outline. The same is true of table 8–2, which lists basic cardiopulmonary equipment and drugs. Notice that a tracheostomy kit has not been included. I believe this procedure should be done only in a hospital. Because improper insertion can result in vocal-cord fibrosis, I also feel that the use of a cricothyreotomy kit should be a last-chance-effort to obtain an airway.

Normally, the equipment listed in table 8–3 should be provided by the school. However, if it is an away game and the availability of such equipment is less than certain, it is advisable to pack your own bolt cutter, aluminum backboard, knee splint, and forearm immobilizer.

Table 8–1   Contents of the Team Physician's Bag—Acute Phase

ABD pads
Ace bandages (2-, 3-, 4-, and 6-inch widths)
Alupent inhaler for asthmatic or allergic attack
Anaphylaxis kit
Aneroid manometer
Bandage scissors (8-inch heavy duty)
Bandaids, all sizes
Betadine ointment
Betadine solution
Cotton web roll (4-inch width)
Dexamethazone (Decadron) 24 mg/mL, 5-mL vial for spinal-cord injury
Diazepam (Valium) 10 mg in prefilled syringe for convulsion
Disposable flashlight
Elastic tape (1- and 3-inch width)
Eye-injury assessment and treatment including
    erythromycin eye ointment
    magnifying glass
    metal or plastic protective eye shield
    penlight
    proparacaine (0.5% dropperette)
    sterile adhesive strips, cotton swabs, eye patches, fluorescine strips, irrigating solution
    vision card
Felt padding
Medicine cups
Moleskin (6 × 6 inch)
Ophthalmoscope/otoscope
Orthoplast sheet for splinting fingers (6 × 6 inch)
Padded tongue blade for convulsions
Plastic foam sheet (⅜ inch thick)
Plastic suture material with swaged PRE and 2 needles
Prewrap foam bandage (3-inch width)
Skin lubricant (Cramer)
Sterile gloves
Sterile gauze pads (2 × 2, 3 × 3, and 4 × 4 inch sheets)
Ster-I-Strip (¼ and ½ inch widths)
Stethoscope
Super glue
Swiss army knife with as many gadgets as possible
Tape (adhesive)
Tetracaine or Xylocaine (0.5%, 2-mL ampule)
Thermometers (oral and rectal)
Thermometer to measure air and water temperature (sling psychrometer to determine
    heat-stress index is advisable)
Tufskin (Cramer)

Table 8–2 Cardiopulmonary Resuscitation (CPR) Equipment and Drugs

Equipment
Ambu bag with face mask and adapter for endotracheal tubes
Aneroid manometer
Backboard with strap restraints
Cricothyreotomy kit
Endotracheal tubes (cuffed, small, medium, and large)
Laryngoscope with light source (preferably disposable)
Mouth screw to open mouth
Nasal airways (medium and large)
Oral airways (small, medium, and large)
Padded tongue blade
Stethoscope
Syringe (50 mL) and large catheter for suction
Towel clip

Medication
Atropine sulfate 1.0 mg in Abboject prefilled syringe (10 mL)
Demerol 100 mg in 2-mL ampule
Epinephrine 1:10,000 in Abboject prefilled syringe (10 mL) to be given if chest massage
    unsuccessful
Epinephrine 1:1,000 in Abboject prefilled syringe (10 mL) to be given through endotracheal
    tube
Lactated Ringer's solution 500 mL with tubing and needles
Lasix 40 mg IV ampule
Lidocaine hydrochloride 100 mg in Abboject prefilled syringe (50 mL) for prevention or
    treatment of arrhythmia
Morphine sulfate 15 mg Tubex with syringe
Nitrostat 0.4 mg sublingual tablets
Sodium bicarbonate 50 mEq in Abboject prefilled syringe (50 mL)

Table 8–3 Equipment Usually Provided by the School

Backboard (one piece with attached strap restraints)
Blankets (two regular army blankets)
Bolt cutter, double-action (used to quickly remove a face mask to establish an airway without
    removing the helmet)
Crutches (two pairs with adjustable lengths to aid in moving an athlete from the field to bench
    or dressing room)
Ice bags (invaluable for cooling off players and injured areas; cheaper and more practical than
    chemically activated cold packs)
Rubberized elastic bandages (12 each in 3-, 4-, and 6-inch widths)
Sandbags (four of 5-lb size to immobilize an athlete during transportation)
Slings (three large muslin triangles with two safety pins each)

Sling psychrometer or a device to measure wet-bulb, globe, and dry air temperatures
(heat-stress index should be determined before and during contests on extremely hot,
humid days)
Splints (two each upper and lower) (plastic air splints are preferable)
Stretcher (a metal rescue stretcher that can be assembled under the athlete without lifting is
optimal)

The final item for the team physician is a two-way radio pager that can be used
to summon an ambulance and relay pertinent information to the hospital emergency
room. If an ambulance in attendance at a game has its own two-way radio, this will obviate
your need for a separate one.

Suggested Reading

Loomis, J. L., Johnson, D. A., Hochberg, W. J., et al. Equipment update: Penn State's foldable
rigid stretcher. *Physician Sportsmed.* 7:135–136, 1979.
Mayne, B. A. If sports medicine is your bag—equip it well. *Physician Sportsmed.* 3:67–69, 1975.
Mayne, B. A. A team physician's bag. *Physician Sportsmed.* 9:85–87, 1981.
Vinger, P. F. and Hoerner, E. F. Contents of the sportsmedicine bag. In P. F. Vinger and E. F.
Hoerner (Eds.) *Sports Injuries: the Unthwarted Epidemic.* Littleton, Mass.: PSG Publishing Co.,
Inc., 1980.

III / Sports Injuries: Prevention, Treatment, and Specialist Referral

9 / Head and Neck Injuries

The central nervous system (brain and spinal cord) is unique in that nerve cells are not capable of regeneration. Injury to these structures takes on a singular importance, since cells that die are forever lost. While virtually every major joint (ankle, knee, hip, elbow, shoulder) and most of the body's organs can be replaced, the central nervous system housed in the skull and spine is not capable of regrowth, transplantation, or replacement with artificial hardware. With these sobering facts in mind, clinical evaluation of the head- or spine-injured athlete must be expeditious and precise, and the physician must be forever mindful of the Hippocratic prohibition: "First, do no harm."

Whenever an injury involves a loss of consciousness, several important simultaneous observations and assumptions must be made. It must be assumed that the patient has a fractured neck and the examination must be carried out with this in mind. First, it must be established that the patient has an adequate airway; then a rapid baseline medical and neurologic examination should be conducted. This should include blood pressure, pulse, respiratory rate, state of consciousness (alert, stupor, semicomatose, or comatose), pupillary size and reactivity, extremity movement spontaneously and in response to painful stimulation, and deep-tendon and Babinski reflexes.

This initial examination is crucial to subsequent evaluation and treatment. If the patient shows improvement within a few minutes, subsequent transportation and diagnostic evaluation can proceed in a routine manner. If, however, deterioration is seen, especially in the state of consciousness, transportation and subsequent treatment must be precipitous. Every unconscious athlete should be transported on a fracture board. The head should be secured in a neutral position with sand bags, four-poster collar, or traction device if available.

If the unconscious athlete is wearing a helmet and has a good airway, the helmet

All of the tables and figures and some of the text in this chapter are reproduced with permission from Robert C. Cantu (Ed.), *Health Maintenance through Physical Conditioning,* © 1981 by PSG Publishing Company, Inc., Littleton, Massachusetts.

should not be removed, since this may precipitate quadriplegia if an unstable cervical fracture is present. The helmet should be removed only if the airway is questionable, and then never forcibly and always with the neck in a neutral (neither flexed nor extended) position. The helmet can be used for cervical traction, with the chin strap serving as the halter and the earholes and/or immediately adjacent edge of the helmet as a site for attaching neutral traction. While the unconscious athlete is being moved onto the spine board, the earholes of the helmet may also serve as a convenient site to insert one's index finger to effect gentle neutral cervical traction. Only after appropriate cervical-spine x-rays have excluded a cervical-spine fracture, malalignment, or instability, can the helmet be safely removed from the unconscious athlete.

If a fracture board is not readily available to transport the unconscious athlete from the site of injury, a decision must be made to either wait for the ambulance to arrive with its stretcher or move the athlete using the locked-arm technique. While I generally favor the former, it is true that if adequate players or spectators are present, locking hands to elbows of individuals standing opposite each other provides a secure surface for moving an injured athlete a short distance. When transporting an unconscious athlete in this manner, one person applies neutral traction to the helmet or otherwise secures the head in a neutral position.

Sports Most Hazardous to the Head and Cervical Spine

Table 9–1 lists those athletic pursuits most likely to cause serious head and spine injuries. One study of automobile racing showed that during their first two years, 30% of new participants were either killed or so seriously injured they could not compete again. [1,3] Motorcycles (or as I prefer, suicycles) are even more dangerous. Eighty percent of the serious injuries occur to those riding six months or less. Hang gliding ranks at the top of the list in terms of fatalities or serious injuries per participant. Amazingly, the use of adequate helmets is not even uniformly seen in this "sport."

Table 9–1 Sports Most Likely to Cause Serious Head and Spine Injury

Maximal Risk	*High Risk*
Automobile racing	Gymnastics
Diving	Horseback riding
Football (the only team sport)	Mountain climbing
Hang gliding	Parachuting
Motorcycle racing	Ski jumping
	Skydiving
	Sky gliding
	Snowmobiling
	Trampolining

The mechanism of cervical-spine injury is illustrated in figures 9–1 and 9–2. In neutral posture, the neck has a gentle S-shaped curve (figure 9–1). When the neck is flexed, the spine becomes straight (figure 9–2). With the vertebral bodies lined up straight, vertical-impact force is directly transmitted from one vertebra to the next, allowing for minimal dissipation of the impact force to be absorbed by the muscles. If the impact force exceeds the strength of the bone, it compacts the bone at one or more levels, causing a compression fracture. If the fractured vertebra malaligns and is driven back into the spinal cord, quadriplegia may result.

It is when tackling with the head, especially in the open field where momentum is greatest, that most serious neck injuries occur [6]. The small defensive back is the most susceptible player. The fast but light safety is injured trying to bring down a larger, heavier back with a head tackle. The high-school athlete, who has the greatest degree of variation in physical maturation and athletic ability, is at greatest risk. Tables 9–2 to 9–5 show the breakdown of injuries caused by football.

Presently, catastrophic football head and neck injuries are at the lowest level in the last eighteen years, approximately 0.5 per 100,000 athletes[6]. This represents a reduction of over 600% from peak years in the late 1960s, and directly reflects the 1976 rule change to prohibit butt-blocking and face-tackling. It is also due to the football-helmet standard established by the National Operating Committee on Standards for Athletic Equipment (NOCSAE), improved conditioning programs, and improved supervision by team physicians and trainers.

Figure 9–1   A and B. Normal neutral neck posture. Reproduced with permission from *Health Maintenance through Physical Conditioning* edited by Robert C. Cantu. Copyright © 1981 by PSG Publishing Company.

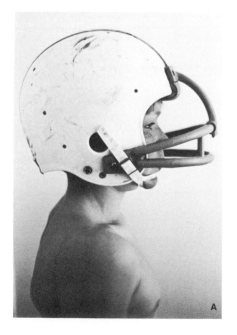
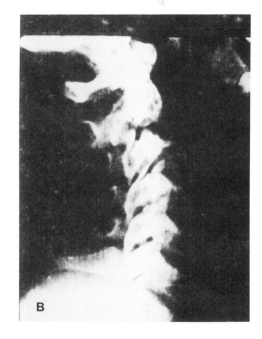

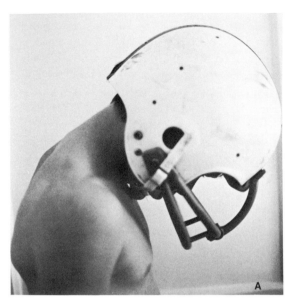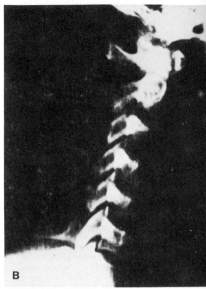

Figure 9–2 A and B. Flexed spearing neck posture. Reproduced with permission from *Health Maintenance through Physical Conditioning* edited by Robert C. Cantu. Copyright © 1981 by PSG Publishing Company.

Table 9–2 Cervical-Spine Injuries Caused by Football, 1971–1975

	Fracture/Dislocations	*Permanent Quadriplegias*
High school	182	77
College	64	18
Other	13	4
TOTAL	259	99

While football fatalities and catastrophic injuries will never be totally eliminated, their occurrence is now rare. Most football conferences go for decades without such an occurrence, while almost every participating school has one or more fatalities or catastrophic injuries attributed to a car or motorcycle accident per year. For the high-school student, it is clearly more dangerous to drive a car or motorcycle than to play football.

Table 9–3 Permanent Cervical
Quadriplegia Caused by Football,
1971–1975

Mechanism of Injury	No. of Injuries
Hyperflexion	10
Hyperextension	3
Vertical compression (spearing)	52
Knee/thigh to head	15
Collision/pile/ground contact	11
Tackled	7
Machine-related	3
Face mask acting as lever	0

Table 9–4 Football Injuries by
Position, 1971–1975

Position	Permanent Cervical Quadriplegia (%)	
	High School	College
Defensive back	52	73
Linebacker	10	0
Specialty team	13	7
Offensive back	11	7
Defensive line	10	0
Offensive line	4	13

Table 9–5 Football Injury by Activity,
1971–1975

Activity	Permanent Cervical Quadriplegia (%)	
	High School	College
Tackling	72	78
Tackled	14	22
Blocking	6	0
Drill	3	0
Collision/pileup	3	0
Machine-related	2	0

Cranial Injuries

Concussion

The most common athletic brain injury is concussion. While physiologically defined as a transient alteration of brain function (usually with a period of unconsciousness) followed by complete brain recovery, many concussions occur without a lapse in consciousness. This has led to a clinical grading of concussion. In the most mild form (grade I), there is no loss of consciousness but only lapse of memory after the head trauma. Many boxers have instinctively won fights after blows to the head rendered them amnesic for events following an early round. Also, it is not uncommon for a football player to have his "bell rung" during a given play, and then to play the rest of the game without subsequent recall.

In the more severe grades of concussion, one is unconscious transiently (grade II) or for a more prolonged time (grade III). In this instance the head trauma causes alterations in the function of the reticular activating system that runs from the upper cervical spinal cord to the thalamus, resulting in unconsciousness and associated changes in pulse, respiration, and blood pressure. Consciousness, motor power, and coordination are regained as the reticular activating system resumes normal function.

Generally speaking, the degree and duration of amnesia correlates with the severity of the concussion. In grade I, the amnesia is usually only for events immediately after the head trauma (retrograde amnesia). However, in grade III, events preceding the trauma may also be lost (anterograde amnesia). For the student-athlete, a grade II or III concussion requires removing the student from the game, obtaining skull x-rays, and placing him or her in a medical facility for 24 hours neurologic observation. With a grade I concussion, in certain instances where the player is fully lucid with no headache, return to play is permissible. However, that player should be observed closely over the next 24 hours in case an expanding intracranial mass (blood clot) is developing. The player should be awakened every two hours during the night and should not be left alone that first night.

Occasionally head trauma will be sufficient to produce a degree of brain swelling (edema) over the ensuing 24 hours, which may result in headache. An athlete should be free of headache at rest before resuming play, and free of headache at maximal-intensity training before returning to competition.

The question of allowing an athlete to return to competition after repeated concussions is still controversial. For the nonprofessional student-athlete, it is generally agreed that two concussions of grade II or III severity during any one season should exclude that athlete from further participation that season. When the athlete is free of headache at maximal exertion and has a normal electroencephalogram (EEG), he or she may safely resume competition after a first concussion. However, before this is allowed, there should be a thorough review of the circumstances resulting in the concussion. If available, videotapes or game films should be reviewed by the player, coach, and trainer. It should be determined if the player was using his or her head unwisely, illegally, or both. It will also reveal if the player is wearing the equipment correctly. Finally, the equipment itself should be checked to be certain it is worn properly and fits correctly.

Intracranial Hemorrhage

The leading cause of death from athletic head injury is intracranial hemorrhage. There are four types of hemorrhage the examining trainer or physician must look for in every instance of head injury. Since all four types may be fatal, rapid and accurate initial assessment as well as appropriate followup is mandatory after an athletic head injury.

1. An epidural or extradural *hematoma* is usually the most rapidly progressing intracranial hematoma. It is frequently associated with a fracture in the temporal bone, and results from a tear in one of the arteries supplying the covering (dura) of the brain. The hematoma accumulates inside the skull, but outside the covering of the brain. It may progress quite rapidly and reach a fatal size in 30 to 60 minutes. Although not always present, there may be a lucid interval; that is, the athlete may initially regain consciousness after the head trauma, before starting to experience increasing headache and progressive deterioration in level of consciousness, as the clot accumulates and the intracranial pressure increases. This lesion, if present, will almost always be apparent within an hour or two after the time of injury. The brain substance is usually free from direct injury; thus, if the clot is promptly removed surgically, a full recovery is to be expected. Because this lesion is rapidly and universally fatal if missed, all athletes receiving a head injury must be very closely observed for the next 24 hours, preferably where full neurosurgical services are immediately available.

2. A subdural hematoma occurs between the brain surface and the dura, that is, under the dura and directly on the brain. It often results from a torn vein running from the surface of the brain to the dura. It may also result from a torn venous sinus or even a small artery on the surface of the brain. With this injury, there is often associated injury to brain tissue. If a subdural hematoma requires surgery in the first 24 hours, mortality is high, not due to the clot itself, but to the associated brain damage. With a subdural hematoma that progresses rapidly, the athlete usually does not regain consciousness, and immediate neurosurgical evaluation is obvious. Occasionally the brain itself will not be injured, and a subdural hematoma may slowly develop over a period of days to weeks. This chronic subdural hematoma, although often associated with headache, may initially present with a variety of very mild, almost imperceptible mental, motor, or sensory signs and symptoms. Since its recognition and removal will lead to full recovery, it must always be suspected in an athlete who has previously sustained a head injury and who appears somewhat abnormal days or weeks later. A CT scan of the head will definitively show such a lesion.

3. An intracerebral hematoma is the third type of intracranial hemorrhage seen after head trauma. In this instance, the bleeding is into the brain substance itself, usually from a torn artery. It may also result from the rupture of a congenital vascular lesion such as an aneurysm or arteriovenous malformation. Intracerebral hematomas are not usually associated with a lucid interval and may be rapidly progressive. Death occasionally occurs before the injured athlete can be moved to a hospital. Because of the intense reaction such a tragic event precipitates among fellow athletes, family, students, and even the community at large, and the inevitable rumors that follow, it is imperative to obtain a complete autopsy to fully clarify the causative factors. Often the autopsy will reveal

a congenital lesion, indicating that the cause of death was other than presumed and ultimately unavoidable. Only by such full, factual elucidation will inappropriate feelings of guilt in fellow athletes, friends, and family be assuaged.

4. The fourth type of intracranial hemorrhage is subarachnoid or confined to the surface of the brain. Following head trauma, such bleeding results from disruption of the tiny surface brain vessels, and is analogous to a bruise. As in intracerebral hematoma, there is often brain swelling, and such a hemorrhage can also result from a ruptured cerebral aneurysm or arteriovenous malformation. Bleeding is superficial, and surgery is not usually required unless a congenital vascular anomaly is present.

All types of intracranial hemorrhages usually cause headache and, not infrequently, associated neurologic deficit, depending on the area of the brain involved. The irritative properties of the blood may also precipitate a seizure. If a seizure occurs in a head-injured athlete, it is important to log-roll the patient onto his or her side. By this maneuver, any blood or saliva will roll out of the mouth or nose, and the tongue cannot fall back obstructing the airway. A padded tongue depressor or oral airway can be inserted between the teeth. Under no circumstances should fingers be inserted into a seizing athlete's mouth, as a traumatic amputation can easily result from such an unwise maneuver. Traumatic seizure will usually last only for a minute or two, the athlete will then relax, and can be transported to the nearest medical facility.

Cervical-Spine Injuries

The same traumatic lesions discussed for the brain, that is concussion, contusion, and the various types of hemorrhage, may also occur to the cervical spinal cord. The major concern with a cervical-spine injury is the possibility of an unstable fracture that may produce quadriplegia. There is no way to determine the presence of an unstable fracture until appropriate x-rays are taken. There is also no way of determining a full recovery from a permanent case of quadriplegia. If the patient is fully conscious, the presence of a cervical fracture or cervical-cord injury is usually accompanied by rigid cervical muscle spasm and pain, which immediately alerts the athlete and physician to the presence of such an injury. It is the unconscious athlete, unable to express pain and whose neck muscles are not in protective spasm, who is susceptible to potential cord severence if the possibility of an unstable cervical-spine fracture is not considered. It is imperative that no neck manipulation be carried out on the field. Definitive treatment should await appropriate x-rays at a medical facility, and all precautions previously discussed must be carried out.

In addition to neck injuries, a stretch or traction injury to the brachial plexus or a nerve root must be considered. This condition, called a "burner" by athletes, usually results from a forceful blow to the head from the side, but can also result from head extension or by depression of the shoulder while the head and neck are fixed. The athlete experiences a shock-like sensation of pain and numbness radiating into the arm and hand. Repeated injury of this type over a period of years may lead to weakness of the deltoid, biceps, and teres major muscles, as well as constant pain. The use of a high cervical collar that limits lateral neck flexion and extension, changing the athlete's hitting technique, or moving the athlete to another position may eliminate this problem. If it recurs repeatedly, however, the athlete should stop playing the responsible contact sport and move to another athletic pursuit.

If the athlete sustains burner-like symptoms, but the pain, numbness and/or weakness persist, usually with neck pain and spasm, a ruptured cervical disc is to be suspected. Such a lesion often exists in a young athlete without any abnormality on routine cervical spine x-rays.

A final uncommon, but very serious, neck injury involves the carotid arteries. The inner layer (intima) of the carotid may be torn by extremes of lateral flexion or extension or by a forceful blow from a relatively fixed narrow object such as a stiffened forearm or a cross-country-ski tip impaling one's neck in a forward fall. This can lead to clot formation at the site of injury, resulting in emboli to the brain or, more commonly, a complete occlusion of the artery, causing a major stroke.

It is recommended that an athlete not return to competition after a neck injury until free of any neck or arm pain at rest, and with a full range of neck motion without discomfort or spasm. Rockett has described further criteria used at Harvard University [4]. Each athlete is measured as to the maximum weight he or she can pull with neck in flexion, extension, and to each side. This becomes the neck profile for that person. An athlete with a neck injury is not allowed to return to competition until he or she can perform to the level of the neck profile.

Prevention of Head and Neck Injuries

Prevention of athletic head injuries is largely limited to using appropriate protective headgear such as the NOCSAE football helmet, then taking one's chances. The brain cannot be preconditioned to accept trauma. Rather, the reverse is true: once the brain is injured, it is more susceptible to future injury.

In contrast to the brain, the neck can be strengthened and the risk of injury reduced. Nautilus machines are now available that strengthen the neck in all four movements: flexion, extension, lateral bending, and rotation. These same exercises can be carried out without machines using the resistance of a fellow colleague's wrist. While controversy exists as to whether the neck can be conditioned to withstand the maximum forces to which it may be subjected in contact sports [2], it is universally agreed that a neck-exercise program minimizes the risk of neck injury.

Finally, since most serious neck injuries occur in diving accidents, almost all in unsupervised recreation, the following tips from Shields et al [5] should be made available:

1. Never dive into unfamiliar water.
2. Do not assume the water is deep enough. Even familiar lakes, rivers, and swimming holes change levels.

3. If you are present when a spinal-cord injury occurs, keep the victim's head and neck from bending and twisting.

4. Never dive near dredging or construction work. The water level may have dropped, and dangerous objects may be just beneath the surface.

5. Do not drink before diving or swimming. Alcohol distorts judgment.

6. Water around a raft can be dangerous, especially if the water level is down. A slackened cable permits the raft to drift, putting the cable and anchor into the diving area.

7. Cloudy water can conceal hazardous objects. Check the bottom.

References

1. Bodnar, L. M. Sports medicine with reference to back and neck injuries. *Curr. Pract. Orthop. Surg.* 7:116–153, 1977.
2. Cushing, D. NFL expands roughness rules. *Physician Sportsmed.* 7:17, 1979.
3. Mueller, F. O. and Blyth, C. S. Catastrophic head and neck injuries. *Physician Sportsmed.* 7:71–74, 1979.
4. Rockett, F. X. Injuries involving the head and neck: Clinical and anatomic aspects. In P. F. Vinger and E. F. Hoerner (Eds.) *Sports Injuries: The Unthwarted Epidemic.* Littleton, Mass.: PSG Publishing Co., Inc., 1981.
5. Shields, C. L., Jr., Fox, J. M., and Stauffer, E. S. Cervical cord injuries in sports. *Physician Sportsmed.* 6:71–76, 1978.
6. Torg, J. S., Quedenfeld, T. C., Burstein, A., et al. National football head and neck injury registry: Report on cervical quadriplegia. *Am. J. Sports Med.* 7:127–132, 1979.

10 / Lumbar-Spine Injuries

Low-back pain is a common ailment in both athletes and nonathletes [3,6]. It is the second most common medical symptom (the first is headache), and runner-up only to the common cold in days missed from work. It is a major health problem today, with over $15 billion expended annually on treatment and compensation [5]. In industry, compensation for low-back disorders represents an amount exceeding that of all other injuries combined [2]. Approximately 80% of adults will suffer from low-back pain at some time in their lives.

What causes low-back pain? Why are young, vigorous, physically fit, elite men and women athletes suffering the same symptoms so prevalent in unfit, sedentary middle-aged persons? Understanding the anatomy and pathology of low-back pain will help to answer these questions and eliminate the problem.

The lower back is composed of five mobile lumbar vertebrae with cartilaginous cushions (discs) between them and the fused bones of the sacrum and coccyx that form the back of the pelvis. Ligaments (thick, dense, tough strands of connective tissue) hold the foundation blocks of the lower back, the vertebrae, sacrum, coccyx, and pelvis together. These ligaments have some elasticity and provide the back with mobility. The five major groups of low-back ligaments and their mechanism of injury include:

Annuli fibrosi. These are the hard, outer circumferential coverings of the nuclei pulposi (discs). The radial relationship of the fibers adds strength, and has been copied by industry with the radial-ply tire. The annuli restrict excessive motion between the vertebrae and hold the discs in place with their resultant cushion effect.

Anterior and posterior longitudinal ligaments. These ligaments run along the front (anterior) and back (posterior) longitudinal surface from one vertebra to another. They

All of the tables and figures and some of the text in this chapter are reproduced with permission from Robert C. Cantu (Ed.), *Health Maintenance through Physical Conditioning,* © 1981 by PSG Publishing Company, Inc., Littleton, Massachusetts.

135

blend with and reinforce the annuli fibrosi. The anterior ligament is much stronger than the posterior; the posterior ligament ruptures more often.

Ligamenta Flava. This group forms the roof of the spinal canal and binds rear segments of vertebrae. They are more elastic than other ligaments and are rarely torn.

Interspinal ligaments. These ligaments extend from one spinous process to another and limit forward bending. They relax in extension and are torn or ruptured by extremes of forward-bending motion (flexion).

Intertransverse ligaments. These ligaments extend from one transverse process to another and limit sideward bending. They are torn or ruptured by extremes of sideward bending.

The muscles of the back, abdomen, and hip are responsible for support and movement of the back. There are four groups of muscles essential for support of the back that can play a major role in back pain. It is convenient to think of the lower back as a pole held erect by four guy-wire muscle groups: the abdominal, the extensor, and the two sides.

Abdominal muscles. These anterior guy wires are the rectus abdominus, internal oblique, external oblique, and transverse abdominus muscles. They extend from the rib cage to the sides and front of the pelvis where they attach by strong, rough connective tissues called tendons. They support the abdominal cavity and control bending movements of the spine. When they are tensed, they relieve strain on the back. Investigators have demonstrated that it is the strong abdominal muscles that allow one to lift weights that would otherwise crush the spine.

Extensor muscles. These posterior guy wires consist of many layers, some spanning a single vertebra and others many vertebrae, from the lower back to the neck. Their tendons attach to the spine, pelvis, ribs, and head. These muscles are maximally used for pulling or pushing a heavy object. They are injured by posterior (arching) movements of the back.

Side muscles. The two lateral guy-wire muscle groups control the sideward bending of the back by contraction of the quadratus lumborum and the psoas major. The psoas major is one of the body's largest muscles, running from the side of the spine through the pelvis to attach to the anterior surface of the femur just below the hip joint.

These three groups of muscles support the back. The hips, however, by virtue of their relationship to the pelvis and, thus, to the spine, can have a very significant effect on the back. The flexor muscles lift hips up, abductors turn hips out, adductors turn hips in, and extensors lift hips back. The hip-extensor muscles as a group control lumbar lordosis, a condition that when excessive is called "swayback" by the layperson; this condition is a major cause of back pain. The hip extensors, in combination with the hip flexors, are essential to good posture.

Common Causes of Low-Back Pain in the Athlete

Less than 5% of athletic back injuries involve a ruptured disc or spine fracture. The definitive medical treatment of these disorders is beyond the scope of this book, but early recognition and emergency care are vital.

Almost all athletic injuries to the lower back involve either a contusion (a bruise from a direct blow), a sprain (a pulling with stretching and tearing of the muscles or their tendons), or a strain (tearing of a ligament). In general, a strain is most painful when the back is forced in the opposite direction, and a sprain produces pain when the affected muscle is contracted. There is an intricate relationship among the muscles, tendons, and ligaments of the back, and most injuries involve two or all three entities.

The cause of most back strains and sprains in athletes and nonathletes is weak muscles (especially the abdominal muscles and hip flexors) or lack of flexibility (especially in the hamstring hip extensor muscles). One wonders how world-class athletes could have weak muscles. During intensive training world-class athletes often neglect anatomic areas (the back, abdomen, or hip) that do not seem to require development for success in their sport. At the 1976 Olympics, the Canadian medical team found the abdominal muscles underdeveloped in many world-class athletes [5]. Some of Canada's top athletes had trouble executing more than one or two bent-knee sit-ups. In general, athletes have strong extensor muscles (the back and hip), and the flexor muscles in one or both regions are frequently underdeveloped.

Mechanisms of Back Strain and Sprain

Most strains and sprains develop in one of two ways. The first is by a sudden, abrupt, violent extension/contraction of an overloaded, unprepared, or underdeveloped spine, especially when there is some rotation in the attempted movement. This can result in stretching a few fibers, a complete tear, or an avulsion fracture of a spinous or transverse process.

The second mechanism involves a chronic strain, often with associated poor posture—excessive lumbar lordosis. There is a continuation of the underlying disease with recurring injury to the original and/or adjacent sites.

Through the repetition of training, many sports predispose to low-back pain. Most sports involve either strong back-extension movements, as opposed to strong flexion, or external forces that produce extension. Track athletes run in forced extension. The discus thrower, shot-putter, and weight lifter propel heavy weights with the back extended. Gymnasts repeatedly dismount with a hyperextended low back as the feet hit the mat. The diver hits the water in extension with foot-entry dives.

Examination of Back Injuries

The back examination of an acutely injured athlete seen on the athletic field will be discussed separately from the ambulatory back-injured patient seen in the office or clinic. The essential medical equipment for an office examination includes your hands, a pin, and a reflex hammer. Ice or ethylene chloride freezing spray, and a fracture board or rigid stretcher are the primary on-the-field treatment aids.

Acute

When an athlete receives a back injury during competition, whether it is due to a tackle in football, a slide in baseball, a fall in basketball, or from riding the pole back down to the ground after a pole vault (this did happen to a high-school jumper who froze with the pole in his hands), the initial examination should be done on the spot. Although unstable fractures and fracture/dislocations (with and without neurologic involvement) are uncommon in the lower back, a careful examination to eliminate their presence is essential. When one arrives at the side of the conscious injured athlete, the first question asked is, "where does it hurt?" For the back-injured athlete—even before examining the back—the next question is whether there is any loss of feeling or weakness in the lower extremities. The spinal cord ends at the lower border of the first lumbar vertebra in most adults. Injury to the spinal cord usually implies a fracture/dislocation or dislocation of the vertebra at the instant of impact, with spontaneous relocation. Both should be considered unstable, and the athlete should be transported off the field and to a hospital on a fracture board.

Injury to the spinal cord may produce either complete or incomplete loss of function of the nervous system below the level of the lesion. In a complete lesion, sensation, motor power, and reflexes in the legs are lost, as well as bowel and bladder control. In an incomplete lesion, varying degrees of these functions are retained. The seriousness of either a complete or incomplete lesion of the spinal cord requires an immediate neurologic evaluation of sensation, movement, and knee and ankle reflexes. If any neurologic deficit is recorded, the patient must be transported from the field on a fracture board to the nearest medical facility where neurosurgical consultation is available.

Fortunately, few back injuries have neurologic impairment. After determining that there is none, the back muscles themselves should be examined. Palpation of the back should start in the midline, with a thumb pressing over each spinous process. Exquisite pain over one spinous process suggests a possible fracture or tear of the interspinal ligaments. Such a fracture rarely has associated vertebral instability. Pain described as deep in the back, with localized tenderness over one or in between two spinous processes, could mean a compression fracture of a vertebra. Most compression fractures involve either the eleventh or twelfth dorsal vertebra or one of the first two lumbar vertebrae. The young pole vaulter who did not let go of his pole and rode it back down to the ground incurred a fracture/dislocation of the first and second lumbar vertebrae. While most compression fractures, like spinous or transverse process fractures, are stable, if there is focal midline tenderness on palpation, it is wise to transport the injured athlete on a fracture board until x-rays clearly establish that the fracture is stable.

After eliminating the most worrisome back injuries, it is important to continue palpating the back paraspinal muscles and around the abdominal wall, including the side flexor and rotator muscles. Areas of focal tenderness may be found that indicate local spasm. A large swelling usually represents a contusion with hemorrhage into the muscle. A slight swelling could indicate contusion, strain, sprain, or a combination. The immediate treatment is application of cold to the trigger point, either by an ice pack or freezing spray. Later treatment will involve heat, rest, and analgesic and anti-inflammatory medication. In virtually all of these injuries, the athlete can safely walk from the field.

Nonacute

A small percentage of athletes with low-back problems will not only have low-back pain, but also pain that radiates from the back into the buttocks or down one or both legs. Coughing, sneezing, or straining to pass urine or bowel movements usually makes the leg pain worse. Numbness may also be felt, usually in the foot, over the medial half or along the lateral side. This pattern of pain is called sciatica and suggests that a ruptured disc is pressing on a nerve root. Discs are the fibrocartilaginous cushions between the vertebrae. As the body ages, the discs lose fluid content, becoming slightly narrower and causing a slight shrinkage in height. The outer, more-fibrous capsule of the disc, called the annulus fibrosus, may also tear, allowing the disc to rupture posteriorly out of the disc space and compress the nerve root as it exits from the spine. Most simple ruptures can be treated successfully with a period of bedrest, muscle relaxants, anti-inflammatory medicines, analgesics, and later, exercise. A minor percentage with neurologic deficit such as an absent reflex at knee or ankle, weakness of ankle or great toe extension, or persistent pain and numbness, will require surgical excision of the ruptured disc. With careful selection, the success of such surgery should exceed 90%. Following surgery, the athlete should adhere to the exercises and advice given in this chapter, and should be able to resume competition. Neurosurgical or orthopedic referral is recommended in athletes with persistent sciatica, especially if neurologic deficit is present.

A third group of athletes with low-back problems suffer from mechanical malalignment of the vertebrae—spondylolisthesis [8]. This diagnosis is established by x-ray of the back. If there is instability documented by further malalignment as the back is placed through flexion and extension maneuvers, a surgical procedure of lumbar fusion may be indicated [6,7]. An abnormal lateral curvature of the spine (scoliosis) is another cause of low-back pain. If it is severe in children, it may require surgical correction that is a very extensive and time-consuming procedure. Severe scoliosis renders athletic excellence very remote. The mild form seen in some athletes can be pain-free if the exercises and recommendations in this chapter are followed. If neurologic deficit, spinal instability, malalignment, or significant scoliosis is present, orthopedic or neurosurgical referral is suggested. The exercises and advice in this chapter are primarily directed to the athlete with low-back pain but without neurologic deficit, or who has already had concern about a ruptured disc or spinal instability eliminated by appropriate neurosurgical or orthopedic consultation.

The vast majority of athletes with low-back pain will have no neurologic symptoms, deficits, or spinal instability. Palpation, as with the acute injury of the paraspinal, side flexor and rotator, and abdominal muscles, usually reveals segmental spasm, tenderness, or an area of point tenderness.

Athletes are usually thin and quite physically fit, but have an accentuated lumbar lordosis when walking. The posterior erector spinal muscles are strong, but the abdominal (flexor) muscles, although flat, are quite weak in comparison. A good test of abdominal muscle strength is a slow bent-knee sit-up. An athlete should be able to do 20 or more, but some Olympic-class athletes with back problems have trouble doing one [6]. The back extensor muscles are tested with the athlete on his or her abdomen with a pillow under the hips as a cushion. To test the upper back, with the hands behind the head, the elbows, chin, and trunk should be raised off the floor as long as possible. Low-back strength is tested by keeping the head down with hands behind, while both legs held together with knees straight are raised off the floor. In both exercises, 20 seconds indicates strong muscles and under 10 seconds indicates weak muscles.

Frequently, back rotation is weak. When the overdeveloped extensors are tight, both flexion and rotation are compromised. In some athletes the hip flexor and hamstring muscles will be tight. In such cases, one cannot touch the floor with fingertips with the knees straight. Ideally, the hamstring muscles should be at least 60% to 80% as strong as the quadriceps; the closer to 80%, the fewer back problems encountered. To test the strength of the hip flexor muscles, the athlete should lie on his or her back, legs extended, hands clasped behind the head. With legs touching, the athlete should lift the feet about ten inches off the floor and hold this position for as long as possible. Over 20 seconds indicates strong muscles, under 10 indicates quite weak hip flexor muscles.

Treatment

The successful treatment of low-back pain in athletes involves a three-step program: (1) relief of pain and spasm; (2) adoption of an appropriate exercise program that includes both stretching and strengthening exercises; and (3) an educational program that considers the training program and is tailored to prevent future injuries.

Relief of Pain and Spasm

Ice, analgesics, muscle relaxants, anti-inflammatory agents, and rest are used in acute stages, while heat, muscle stimulation, ultrasound, physical therapy, and the same pharmacologic agents are used 12 or more hours after injury. Ultrasound and gentle muscle stimulation seem to dissipate muscle spasm, point tenderness, and general soreness more rapidly. This is probably due to enhanced muscle circulation and exchange at the cellular level of prescribed pharmacologic agents plus elimination of toxic cellular products [4]. Actually, while modes of pain relief exist, no one treatment has been clearly demonstrated to accelerate actual tissue healing.

Stretching and Strengthening Exercises

Medication, manipulation, massage, ultrasound, and hot and cold applications do not strengthen a weakened or compromised part of the body. Low-back pain is usually due to muscles that are weak, tense, fatigued, or all three. Once the healing process has occurred, it is essential to begin an exercise program to rebuild the back and abdominal musculature.

Before beginning strengthening exercises, it is important to first execute specific stretching exercises for the lumbar extensor and pelvic rotator, hip flexor, and hamstring and hip extensor muscles.

Stretching. Athletes can stretch their lower-back muscles by lying on a mat and bringing the feet up over the face to touch extended toes beyond the head. It is important that these movements are executed fluidly, with no sudden jerking. A good exercise to stretch the hip flexor muscles is to lie on one's back with knees bent and feet under the buttocks. When the arms reach as far toward the knees as possible, the back arches and the hips are thus maximally extended. The straight-leg raise and nose-toe touch, while standing with one leg on a waist-high table are good flexibility exercises for the hamstrings, while the single-knee raise and double-knee hug stretch the hamstrings, lower back, and hip extensors. The athlete must work daily on flexibility exercises to maintain a good range of motion. These exercises should become a routine part of the daily warm-up and cooling-off exercises.

Strengthening. Exercises that strengthen the lower back and abdominal muscles include some of the same exercises that stretch the hamstring and hip flexor muscles. Ten of these exercises are the back flattener, single-knee raise, single-knee hug, double-knee hug, single-leg raise, partial sit-up, advanced sit-up, sitting bend, deep-knee bend, and posture check. Illustrations and descriptions of these exercises appear in appendix 4A. The exercises should be carried out on a hard, flat surface with adequate padding. A tumbling mat is ideal, but a thick rug with underpadding may suffice. For exercises done in a supine position most people find that a small pillow placed under the neck provides more comfort. One should wear loose, unrestrictive clothing. The exercises must always be started slowly to allow muscles to loosen up gradually. At no time should there be jerking or snapping movements. Most persons find relaxing before exercise beneficial, and heat treatment to the lower back aids in loosening tight muscles. Slight discomfort may occur while the exercises are performed, but if frank pain is experienced, the exercise period should be terminated. The exercises should be done daily, ideally twice a day in the beginning. Each athlete should progress at his or her own pace. Initially, five repetitions are usually enough; then, one repetition or two can be added daily to each exercise that can be accomplished with relative ease. If an exercise results in appreciable discomfort, it should be abandoned. An exercise should only be resumed when it can be done without discomfort.

Educational Program

The final link in the low-back-pain elimination triangle involves educating the athlete to avoid back problems, both in training and in daily life. Good posture is achieved by rotating the top of the pelvis backward, which flattens the curve in the lower back. Common everyday tips to avoid the occurrence of low-back pain include:

Standing and walking. Stand with lower back erect and as flat as possible. By squeezing buttocks and sucking in and tensing abdomen, the lower back is straightened. Walk, stand, and sit as tall as possible.

Bend knees when leaning, as when over a wash basin. Avoid leaning whenever possible and squat with a straight lower back.

Avoid high-heeled shoes. They shorten Achilles tendons and increase lordosis.

Avoid standing for long periods, but if it is necessary, alternate leaning on the left foot and the right foot; if possible, use the bent-knee position, as on a stool. This flattens the lower back.

When standing, do not lean back and support the body with the hands. Keep hands in front of the body and lean forward slightly.

When turning to walk from a standing position, move the feet first and then the body.

Open doors wide enough to walk through comfortably.

Carefully judge the height of curbs before stepping up or down.

Sitting. Sit so that the lower back is flat or slightly rounded outward, never with a forward curve.

Sit so that knees are higher than hips; this may require a small footstool for a short person in a high chair.

Hard seat backs that begin contact with the back four to six inches above the seat and provide a flat support throughout the entire lumbar area are preferred.

Do not sit in a soft or overstuffed chair or sofa.

Avoid sitting in swivel chairs or chairs on rollers.

Do not sit with legs out straight on an ottoman or footstool.

Never sit in the same position for prolonged periods; get up and move around.

Driving. Move front seat forward so that knees will be higher than hips and the pedals can be easily reached without stretching.

Sit back with back flat; do not lean forward; sit tall;

Add a flat back rest if car seat is soft or if travelling a long distance.

On a long trip, stop every 30 to 60 minutes, get out of the car and walk around, and tense the buttocks and abdomen to flatten the back for several minutes.

Always fasten seatbelt and shoulder harness.

Be sure car seat has a properly adjusted headrest.

Bedrest. Sleep or rest only on a flat, firm mattress. If one is not available, place a bedboard of no less than three-quarter-inch plywood under the mattress. A board of less thickness will sag, preventing proper spine alignment.

The preferred sleeping position is on the side, both arms in front, with the knees slightly drawn up toward chin.

Do not sleep on stomach.

When lying on the back, place a pillow under the knees; raising the legs flattens the lumbar curve.

When lying in bed, do not extend arms above head; relax them at sides.

If the doctor prescribes absolute bedrest, stay in bed. Raising the body or twisting and turning can strain the back.

Sleep alone or in an oversized bed.

When getting out of bed, turn over on side, draw knees up, then swing legs over the side of the bed.

Lifting. When lifting, let the legs do the work, using the large muscles of the thighs instead of the small muscles of the back.

Do not twist the body; face the object.

Never lift with legs straight.

Do not lift heavy objects from car trunks.

Do not lift from a bending-forward position.

Do not reach over furniture to open and close windows.

Tuck in the buttocks and pull in the abdomen when lifting.

Hold the object being lifted close to the body.

Lift a heavy load no higher than the waist, and a light load no higher than the shoulders; greater height increases lumbar lordosis.

To turn while lifting, pivot the feet, turning the whole body at one time.

In training, to minimize back injuries, the athlete should always warm up slowly and cool down after the main workout. Both the warm-up and cooling-off periods should include back-stretching exercises. Calisthenics that involve hyperextension of the back, such as back bends, straight-leg sit-ups, or straight-leg raises, should be avoided when possible. By faithfully carrying out a daily program of back exercises, the athlete can pursue a variety of potentially hazardous sports with minimal risk of back injury.

Sports Most Hazardous to the Back

Football is felt by some to be legalized assault, often between physical unequals. It is one of the most hazardous sports to the body, particularly to the back. This is especially true for the interior linemen (defensive ends, guards, tackles, and centers). A report from a major university with a number-one national ranking stated that during one year 50% of interior linemen sought medical attention for low-back pain[1]. This report postulated the biomechanics of back injury. As the lineman drives forward attempting to push the opponent backward, the lumbar spine is extended; this converts more of the force to a shearing force that can lead to pars interarticularis injury. The report concluded that the high incidence of spondylolisthesis and spondylosis seen in interior linemen is the result of repeated forces being transmitted to the pars interarticularis while players are in the lumbar-extended posture.

Weight lifting, especially the overhead military press and the clean and jerk, is another high-risk back-injury sport. Severe lordotic postures are also assumed when spiking a volleyball, hitting a twist serve or deep overhead stroke in tennis, putting the shot, throwing the discus or hammer, or even stretching for the tape in track. Extreme backward arching movements are required by the gymnast (especially in dismounts), diver, trampolinist, and squash, soccer, handball, and racquetball enthusiast. Sledding, downhill skiing, and snow- and water-ski jumping can also result in excessive stress to the lower back. Both the hang-glider and pole-vaulter occasionally have precipitous descents in awkward postures that can result in back strain and even compression fractures.

Sports that are less likely to result in back injury include baseball, basketball, bowling, golf, figure skating, softball, ping-pong, waterskiing, canoeing, rowing, fencing, cross-country skiing, badminton, and archery. Sports least likely to result in back injury include bicycling, hiking, swimming, fishing, curling, darts, skin diving, boccie, billiards, pool, and sailing.

In some sports, the most hazardous maneuvers can be modified. For example, the serve and the overhead are the two tennis strokes most strenuous to the back. By tossing a serve slightly forward, less back extension is required, causing less back strain. For those who play a serve and volley game, it will also aid in gaining forward momentum toward the net. When hitting the overhead, the player should go up to the ball, hitting it slightly in front of the body. When trying for a low ball, as in tennis, handball, volleyball, softball, or baseball, the athlete should bend the knees rather than the back, whenever possible. Most gymnastic sports and diving stress good posture. The athlete should sit and stand as tall as possible at all times. The runner, equestrian, diver, and gymnast should keep the lower back flat by tensing the buttocks and abdominal muscles whenever possible.

References

1. Ferguson, R. J. Low back pain in college football linemen. *J. Sports. Med. Phys. Fitness* 2:63–80, 1974.
2. Friedmann, L. W. and Galton, L. *Freedom from Backaches.* New York: Pocket Books, 1973.
3. Harris, W. D. Low back pain in sports medicine. *J. Arkansas Med. Soc.* 74:377–379, 1978.
4. Nachemson, A. The lumbar spine: An orthopedic challenge. *Spine* 1:59–71, 1976.
5. Root, L. and Kiernan, T. *Oh, My Aching Back.* New York: New American Library, 1975.
6. Smith, C. F. Physical management of muscular low back pain in the athlete. *Can. Med. Assoc. J.* 177:632–635, 1977.
7. Wiltse, L. L. Etiology of spondylolisthesis. *Clin. Orthop.* 10:48–60, 1957.
8. Wiltse, L. L. Spondylolisthesis: Classification and etiology. In *American Academy of Orthopedic Surgeons Symposium on the Spine.* St. Louis: C. V. Mosby, 1969.

11 / Eye, Mouth, and Face Injuries

Paul Vinger, M.D.

Lance Junior is the allstar halfback on the college team where you are the team physician. Lance Senior, a successful attorney on the board of trustees of the college, is eagerly watching the final minutes of the "Big Game." It is third down, goal to go with 33 seconds on the clock. Lance Junior gets the ball and is stopped short of the goal by a foot. During the play, he gets poked in the eye with a finger. You examine him—the eye is somewhat red, but Lance Junior assures you it feels okay as he runs back to the line of scrimmage. This try, Junior makes the score and is rewarded with a trip to Hawaii by his joyous father. While in Hawaii, Junior suffers a total retinal detachment as the previously undiagnosed giant retinal tear leaks vitreous into the subretinal space. Several operations by the best surgeons fail, and Junior loses useful vision in the injured eye. At this time, you learn that Junior had dense amblyopia in the uninjured eye from a small esotropia. Lance Junior's career in his father's law firm will be virtually impossible, since he cannot read with finger-counting vision. Lance Senior will: A. Put his arm around you and thank you for all the years of great service to the team. B. Sue you for the value of Lance Junior's career, with the thrust of his case built on the "rule of forseeability."

Impossible? A scare case that could never happen? I do not think so. From my experience studying the mechanism of eye injury in hundreds of injured athletes, the probability of an occurrence similar to this is almost inevitable—many team physicians do not check preplay vision; even more allow play to continue after an injury that is not given adequate follow-up referral by an appropriate specialist. All eye and teeth injuries and most significant facial injuries are beyond the competence of the primary-care physician to evaluate and treat. Referral to a dentist, oral surgeon, otolaryngologist, plastic surgeon, or ophthalmologist as appropriate is the only way to assure that no reversible, potentially permanent injury escapes the scrutiny of the primary physician. This chapter is not intended to cover all the possible eye, teeth, and face injuries with details of definitive treatment by the specialist. This type of information is available elsewhere [2]. Rather, this chapter will provide the means of recognizing significant injuries to these areas, when to refer to a specialist (immediately or on a delayed basis), and the protective devices available for various sports. The role of the primary-care physician in the treatment and prevention of eye, face, and teeth injuries is vital, since prompt primary care will often be the difference between loss of function and successful repair by the appropriate specialist.

The most important task for the team physician takes place well before the athletes have their first practice—appropriate protective devices must be chosen. The use of protective devices can eliminate most eye, teeth, and facial injuries.

Even with the best protection and with rigid enforcement of the rules, injuries will occur—often in rain or snow or during the heat of competition—with only primitive diagnostic facilities on the site. The primary physician must be able to recognize that a potentially significant injury has occurred, administer appropriate first aid, and institute referral to a specialist (if necessary), while remembering that the rest of the team is still exposed to injury. Under these conditions, the clues to serious injury should be easily noted with simple diagnostic methods.

Necessary Equipment for Diagnosis and First Aid

1. A player book, with the name and any special medical problems of each athlete should be brought to all practices and games. This is especially important for the notation of any preexisting visual impairment, dentures, or allergies.

2. Phone numbers of hospitals and covering physicians, especially for away games, should be in the player book. The primary physician has the right to expect full and immediate coverage from colleagues specializing in dentistry, ophthalmology, otolaryngology, and plastic surgury. Access to a phone is often overlooked at strange fields.

3. A way to transport an athlete, on a stretcher, to a hospital is necessary (station wagon or van if ambulance is not at site). No meaningful definitive treatment can be done for eye, face, and teeth injuries on an athletic field.

4. Contents of the sports-medicine bag should be on hand (chapter 8).

The Eye

Preseason Evaluation

Any history of prior eye disease or trauma should be recorded, and appropriate letters from the ophthalmologist should attest that the athlete is fit to resume play if the injury or disease was significant. The vision in each eye, tested separately for near and far, should be measured and recorded. If the vision in either eye is less than 20/40 with glasses, referral to an ophthalmologist before practice is necessary. The ophthalmologist may find a refractive error, in which case spectacles or contact lenses may be needed for adequate visual performance. If the vision cannot be corrected with glasses, the ophthalmologist should give the diagnosis, prognosis, and any ocular contraindications to the coach or trainer of the intended sport.

If one eye is normal, and the other has subnormal vision that cannot be corrected with glasses or contact lenses, the decision for athletic participation rests on the quality of vision in the poor eye and the chances of leading a normal life with the vision in the poor eye if a catastrophic injury occurred to the good eye. Best correctable vision of 20/40 or better is consistent with most normal activities. Best correctable vision between 20/50 and 20/200 makes it impossible to drive a car in most states and makes many jobs that require good vision impossible, yet the person may still lead a productive life with the remaining vision. Best correctable vision below 20/200 is considered legally blind in most states, and qualifies the patient for the benefits given the blind by society.

The One-Eyed Athlete

An athlete should be considered one-eyed if the best corrected vision in the involved eye is 20/200 or less, with the other eye found normal by an ophthalmologist. Since the loss of the good eye would result in legal or total blindness, the athlete and the parents must be informed of the potential long-term consequences if the good eye is lost. They should also be informed of the risks of injury, the effectiveness of available protective devices, and the possibilities of repair of injuries typically seen with the sport in question. Boxing should be totally excluded from consideration since there is no possibility of protecting the remaining eye. Collision and contact sports should be discouraged, since even with the best protectors, catastrophic eye injuries are possible. However, if the player, parents, and their lawyers (one cannot discriminate against the handicapped) are persistent after an informative discussion, they should sign appropriate waivers provided by the school-committee legal staff. No waiver should be given for boxing—the protection of the athlete is worth a court appeal. The waiver should include mandatory use of protective devices. Class I or Class II sports eye protectors must be worn at all times while participating in *any* sport. In addition, appropriate helmet/face-mask protection is to be used for all practices and games.

In general, any person considered one-eyed should wear safety glasses most of the time to protect the good eye. This is especially true of young active people who are subject to injury on or off the athletic field.

Evaluate pupillary reactions. The most sensitive, quick screening test available for injury to the optic nerve or retina is the swinging light test for afferent-conduction defect. An ophthalmologist should demonstrate the normal and abnormal reactions, since proper execution of the test requires a "feel," which is easy to demonstrate but difficult to describe. A pocket flashlight is swung from eye to eye—shined onto the right pupil, then the left, then back to the right, then to the left. As the light is swung from eye to eye, at the rate of once per second or two, the physician observes the reaction of the pupil being illuminated. Only the initial pupillary reaction is considered, since the pupil will frequently dilate and constrict slightly while under the light stimulus (hippus). In the normal person, the initial reaction of the pupil being illuminated is constriction. If the initial reaction is dilation, no matter how slight, the test is positive and the patient has a conduction defect in the afferent pupillary system of the eye in which the pupil dilates. A positive swinging light test always indicates a lesion in the retina or optic nerve, and a full evaluation by an ophthalmologist is required before beginning athletic participation. If the swinging light test is normal, the pupils should be evaluated for equality in size, reaction to light and accommodation, symmetry, and centration. Since pupillary findings are of prime importance in the evaluation of injury on the field, any abnormality, no matter how small, should be evaluated by an ophthalmologist and the finding noted in the player book.

Check Extraocular Motion. The six cardinal gaze positions (right, left, up and right, up and left, down and right, and down and left) should be checked while asking the athlete if any diplopia is experienced in any gaze position. The presence of nystagmus or any unusual facial asymmetry should be noted. Any questionable findings and all ptosis should be referred for evaluation.

Evaluate the fundi. The pupils should be dilated if the fundi cannot be seen (2.5% phenylephrine plus 1% tropicamide will dilate most pupils within 20 minutes). Do not dilate the pupils after injury; dilated pupils may interfere with neurologic observation. Although evaluation of the fundi is an important preseason evaluation, it is relatively unimportant at the time of injury because (1) the fundi are often difficult to see under game conditions, especially if the media are hazy or the athlete is in pain; (2) the pupils should not be dilated at the time of injury; and (3) most fundus injuries from ocular contusion require specialized equipment (indirect ophthalmoscope with scleral depression) to visualize. In all contused eyes, the fundi should be evaluated by an ophthalmologist. Under the best conditions, somewhat less than one-half of the retina can be seen with the hand-held (direct) ophthalmoscope. This instrument is essential for the preseason evaluation, but may be left in the office at practice or game time.

Choose and Properly Fit Eye Protective Devices. One of the most important, yet neglected, roles of the primary team physician is his or her involvement in the choice of protective equipment. Eye, face, and head protectors should be chosen and properly fitted to each athlete. Well-made, properly-fitted protective devices are as important to the freshman team as they are to the varsity. If used equipment is recycled to less-skilled players, it should be first-quality and well-fit. There is no place for obsolescent protective equipment in any athletic program.

If the athlete wears glasses, the type of lens and frame should be specified by the optician. Streetwear glasses may be unsafe for many sports, and a Class-II eye protector should be required before athletic participation. If an athlete wears contact lenses, a back-up pair of eyeglasses should be required at all games and practices. Since contact lenses offer no eye protection, an appropriate eye protector must be worn for those sports where protection is necessary.

Athletes should be instructed on the importance of proper use and maintenance of protective gear. Failure to use the protective devices should result in a strict penalty, such as benching for the remainder of the practice or game, and removal from the team for repeated offenses. The attitude of the team physician is that injuries will be reduced as much as possible; the athletes and coaches must understand and acknowledge the physician's authority in insisting on the proper use of preventive measures.

The physician's responsibility does not start only after an injury occurs. This position will be resisted by some coaches, who tend to minimize the necessity of protective equipment, especially in practice sessions. The authority of the physician must be spelled out by the athletic director before the season begins and clearly articulated to the coaching staff. If the physician has no control over the choice and use of protective equipment, he or she is vulnerable when injury that could have been prevented with better-designed or better-fitting devices occurs. A physician who is expected to treat injury but not in a position to prevent injury should resign from service to the team.

Field Evaluation for Injury

The general principle for treating all significant eye injuries is *patch and refer.* More harm than good will result from improper attempts at treatment on the athletic field.

When an athlete suffers a blow to the eye, the integrity of the globe should be ascertained immediately. If the lids are swollen shut, it should be assumed that the globe is ruptured. The lids should not be forced open, as the rise in intraocular pressure can cause extrusion of the ocular contents if there is a corneal or scleral laceration. If there is any suspicion of a ruptured globe, the patient should be kept calm and urged not to squeeze the lids tightly closed. Forced lid closure can elevate the intraocular pressure from a normal 15 mm Hg to over 70 mm Hg, with potentially disastrous results. The injured eye should be covered with a sterile eye patch (moderate pressure by single patch), a hard-metal or plastic shield should be put over the patch with tape, and the athlete should be moved at once to ophthalmologic care. The majority of ruptured globes can be salvaged, provided the retina and choroid are not extruded. Loss of aqueous and vitreous alone do not preclude return of visual function. Therefore, every attempt must be made to avoid increases in intraocular pressure from examination techniques, the patient's forced lid closure, or the patient's inadvertent rubbing of the injured eye. Lacerations of the cornea may be extremely subtle.

If the globe is not ruptured, the lids and periocular structures should be examined for lacerations and edema. Crepitus (air beneath the skin) always indicates a fracture into one of the sinuses, usually the floor or medial wall of the orbit into the maxillary or ethmoid sinuses. Vision in both eyes should be measured (near card will suffice). The eye not being tested must be completely occluded, as the athlete may try to cheat to remain in competition. The pupils should be examined carefully, using the swinging-light test. Very minimal pupillary changes may indicate significant intraocular pathology. The cornea and anterior chamber must be examined. The cornea should be crystal clear, and the iris details should exactly match those of the other eye. Blood or inflammatory debris in the anterior chamber is often manifest by a barely detectable haze of the iris details.

The extraocular movements in the six cardinal gaze positions should be evaluated while questioning the athlete for diplopia.

Immediate referral to the ophthalmologist is required for:

imbedded corneal foreign bodies

haze or blood in the anterior chamber

decreased vision, constriction, or loss of a portion of the visual field

irregular, asymmetric, or poorly reacting pupil

diplopia in any field of gaze

lacerations involving the lid margin, or impaired lid function

suspected perforation or laceration of the globe

broken contact lens or shattered eyeglasses

unexplained eye pain or visual complaints

In addition, the ophthalmologist should examine at a later date all blunt trauma to the eye and orbit. Only a complete eye examination can rule out internal ocular injury. Many injuries, easily treated in their early stages, result in loss of vision if left to their own course.

A topical anesthetic should never be used to relieve eye pain so that the athlete may continue play.

Teeth

Preseason Evaluation

Since the teeth have the lowest potential to return to a normal, healthy state than any other part of the body and since attempts at reconstruction are costly and time consuming, the main preseason emphasis should be on the choice of adequate protection. Full face protectors (when indicated) should be chosen and well fitted to the helmet and face. For internal protection, a protector custom-made by a dentist (figure 11–1) is preferred over the stock-type and mouth-formed protectors. Most teams can enlist the assistance of a sports-minded dentist who will mold these guards for the entire team at lower cost as a service to the school. If the custom-made mouth guard is not within the team budget, the services of a dentist to aid in the forming of the kit-type mouth protectors (figure 11–2) will help assure proper fit and protection. Internal mouth protectors help reduce the incidence of tooth fracture, protect the jaw, and possibly aid in preventing concussion from blows to the chin. They should be made with a fail-safe strap to attach to the face guard for use in football and hockey to prevent possible aspiration of the protector.

A record should be made in the player book of any dental prosthesis the athlete may use. A note from the dentist should indicate proper use of the prosthesis and if it

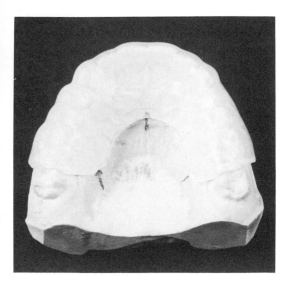

Figure 11–1. A custom-made mouth protector. A piece of clear vinyl plastic is heated and vacuformed to a plaster model made from a dental impression of the upper jaw.

Figure 11–2 A finished mouth-formed protector. Note attachment strap for fixation to headguard.

should be removed for certain types of sports because of the potential of unconsciousness and aspiration of the prosthesis.

The mouth and teeth should be examined by the team physician. Any significant dental disease should be corrected before the onset of athletic participation.

Field Evaluation for Injury

The teeth and the stability and motion of the jaw should be examined after all blows to the mouth and chin. Players may resume play after a partially fractured (angle or corner) stable tooth with no pain or bleeding, but they should be seen by a dentist as soon as possible. Partially dislodged teeth require immediate dental evaluation for alignment and stabilization. Completely dislodged teeth should be repositioned into the gum by the physician on the field if there appears to be no root fracture. If this cannot be done, the best chance of maintaining viability is to have the injured athlete hold the tooth in his or her mouth under the tongue to keep it moist until splinted by a dentist. A dislodged tooth should not be carried outside the mouth. If kept out of the mouth dry for 30 minutes, there is almost no chance of retention after replacement. If the athlete is unconscious or disoriented, the tooth should be carried in gauze moistened with saline. Bleeding in the mouth and perioral tissue can be controlled with direct pressure while awaiting definitive care. A chest x-ray is necessary to rule out aspiration if missing teeth or dental prosthesis cannot be found on playing field.

Face

Preseason Evaluation

Any history of prior surgery and any wires or prosthetic devices should be noted. Significant prior injury requires a detailed letter from the surgeon, listing potential contraindications to certain sports and the need for properly fitted special protective equipment.

Field Evaluation for Injury

Since the facial skeleton is the supporting structure for the digestive tract, the most important consideration with any facial injury is the maintenance of an adequate airway. After a blow to the jaw or neck, a fractured larynx should be suspected if there is any change in the quality of the voice, shortness of breath, or hemorrhage. Fractures to the frontal bone, midface nose, zygoma, and jaw require stabilization of the patient, maintenance of the airway, control of bleeding, and referral to specialist care.

Sports Guidelines for Eye, Face, and Teeth Safety

Data from the Consumer Product Safety Commission and the National Society to Prevent Blindness document an ever-increasing rise in the number of eye injuries from sports, with over 26,400 visits to hospital emergency rooms in 1978. That most eye injuries can be prevented with proper protective devices (with great savings in medical costs) has been proven by detailed study of the medical and economic effects of full-face hockey protectors [2,3,4]. Hospital studies show that sports are responsible for 48% of hyphema (hemorrhage into the anterior chamber of the eye) (table 11–1). Most of these injuries can be prevented with use of proper eye (and face) protective devices (see appendixes 11–A, 11–B, and 11–C for types of protectors, spectacle classification, and protector recommendations). Protective devices do not provide a guarantee against injury but are de-

Table 11–1 Causes of Hyphema at Massachusetts Eye and Ear Infirmary (February 1, 1980 to September 30, 1980)[a]

Cause	Number of Cases
Traumatic	
Sports (see summary below)	45[b]
Accidental	31
Mechanical/Household/Handyman	5
Alleged Assault	9
Spontaneous	
Secondary to Vitreous Hemorrhage	2
Unknown	2
	—
	94
Summary of Sports Injuries[c]	
Racquetball (ball)	10
Racquetball (racket)	1
Tennis (ball)	9
Squash (ball)	2
Baseball (ball)	4
Baseball (bat)	1
Softball (ball)	4
Wiffle ball (ball)	2
Hockey (stick)	3
Street hockey (ball)	1
Frisbee	2
Bicycle (fell off)	1
Basketball	1
Volley ball	1
B-B	1
Ball not specified	2

[a]Data collected by Harvey H. Slansky, M.D., Stephen Depperman, M.D., Frank Berson, M.D., and Joel A. Kraut, M.D.

[b]Of the 45 cases caused by sports, 43 had no eye protection. Of the 2 with eye protection, one was in baseball, where the ball squeezed through the catcher's mask; the other was in racquetball, where the ball squeezed through a protector without lenses.

[c]Observations: (1) Sports caused 48% of hyphemas admitted. (2) Prevention of these injuries would have saved $39,029 in hospital expenses alone. Physician fees, time lost from work, late complications, insurance costs, and other problems represent significant additional potential savings. (3) Protective devices are essential for racquet sports. (4) Baseball and softball are responsible for substantial injuries. (5) No injuries were seen to hockey players wearing protective devices.

signed to reduce the incidence or minimize the severity of injuries. So that the efficacy of protective devices can be monitored, a detailed record should be kept of all injuries and should be reviewed on a regular basis to determine particularly hazardous activities. This data is most effectively utilized if pooled in a system such as the National Athletic Injury/Illness Reporting System (NAIRS). Performance standards exist for some protective devices but not for others. Where standards do exist, only devices that meet the specifications of the standard should be used. If no performance standards have been written, the manufacturer should document the efficacy of the protective device (see appendix 11–D for available performance standards).

Suggested Readings

Hinson, D. R. Legal aspects of sports eye injuries: Lawyer's perspective. In P. F. Vinger (Ed.). *Ocular Sports Injuries.* Boston: Little, Brown and Company, 1981.

Tolkin, H. G. and Bentkover, J. D. Economics of sports injuries. In P. F. Vinger and E. F. Hoerner (Eds.). *Sports Injuries: The Unthwarted Epidemic.* Littleton, Mass.: PSG Publishing Co., Inc., 1981.

Vinger, P. F. Sports eye injuries: A preventable disease. *Ophthalmology* 88:108–113, 1981.

Vinger, P. F. and Hoerner, E. F. (Eds.). *Sports Injuries: The Unthwarted Epidemic.* Littleton, Mass.: PSG Publishing Co., Inc., 1981.

Appendix 11-A
Types of Protectors

Total-Head-Protection Concept. Several sports (football, hockey, lacrosse) have such high potential-energy levels that the head, brain, face, eyes, teeth, jaw, and in some cases, the larynx must be protected as a unit, wherein forces are transmitted through a helmet-mounted face protector to a helmet designed to protect the brain (figure 11–3).

Full-Face Protector. Some sports (fencing) have the potential for injury to the entire facial structure, but the forces are directed mostly from the front, with little threat to the brain. Energy is transmitted to the buttress bones of the face (frontal, zygoma, and maxilla) and the mandible by padding at the periphery of the protector.

Figure 11–3 Hockey helmet/face mask combination.

155

Sports Eye Protector. This device is designed to protect the eyes only. Several design options are available:

(1) *Class-I:* A protector with the lens and frame frontpiece molded as one unit. Frame temples or other devices (such as straps) to affix to the lens/frontpiece may be separate pieces (figure 11–4).

Figure 11–4 Class-I sports eye protector

Figure 11–5 Industrial safety glasses with clear side shields

(2) *Class-II:* A protector with a lens, either nonprescription or prescription, mounted in a frame that is manufactured as a separate unit. Industrial safety glasses (figure 11–5) as well as specifically-designed sports eye-frame/lens combinations (figure 11–6) are available.

(3) *Class-III:* A protector without a lens, designed for use by itself (figure 11–7) or over spectacles.

Larynx Protector. This device, worn separately or mounted onto a face protector, is designed to prevent blows to the larynx.

Figure 11–6   A and B. Class-II sports eye protectors

Figure 11–7   Class-III sports eye protector

External Mouth Guard. Worn over the mouth, this protector is designed to transmit forces away from the teeth to the maxilla and mandible.

Internal Mouth Guard. This device is worn between the teeth, to prevent fracture of the teeth and jaw. Several types are available:

(1) stock
(2) mouth-formed
(3) custom fabricated over a model

Appendix 11-B
Spectacle Classification

Streetwear (FDA specification for impact resistance). Streetwear spectacles are the glasses a person receives from an optician when there is no need for impact resistance, other than the ordinary hazards of daily living. Streetwear spectacles should not be used in any sport where there is a potential for eye contact by an object or competitor.

Industrial Safety Spectacles (American National Standards Institute [ANSI] Z 87.1). Impact-resistance and lens-retention characteristics of both lenses and frames must withstand the energy potential in many industrial settings. As a general rule, athletes participating in sports that involve a ball, racket, poking fingers, fists, or elbows (basketball, racket sports, baseball,) could obtain adequate protection with industrial-safety spectacles. Clear sideshields provide additional protection to the exposed lateral side of the eye. Polycarbonate is the lightest, strongest plastic available for lenses but is not available in all prescriptions. If the prescription is not available in polycarbonate plastic, CR-39 plastic lenses should be used. Glass spectacle lenses should never be used by an athlete unless the prescription cannot be ground in polycarbonate or CR-39.

Sports Eye Protectors. Many eye protectors are being designed for specific sports. Those designed to hold a prescription lens should have polycarbonate or CR-39 lenses mounted. Plano (nonprescription) protectors should be molded of polycarbonate plastic and coated for scratch resistance.

Appendix 11-C Protector Recommendations

Total Head Protection (helmet, full face protector, internal mouth guard)

- Essential for football, hockey, (forwards, defensemen, and goalies) lacrosse (men and women), box lacrosse, baseball catcher (although it is common practice for baseball catchers to use only face protectors, the bat to the rear of the head in overswing is also a hazard)

- Highly suggested for field hockey and baseball batters (especially little league)

Helmet with Separate Eye Protector (helmet-mounted shield may be preferred by some athletes for some sports)

- Essential for horseback riding, ski racing, cycling, motorcycling, auto racing, and snowmobiling

- Suggested for polo and cricket

Helmet Alone (designed to give at least partial eye protection)

- Essential for boxing

Face Protector

- Essential for fencing

- Not adequate for hockey goalie unless affixed to helmet

Eye Protector Alone

- Essential for racket sports

- Highly suggested for baseball (fielders), softball, soccer, basketball, and cross-country skiing)

161

Appendix 11-D
Available
Performance
Standards

Helmet

1. Standard Method of Impact Test and Performance Requirements for Football Helmets. Prepared by National Operating Committee on Standards for Athletic Equipment. Sept. 1973; revised Sept. 1977; revised Jan. 1980.

2. Standard Test Method for Shock-Attenuation Characteristics of Protective Headgear for Football. ANSI/ASTM F 429–79. American Society for Testing and Materials (ASTM). Dec. 1979.

3. Specification for Shock Attenuation of Football Helmets. ASTM F 717 (in committee).

4. Hockey Helmets. Canadian Standards Association (CSA) Z262.1–1975; Supplement No. 1 Z262.1S1–1976.

5. Hockey Helmets. ASTM (in committee).

6. Standard Method of Impact Test and Performance Requirements for Polo Helmets. Prepared for United States Polo Association by Wayne State University Department of Neurosurgery. Jan. 15, 1979.

7. Specification for Protective Helmets for Pedal Cyclists. British Standards Institution BS 4544. 1970.

8. General Purpose Protective Helmets (for use in Pedal Cycling, Horse Riding and Other Activities Requiring Similar Protection). Australian Standard Specification AS 2063. 1977.

9. Proposed ANSI Standard-Protective Headgear for Bicycle Users. Prepared by Bicycle Helmet Standard Subcommittee, American National Standards Institute (in committee).

10. Motorcycle Helmet. ANSI Z90.1–1971; ANSI Z90.1a–1973; ANSI Z90.1b–1979.

11. Motorcycle Helmets. Helmets Designed for Use by Motorcyclists and Other Motor Vehicle Users. Federal Safety Standard. Motor Vehicle Safety Standard No. 218. March 1974.

12. Standard Protective Helmets, Goggles, Face Shields and Wind Screens for Motorcycles. State of New York—Department of Motor Vehicles. CR–54. March, 1968.

13. Standard for Protective Headgear. Snell Memorial Foundation (crash helmets). 1975.

14. Law Enforcement Standards Program. Riot Helmets. ANSI/NILECJ 0104.00–1974. May, 1977.

Face Protectors for Use When Affixed to a Helmet for Total Head Protection

1. Specification for Eye and Face Protection for Hockey Players. ASTM F 513. Sept. 1979.

2. Face Protectors for Ice Hockey and Box Lacrosse Players (1A). CSA CAN3–Z262.2–M78.

3. Face Protectors for Baseball. ASTM (in committee).

Eye Guards

1. Specification for Eye Protective (Skiing) Devices. ASTM F 659. May 1980.

2. Specification for Eye Protective (Racket Sport) Devices. ASTM (in committee).

Mouthguards

1. Practice for Care and Use of Mouthguards. ASTM F 607. Dec. 1980.

Recommendations

The rules committee for each sport should analyze data on head, eye, face, and tooth injuries for that sport. If injuries are occurring, especially those resulting in permanent disability, protective devices should be examined and possibly changed, or the rules should be changed. If there is inadequate data, a data-collection system should be instituted. Extensive injury data is not essential before the recommendation of protective devices—a high probability of catastrophic eye, face, or tooth injury from a sport is sufficient to recommend protection while the data-collecting process is being set up.

12 / Torso and Genitourinary-Tract Injuries

Injuries to the thorax, abdomen, and genitourinary system can occur with any activity involving rapid deceleration or impact to these regions. Contact sports such as football, lacrosse, or hockey are especially prone to produce torso injuries. The most common thoracic and abdominal injuries include contusion, abrasion, fracture, muscle strain, ligament sprain, and laceration. If the injury is superficial, recognition is usually obvious, but visceral injuries are often very difficult to diagnose.

A primary-care physician in attendance at an athletic event or examining an athlete with a torso injury must be an expert in cardiopulmonary resuscitation (CPR). The first priority with a torso injury, as is true for any major injury, is to make certain there is an adequate airway and the athlete is breathing well. It must be quickly established that the victim is not obstructing the airway with tongue, aspirated gum, mouth guard, or other foreign body. It must be rapidly determine if he or she can breathe deeply and has full chest-wall excursion. The presence or absence of a penetrating chest injury or flail segment of ribs with paradoxical motion in breathing (i.e., retraction of a segment while the remainder of the rib cage expands, and vice versa) must be determined. A quick assessment of circulation must also be part of the initial examination. This includes noting the color of the face and fingernails, palpating peripheral and carotid pulses, and taking blood pressure and pulse rate. This assessment should be orderly, thoughtful, thorough, and rapid, taking 30 to 60 seconds.

First Aid

First aid is very different for open and closed wounds. Players with puncture or penetrating wounds should be transferred to a hospital and referred to a general or thoracic surgeon. Superficial abrasions should be cleansed with a sterile soap and covered with an occlusive sterile bandage. Lacerations should be similarly cleansed, sutured, and bandaged.

Blunt injuries to the chest or abdomen require that the athlete be removed from the playing field and examined for visceral injuries. Ice should be applied to the site of trauma to minimize tissue bleeding and hematoma formation. If pain increases, or pallor, diaphoresis, tachycardia, or hypotension develops, the injured player should be transferred to the hospital for general or thoracic surgical evaluation.

In general, injection of local anesthetics, steroids, or other medications is contraindicated in the initial first-aid evaluation, as serious visceral injuries may be masked. This is especially true of pain medication. Return to play must be the sole decision of the physician, not the coach or player.

Injuries to the Thorax

The components of the chest wall, musculotendinous attachments, bone, soft tissue, and ligaments interact. The function of the upper extremities is also intimately associated with the thorax. Because the manubrium, sternum, and xiphoid are covered only by skin and scant connective tissue, they are especially vulnerable to blunt trauma such as contusion with hematoma formation.

Contusion of the sternum is best treated with ice and anti-inflammatory agents such as aspirin, Bufferin, Butazolidin, Indocin, Motrin, Tolectin, or Clinoril, for the first 24 hours. Then heat (wet or dry) may replace the ice while the anti-inflammatory agents are continued. Activity should be limited until full range of motion of the upper extremities and thorax is possible without pain. If a contact sport is being played, protective padding is recommended with resumption of contact.

Fractures of the sternum are uncommon. If present on x-ray, referral to a thoracic surgeon is suggested, as torso traction or realignment may be indicated.

Costochondral or costosternal subluxation or dislocation occur with deformity, and referral to a thoracic surgeon should be made. While easy to reduce manually, reduction is usually difficult to maintain. Costovertebral subluxation is painful and disabling, and occasionally requires open reduction or resection. The initial treatment is ice, anti-inflammatory pain medicine, and use of a rib belt. The athlete should not return to play until pain and tenderness are gone, usually in two to four weeks. If pain persists longer than a month, referral to a thoracic surgeon is recommended.

Breast injuries are occurring with increasing frequency. This is because more women are participating in sports, and also due to the current fad of not wearing bras. Wearing a firm-fitting bra will protect the breast from blunt trauma and motion that strains the fascial attachments of the breast to the pectoralis-major muscle, resulting in pain. Breast contusions are treated like contusions elsewhere, that is, immediate ice and anti-inflammatory pain medication followed later by heat and padding. Young girls are prone to develop fibrocystic disease and even breast abscess. Fibroadenoma is also common during menstruation. While some team physicians do have the necessary background to treat these injuries, others refer the girls to a gynecologist or general surgeon.

Gynecomastia may occur in young men. Frequently unilateral, the nipple may become sore, tender to pressure, and irritated from rubbing against the shirt. Long-distance women runners who do not wear bras may also suffer from nipple chafing. While wearing a proper bra may prevent this problem in women, men may obtain relief from placing either vaseline or a single layer of plastic tape over their nipples. Gynecomastia is usually a self-limiting problem. If it persists, endocrine referral to assess adrenal, pituitary, and testicular pathology is recommended.

Rib fractures are painful and debilitating, and often coexist with intrathoracic pathology. Any athlete who claims he has lost his breath or can't catch his breath several minutes after injury must be suspected of having sustained an intrathoracic injury such as pneumothorax or hemothorax. The area of trauma should be observed for deformity, edema, or ecchymosis. The ribs should be palpated and compressed in the anterior-posterior and lateral directions to elicit tenderness and demonstrate the crackling sound of subcutaneous emphysema. Such a noise denotes the presence of pleural or bronchial injury, and a thoracic surgery referral is indicated. Which ribs are affected should also be noted, since the kidneys, liver, and spleen lie beneath the lower ribs. Vocal fremitus and breath sounds will both be decreased on the side of a pneumothorax. A chest x-ray is essential for the diagnosis of some cases of pneumothorax, as a child with an excellent cardiovascular system can appear normal yet harbor this lesion. The trachea should be observed for any shift. Cyanosis and tachypnea that do not promptly subside also suggest significant pulmonary pathology and should be referred. A hemothorax will quickly bring on signs of shock.

Rib fractures necessitate removal from competition, and the athlete should return only when (1) rib x-rays show healing of the fracture, (2) tenderness to palpation and compression is minimal, (3) no analgesic agent is required, and (4) full range of motion is possible. The early treatment is an analgesic agent for pain, and while taping is no longer recommended, a canvas rib belt with shoulder straps may afford substantial relief, especially for sleeping. It is removed for bathing. Treating intercostal nerve block with Xylocaine, including two ribs above and below the fracture, may afford temporary relief of severe pain, but must never be used to allow the athlete to return to competition.

The *musculotendinous attachments* to the thorax (pectoralis, latissimus dorsi, trapezius, rhomboid, and rectus muscles) may be strained by vigorous muscular contraction. Treatment, as for strains elsewhere, consists of initial application of ice plus oral anti-inflammatory–analgesic medication and decreased motion through the use of a sling. Rehabilitation can include heat, ultrasound, muscle-resistant exercises, and gradual resumption of activity. Cardiovascular fitness can be maintained during this period by bicycling or jogging.

Costochondritis (Tietze's syndrome) is a self-limiting inflammatory process. Of unknown origin, its symptoms include tenderness, swelling, and pain on motion at the costochondral junction. If oral anti-inflammatory agents do not give adequate relief of pain, an injection of 1 cc 1% lidocaine mixed with 1 cc of a long-acting steroid such as Depo Medrol, may give longer relief.

Injuries to the Abdomen

The abdominal wall is usually not the site of serious injury. This is because the abdomen is largely protected; it is on the flexion side of the torso, and is soft compared to joints and the back, affording some give when it is struck. Also, players such as goalies, catchers, and fencers, who are the targets of thrown or propelled objects usually wear well-designed and well-fitted protective padding. Injuries to the abdominal wall may be defined in several ways: (1) level of injury (skin, subcutaneous tissue, muscles), (2) blunt or penetrating, and (3) individually contracted (strains) or the result of contact with another athlete or immovable object. All penetrating injuries should be referred to a general surgeon. Injuries individually contracted tend to be less severe than those resulting from a collision, thus referral is usually only necessary in the latter case.

Injuries to the *skin* are minor, with abrasions resulting from friction burns being the most common. Thorough cleansing to eliminate surface dirt and debris is mandatory, then covering the wound with a light occlusive, nonadhering dressing. Lacerations of the abdominal wall are uncommon, and their treatment is the same as for lacerations elsewhere. A note of caution is that abdominal subcutaneous fat is less resistant to infection than subcutaneous tissue elsewhere. Thus, there must be meticulous cleansing and removal of foreign debris, an aseptic suturing technique, and tetanus immunization. If there is any question that the laceration extends into the abdominal wall muscle, general surgical consultation is advised.

The only injury of note at the subcutaneous level is a hematoma—arteriolar or venous bleeding into the fatty layer resulting from blunt trauma. Initial treatment should be ice for the first 24 to 48 hours, then heat. Needle aspiration can be attempted if fluctuance develops. If recurrent hematomas develop in a young athlete, he or she should be screened for an underlying blood dyscrasia such as leukemia or idiopathic thrombocytopenic purpura. It is recommended that all young athletes involved in contact sports have a complete blood count and urinalysis as part of their routine preseason physical examination.

The *muscles* of the *abdominal wall* protect the intra-abdominal viscera from most injury but are themselves the site of very painful and debilitating injury. They include the two rectus muscles running parallel from the costal margins to the pelvis, the external and internal oblique muscles, and the transversus abdominis muscle lying closest to the peritoneal membrane. Injuries to the abdominal muscles can be grouped into blunt trauma (contusion), strain, and penetrating injuries. All penetrating injuries should be referred to a general surgeon. A rupture of the deep epigastric arteries and/or veins, creating a deep hematoma in the rectus-muscle sheath until self-tamponading occurs, is the most serious blunt trauma injury of the abdominal wall. If the hematoma continues to enlarge, surgical referral is required, as evacuation of the hematoma and ligation of the epigastric vessel is occasionally required. Treatment of this and lesser contusions of the abdominal wall include ice and anti-inflammatory/analgesic medication initially, then heat. When tenderness has abated and ability to perform all essential maneuvers has returned, the athlete is ready to return to competition. Obviously, no athlete on anticoagulant medication should be allowed to participate in sports where blunt abdominal trauma may occur.

Abdominal-muscle strains usually occur from overstretching a bundle of muscle fibers beyond their normal tensile capability, often when the torso is twisted and hyperextended in contact with another athlete or immovable object. The rectus muscle is essential for a wide variety of movements by hurdlers, ice skaters, rowers, and wrestlers, and is especially prone to strain. Strains can also occur when musculotendinous insertions are pulled away from the bone, such as the iliac crest (hip pointer), or when muscle fibers are pulled away from aponeurotic sheaths or lines. With a hip pointer in a young athlete before epiphyseal closure, the bone may be avulsed. An x-ray to rule out fracture or epiphyseal separation is required. The iliopsoas muscle is prone to strain in divers and gymnasts. Rupture that requires evacuation of a retroperitoneal hematoma and control of bleeding points rarely occurs.

The treatment of muscle strains here is the same as elsewhere: ice to minimize secondary tissue damage from bleeding and pain and anti-inflammatory medication; and after 48 hours, local heat to improve arteriolar blood supply necessary for normal healing. Anesthetic solutions and steroids should not be injected into an area of an acute strain. A chronic strain, however, may be aided by an injection of 1 cc 1% Xylocaine plus 1 cc Depo Medrol into the area of maximal point tenderness.

Injuries to the Abdominal Viscera

Abdominal viscera injuries are less common than abdominal wall injuries. However, failure to promptly recognize such injuries can lead to severe morbidity and loss of life. Early abdominal signs of viscera injury are often subtle, and routine x-rays of the abdomen rarely give early evidence when a major injury has occurred. Finally, diagnostic (peritoneal lavage for intra-abdominal blood, radioisotopic scanning of the liver and spleen, ultrasonography, and CT scanning) and therapeutic procedures must often proceed simultaneously, each giving way to the other, depending on the stability of the patient. With this in mind, if intra-abdominal injury with blunt trauma is suspected, and in all cases of penetrating abdominal injury, referral to a general surgeon or traumatologist is recommended.

After blunt abdominal trauma, a clear history of the mechanism of injury should be obtained, then a physical examination, including blood pressure and the character and rate of the pulse and respirations, should be carried out. If vital signs are unstable, referral is desirable. The most reliable physical finding indicating peritoneal irritation is the presence of voluntary or involuntary spasm, or both. Spasm can best be detected by gently placing the palm of the hand on the abdominal muscle over the rectus muscle, having the patient breathe deeply, and gently depressing the examining hand with the other hand. As the patient exhales, voluntary spasm of the rectus muscle will abate, involuntary spasm will not, and the muscle will feel tense and boardlike. The exact area of tenderness should be localized with one finger and will give a clue as to the viscus injured. In addition, when the hand pressing the tender area is quickly removed, rebound tenderness may be felt in the primary site of pain. This provides further evidence of peritoneal irritation. If any signs of peritoneal irritation, or voluntary or involuntary spasm or rebound tenderness are present, referral to a general surgeon is suggested.

The flanks along and below the lower chest wall should carefully be palpated. It is important to look for masses, hepatic or splenic enlargement below the costal margin, and free fluid in the abdominal cavity. If dullness and tenderness coincide on gentle percussion of the abdomen, a mass is suggested. If any of the above signs of an abdominal mass are present, surgical referral is indicated.

The abdominal viscera that may be injured with blunt trauma include most commonly the spleen, often with left lower rib fractures and in athletes with mononucleosis; the liver, often with right lower rib cage or right upper abdominal blunt trauma; and the jejunum, ileum, colon, duodenum, mesentary, pancreas, stomach, and diaphragm. The diagnosis of visceral torso injuries can be extremely difficult. A high degree of suspicion must be combined with a thorough physical examination, and if suspicions are confirmed, prompt referral is advised.

Injuries to the Genitourinary System

The *kidneys,* although relatively well protected under the rib cage in the upper retroperitoneum, may be injured either by direct trauma to the flank or by contrecoup injury, in which they are violently thrown forward when the athlete abruptly stops. Usually there is pain and tenderness in the flank. In cases of hemorrhage, a flank mass may be felt with or without hypovolemic shock. The presence of such a mass, shock, hematuria, loss of renal psoas shadow on KUB x-ray, adjacent rib or vertebra fracture, or elevation of the diaphragm are all indications to seek urologic or general surgical referral. Infusion intravenous urography combined with nephrotomography affords prompt accurate assessment of the kidneys, ureters, and bladder. The decision as to which kidneys require surgery because of transcortical transcapsular laceration with evidence of perineal extravasation, or no surgery, as with renal contusion, or cortical laceration without extravasation, or intrarenal hemorrhage without capsule rupture, requires the judgment of a skilled genitourinary surgeon.

Ureter injuries, not uncommon with pelvic and vertebral fractures, rarely occur with blunt abdominal trauma. An infusion IVP makes the diagnosis and need for genitourinary referral apparent.

Lower-abdominal blunt trauma may result in contusion or rupture of the *urinary bladder.* Rupture with extravasation into the peritoneal cavity are more common if the bladder is full at the time of trauma, while retroperitoneal rupture and extravasation is more common with fractures of the pelvic ramus. Cystography will establish the rupture and need for genitourinary referral, as rupture with extravasation is usually best managed with exploration and repair. Bleeding from a contused bladder is usually adequately managed with a Foley catheter.

The male *urethra* is divided into two parts. The anterior portion distal to the fixed triangular ligament is mobile and therefore rarely injured. The posterior portion, including the membranous urethra within the triangular ligament and the prostatic urethra, is susceptible to blunt injury, especially with pelvic fractures. Mild trauma may produce obstruction and inability to void, while severe trauma causes tissue damage, hematoma formation, and extravasation. Urethrography and panendoscopy best demonstrate the pathology and are best directed by a genitourinary surgeon.

Because the *female urethra* is short and mobile, injury is uncommon. Blunt trauma from cycling and gymnastics rarely result in contusion, laceration, or frank disruption.

The *scrotum* and its *contents* are very susceptible to blunt trauma, as it lies in an exposed location. It should be carefully protected by appropriate equipment in all contact sports. Contusion is the most common injury and can usually be alleviated by ice and elevation. If there is a mass or suggestion of continued bleeding, or if the athlete has a single gonad—a relative contraindication to contact sports—genitourinary surgery referral is advised.

Suggested Readings

Abrams, H. L. (Ed.) Splenic arteriography. In *Angiography*. Boston: Little, Brown and Co., 1971.

Briggs, B. A. and Hayes, H. R. Cardiopulmonary resuscitation. In E. W. Wilkins, Jr., A. C. Moncure, and J. J. Dineen (Eds.). *MGH Textbook of Emergency Medicine.* Baltimore: Williams and Wilkins, 1978.

Cantwell, J. D. and King, J. T., Jr. Karate chops and liver lacerations. *JAMA* 224:1424, 1973.

Davis, J. J., Cohn, I., and Nance, F. C. Diagnosis and management of blunt abdominal trauma. *Ann. Surg.* 183:672–677, 1976.

Ebert, P. A., Gaertner, R. A., and Zuidema, G. D. Traumatic diaphragmatic hernia. *Surg. Gynecol. Obstet.* 125:59–65, 1967.

Eichelberger, M. R. Torso injuries in athletes. *Physician Sportsmed.* 9:87–92, 1981.

Fischer, R. P., Beverlin, B. C., Engrav, L. H., et al. Diagnostic peritoneal lavage, 14 yrs and 2,586 patients later. *Am. J. Surg.* 136:701–704, 1978.

Frelinger, D. P. The ruptured spleen in college athletes: A preliminary report. *J. Am. Coll. Health Assoc.* 26:217, 1978.

Jones, R. C. and Shires, G. T. The management of pancreatic injuries. *Arch. Surg.* 90:502–507, 1965.

Karmi, S. A., Young, J. D., and Soderstrom, C. Classification of renal injuries as a guide to therapy. *Surg. Gynecol. Obstet.* 148:161–167, 1979.

Madding, G. F. and Kennedy, P. A. *Trauma to the Liver.* Philadelphia: W. B. Saunders, 1971.

Moncure, A. S. and Wilkins, E. W. Jr. Injuries involving the abdomen, viscera, and genitourinary system. In P. S. Vinger and E. F. Hoerner (Eds.). *Sports Injuries: the Unthwarted Epidemic.* Littleton, Mass.: PSG Publishing Co., Inc., 1981.

Perry, J. E., DeMeules, J. E., and Root, H. D. Diagnostic peritoneal lavage in blunt abdominal trauma. *Surg. Gynecol. Obstet.* 131:742–743, 1970.

Persky, L. and Hoch, W. H. Genitourinary tract trauma. *Curr. Probl. Surg.* September:1–64, 1972.

Roman, E., Silva, Y. J., and Lucas, C. Management of blunt duodenal injury. *Surg. Gynecol. Obstet.* 132:7–14, 1971.

Trunkey, D. D., Shires, G. T., and McClelland, R. Management of liver trauma in 811 consecutive patients. *Ann. Surg.* 179:722–728, 1974.

Williams, R. D. and Patton, R. Athletic injuries to the abdomen and thoracic. *Am. J. Surg.* 98:447–450, 1959.

13 / Upper-Extremity Injuries

Shoulder

The shoulder plays an integral role in virtually all athletic activities. The role of the upper extremity in running or skating sports is both power and balance. Many sports that involve the throwing motion (pitching in baseball, quarterbacking in football, the serve and overhead in tennis, and the freestyle and butterfly motions of swimming) demand far more of the shoulder than nature originally intended.

While the upper extremity is a critical end organ in the act of throwing, the coordination and balance of the rest of the body is vital. An inflamed great toe or low-back pain may disrupt the athlete's body muscular rhythm and alter throwing biomechanics, leading to shoulder injury.

Fimrite popularized the Dizzy Dean Syndrome, the situation of creating a second injury by favoring a prior one [5]. Dizzy Dean, an overpowering right-handed pitcher for the St. Louis Cardinals in the 1930s, was struck on the left foot by a line drive and broke his big toe in the 1937 All-Star Game. Two weeks later he attempted to return to pitching, wearing a splint and an oversized shoe. By favoring his injured toe he altered his natural pitching motion, which led to a shoulder injury eventually diagnosed as an inflammation of the deltoid muscle at its insertion on the humerus [5]. From an over-30-game winner, he was to win only 16 games before premature retirement four years later. Smokey Joe Wood is another baseball pitcher who suffered a similar fate. Known for his fastball, and winner of 34 games in 1912, Wood fell fielding a ground ball in the spring of 1913, and sustained a fractured thumb on his pitching hand. He, too, attempted to return too soon and, with an altered delivery, incurred a shoulder injury that claimed his career.

Thus, when evaluating a problem of pain in the shoulder, one must not necessarily assume the entire source of the problem to be within that area.

Anatomy

The shoulder is a complex region consisting of the glenohumeral joint, its static capsular support, and the dynamic muscle groups that control the motion of the shoulder girdle. The shoulder has the widest range of motion of any joint in the body. Normal function at the sternoclavicular joint, at the acromioclavicular joint, and along the scapular thoracic plane are essential for full activity of the upper extremity.

The humeral head articulates with a relatively small biconcave glenoid fossa. The humeral head faces in medial, superior, and approximately 30° posterior directions. The glenoid, which has a surface area only approximately one-third that of the humeral head, faces in anterior, lateral, and slightly superior directions. The cartilaginous glenoid labrum adds additional support to the joint. The angulation of the glenohumeral joint therefore makes the humeral head more unstable anteriorly. The acromion and the coracoacromial ligament protect the joint superiorly. Shoulder abduction and elevation depend upon motion through the sternoclavicular and acromioclavicular joints. The acromioclavicular joint moves in vertical, frontal, and horizontal axes, while the scapula rotates and elevates along the thoracic wall. The coracoclavicular ligaments (conoid and trapezoid ligaments) limit the amount of motion through the acromioclavicular joint.

The capsule of the shoulder joint lends static support to the glenohumeral joint. The coracohumeral ligament extends across the superior aspect of the capsule, and thickened areas within the capsule anteriorly are referred to as the glenohumeral ligaments. The inferior and middle portions of the glenohumeral capsule are particularly important in restraining the humeral head during abduction and external rotation. The muscle groups around the shoulder girdle are very complex and must work in a coordinated fashion to produce smooth motion of the joint. The rotator cuff muscles, the subscapularis anteriorly, the supraspinatous superiorly, and the infraspinatous and teres minor posteriorly, blend with the capsule and attach into the proximal humerus. The biceps tendon extends from the glenoid through the joint superiorly and into the bicipital groove between the greater and lesser tuberosities of the humerus. Scapular elevation and adduction are controlled by the trapezius, levator scapulae, and rhomboid muscle groups. The serratus anterior, which is attached to the inferior pole of the scapula, assists in scapular rotation. The triceps, coracobrachialis, and biceps muscles traverse the shoulder-joint area and extend down the upper arm. The pectoral muscles and latissimus dorsi muscle, originating from the rib cage anteriorly and posteriorly, respectively, fit into the proximal humerus and help control forward flexion and extension. The contributions that these different muscles make vary with the position of the arm at any one time. A complete understanding of the functional anatomy of the shoulder is essential in diagnosing the painful shoulder.

Acute Injuries

Most acute injuries are the result of a single, major, abrupt force. The athlete is able to recall the specific incident, and diagnosis is usually obvious by examination and x-rays taken in two planes at 90° to each other. Deformity is common, and pain is almost always present. These lesions include sprains, dislocations, and fractures that occur about the shoulder girdle.

Sprains, subluxations (partial dislocation), and dislocations are essentially a continuum of the same process: a variable degree of injury to the ligaments and adjacent soft tissues that normally provide for the integrity of a joint. The team physician should be able to care for strains and some minor subluxations, but most subluxations and virtually all dislocations and fractures require orthopedic referral.

Dislocation is characterized by major (75% to 100%) ligamentous disruption and obvious joint deformity and laxity, subluxation with partial (25% to 75%) ligamentous disruption, and sprain with minimal ligamentous tear (less than 25%) with a stable joint. There is moderate sensitivity to palpation over the injured area and mild to moderate swelling. The initial treatment, as with sprains elsewhere, is ice for the first 12 to 24 hours, heat thereafter, rest, and appropriate strapping of the area for one to three weeks. After all pain is gone, an appropriate exercise program should be undertaken. Return to competition should await the return of equal strength in the injured and noninjured shoulders. Throughout the treatment period, a complimentary program for continued general conditioning should be maintained.

The acromioclavicular, glenohumeral, and sternoclavicular joints are the three sites where sprains, subluxations, dislocations, and fractures occur in the shoulder. Most acromioclavicular injuries occur secondary to a direct fall on the elbow or outstretched hand, resulting in a directed force along the extremity to the acromioclavicular joint. Figure 13–1 shows a severe dislocation, and figure 13–2 shows a fracture dislocation

Figure 13–1   Severe dislocation of the acromioclavicular joint.

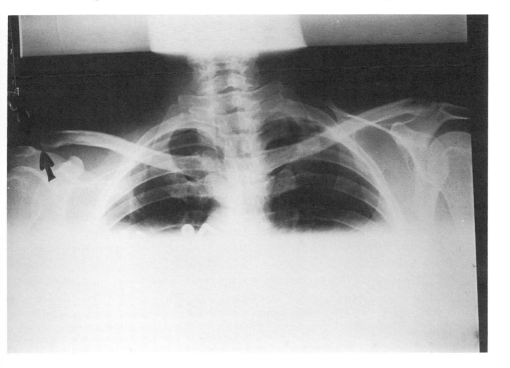

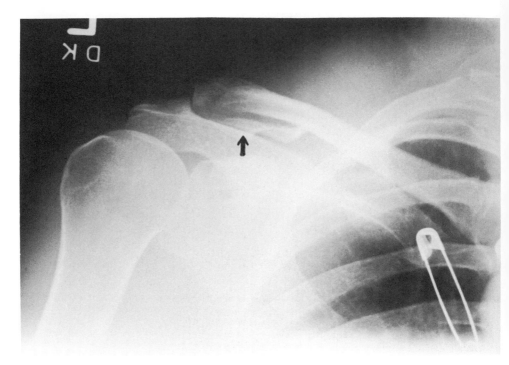

Figure 13–2   Fracture dislocation of the acromioclavicular joint.

of this joint. While the initial treatment is the same as for a sprain—a sling shoulder immobilizer with appropriate compressive padded dressing across the outer end of the clavicle and under the proximal ulna, effecting a compressive force on the dislocated outer clavicle—referral to an orthopedist is recommended.

Of all acute injuries to the glenohumeral joint, 98% to 99% occur to the anterior portion [15]. This is partly because the anatomy has less support anteriorly but also because most injuries occur with the arm abducted and externally rotated. The arm tackle in football and entrapped ski pole with a moving skier are common examples. Forces are directed to the posterior joint only when the arm is adducted, internally rotated, and flexed. Careful determination by examination and x-ray should be carried out to determine if the injury is anterior or posterior. Figure 13–3 illustrates the more common anterior dislocation, and figure 13–4 demonstrates the rare posterior dislocation. If there is a dislocation or if the athlete describes the shoulder as popping forward and then back into place (subluxation), orthopedic referral is advised. When pain only in the anterior or posterior glenohumeral joint is described, a sprain is the diagnosis. Treatment consists of immobilization for 7 to 14 days in a shoulder immobilizer or sling and swathe with elasticized bandages. General conditioning exercises and a postinjury rehabilitation program similar to that for an acromioclavicular sprain are recommended.

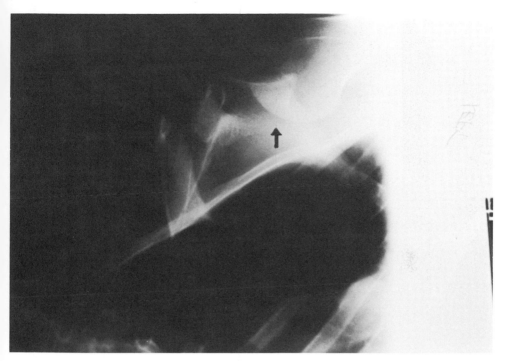

Figure 13–3 Common anterior dislocation of the glenohumeral joint.

Injury to the sternoclavicular joint usually results from forces that drive the shoulder girdle forward, while thrusting the clavicle toward the sternum. They are similarly classified as sprain, subluxation, dislocation, and fracture. All but the sprain should have orthopedic evaluation. The sprain is treated with a sling until pain subsides, as well as with the other measures for sprains previously discussed. The return to competition follows the same guidelines as for acromioclavicular sprains.

Overuse (Chronic) Injuries

There has been a recent increase in the troublesome overuse syndromes involving the shoulder region. The painful pitcher's shoulder has plagued participants, trainers, and team physicians for years, and now similar chronic injuries are frequently seen among recreational, as well as competitive, swimmers and tennis players. Insidious in onset and only annoying in the initial stages, overuse injuries relentlessly increase in intensity and severity and may eventually totally disable the athlete.

An overuse syndrome is defined as a chronic inflammatory condition caused by repeated microtrauma from a repetitious activity. Blazina originally classified these injuries into (1) first degree, those causing pain only after activity, (2) second degree, those pro-

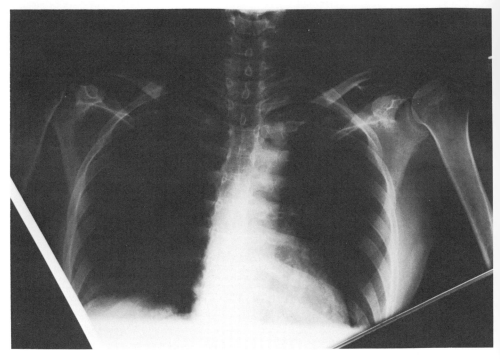

Figure 13–4 Rare posterior dislocation of the glenohumeral joint.

ducing pain during participation and after, but not sufficient to interfere with performance, and (3) third degree, those which result in disabling pain both during and after participation [4].

Overuse syndromes around the shoulder area are particularly common in throwing sports, swimming, and tennis. To appreciate the spectrum of injuries that may occur in throwing, one must comprehend the mechanism of this strenuous activity. Tullos has classified the phases of throwing and has pointed out those structures that are used in each step (figure 13–5) [10]. During the initial cocking motion, the arm is brought back into abduction, extension, and external rotation. Consequently, the middle and posterior aspects of the deltoid are functioning as well as the infraspinatous and teres minor to produce rotation. The trapezius and rhomboids contribute to scapular elevation and adduction. During the cocking stage, the posterior capsule is relaxed, whereas the anterior capsule, subscapularis, and pectoral muscles are passively elongating. The next stage of throwing consists of the acceleration phase, in which the arm begins to move forward again, often preceded by a forward rotation of the trunk. During this activity, the anterior-muscle groups, particularly the subscapularis, pectorals, and anterior deltoid, are contracting while still lengthening (eccentrically). The biceps muscle also may contract, increasing tension on the tendon within the bicipital groove, which is externally rotated.

Figure 13–5 Phases of throwing. A, windup; B, cocking; C, acceleration; and D, follow-through.

It is during this early part of the acceleration phase that the anterior capsule is particularly stretched. As the arm comes forward into the final follow-through position, the posterior capsule and external rotators are relaxed and passively stretched. The various shoulder lesions that can occur during throwing have been enumerated by others [1, 3, 11, 14]. Anteriorly, the capsular ligaments can become attenuated and allow the humeral head to sublux and even dislocate. Sudden contractures of the subscapularis and pectoral muscles can produce tearing and rupture of these muscular tendinous units. Impingement can occur anteriorly around the coracoid, and posteriorly as the humeral head abuts the glenoid. The bicipital tendon and supraspinatous tendon can abut the acromion and coracoacromial ligament, producing impingement syndromes [13]. Small tears in the rotator-cuff muscles, as well as chronic subdeltoid bursitis, frequently follow as a result of these repeated impingements. Bennett has described hypertrophic bony changes along the inferior aspect of the glenoid [2], and Tullos has reported chronic subluxation of the biceps tendon from its groove [10]. Since the acromioclavicular joint contributes to abduction and rotation, chronic degenerative changes at that site may produce pain, felt over the top of the shoulder and radiating both anteriorly and posteriorly. It is obvious that the throwing mechanism is very complex and can cause symptoms and injuries in numerous areas. A great deal of diligence is required when questioning and examining patients with shoulder injuries in order to determine the site of the pathology.

Priest has recently reviewed shoulder injuries in tennis players [16]. He points out that the overhead serve is quite similar to a throwing motion and produces many of the same injuries seen in pitchers.

Kennedy has defined a condition referred to as swimmer's shoulder [7]. Both the freestyle and butterfly stroke produce repeated impingement of the greater tuberosity under the coracoacromial arch [8, 17]. As the arm is brought forward into abduction, forward flexion, and internal rotation, the region of the supraspinatous tendon and biceps tendon in its groove sustain repeated trauma under the acromion and coracoacromial ligament. As the arm is then pulled down into an adducted position in the follow-through motion, the blood flow into the distal portion of the rotator cuff and biceps tendon is impeded by the pressure of the humeral head from below. MacNab demonstrated these areas of avascularity in his microvascular studies of the rotator cuff [12].

A careful history is perhaps the most important step in diagnosing overuse syndromes. A previous history of shoulder subluxation or an acromioclavicular-joint separation should be pursued. One must be familiar with the patient's previous training program. These injuries are frequently seen early in the season and often during periods of double-session workouts. Repeated examinations are often necessary to localize the site of the tenderness and to detect relative weaknesses in the rotator-muscle groups. A complete neurologic examination is needed to rule out cervical radiculitis, entrapment of the suprascapular or axillary nerves, and thoracic outlet syndromes. Vascular problems in the subclavian and brachial systems must also be considered.

Routine x-rays, including the Westpoint view to demonstrate the glenoid, should be obtained. Exostoses along the anterior and inferior aspects of the glenoid may require special views. Degenerative changes at the acromioclavicular joint must also be ruled out. Shoulder arthrograms may be indicated when a rotator-cuff tear is suspected (figure 13–6). An enlarged capsule may also be noted on arthrography in a chronic subluxing shoulder. Jackson has pointed out that chronic impingement syndromes produce thickening and contraction of the subdeltoid bursa [6]. He has performed bursagrams that illus-

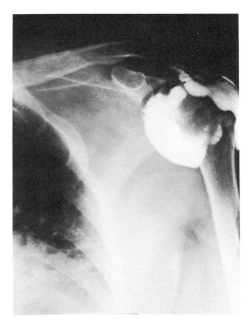

Figure 13–6 Shoulder arthrogram documenting a rotator-cuff tear.

trate this problem. These additional x-ray studies should be done only after a careful examination has been performed to determine the exact site of tenderness, the arc of motion that produces pain, and the presence of any specific weakness.

Treatment of overuse syndromes is directed at reducing inflammation and altering training and performance techniques to prevent recurrence. The type-I and type-II injuries that produce pain primarily after participation and are not disabling should be treated promptly to prevent their progression. Proper warm-up exercises prior to participation, and ice following competition, may help to relieve the inflammatory changes. Oral anti-inflammatory agents such as aspirin or one of the other nonsteroidal medications are often helpful. Reducing the amount of time throwing, swimming, or serving may help to control the pain. It is essential to review the problem with the coach, since minor changes in technique, such as the amount of elevation in the arm in throwing or swimming, may be necessary. Since these injuries frequently lead to contracture and muscle weakness, it is important to seek these problems out and correct them with flexibility exercises and specific strengthening programs. The isokinetic machines are very helpful in detecting relative weakness in the shoulder.

Third-degree injuries usually require a period of rest. During this time, conditioning programs for the other areas of the body may be continued. Local injections of steroids into the involved areas have been helpful in some cases. However, it must be remembered that these injections produce local tissue necrosis and weaken the structures for at least two weeks [9]. During that time, no vigorous participation should be undertaken. Other modalities can be used to reduce inflammation, especially ultrasound and diathermy. Since recurrence of these injuries is very common, the participant must have full range of motion, equal strength, and be free of pain before returning to competition. Since both coordination and endurance are essential in these sports, it is important to progress slowly to avoid future difficulties.

Elbow

Anatomy

The elbow is a hinge joint involving three bones: the lower end of the humerus, the upper end of the radius, and olecranon and coronoid processes of the ulna (figure 13–7). The radius can rotate around the ulna allowing for supination and pronation of the forearm. The annular, ulnar, and radial collateral ligaments and articular capsule maintain joint stability.

Acute Injuries

Hyperextension injuries are quite common in competitive and recreational activities. Subluxation, dislocation (figure 13–8), or fracture may occur as a result of direct trauma. As with the shoulder, subluxation, dislocation, or fracture of the elbow should be ortho-

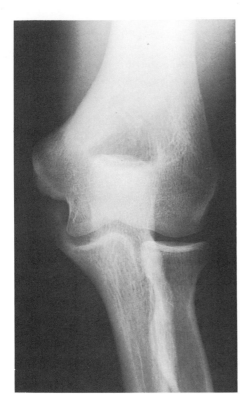

Figure 13–7 Elbow joint.

pedically evaluated, while the team physician should be able to effectively treat sprains.

Treatment of an elbow sprain is similar to that of the shoulder. There is initial application of ice for the first 12 to 24 hours, followed by heat. The elbow should be immobilized in a sling for seven or more days until all pain on motion has ceased. Oral anti-inflammatory medication (aspirin, Indocin, Butazoladine, Motrin, Tolectin, Clinoril) may be used during this period. Thereafter, active flexion, extension, supination, and pronation exercises should be done, and return to competition should await return of strength in the injured arm equal to that of the noninjured arm.

Overuse (Chronic) Injuries

Tennis elbow is the most common overuse syndrome due to recurrent microtrauma at the elbow. While it occurs frequently in tennis players, it is seen in all racquet sports and virtually all recreational activities that involve the arms. The primary site of pain and point tenderness is in the region of the extensor muscle origin from the lateral epicondyle. It is now agreed that the basic pathology is an inflammation of the aponeurosis overlying the extensor carpi radialis and the extensor communis. Overuse and overload

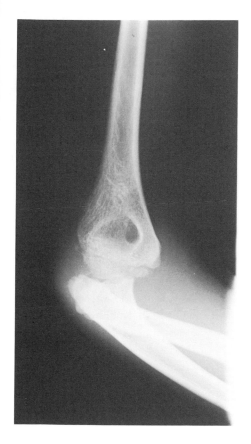

Figure 13–8   Dislocation of the elbow joint.

(often aggravated by improper stroke production), usually associated with a lack of appropriate preconditioning, is the mechanical etiology. Prevention, therefore, includes appropriate advice regarding conditioning and proper technique.

The initial treatment of tennis elbow is rest, ice for the first 24 hours, heat thereafter, and oral anti-inflammatory medication. If symptoms persist, a single injection of local steroid and anesthetic into the area of point tenderness may be tried. If an injection is made, the arm should not be strenuously used for the next two weeks due to the steroid's weakening effect on ligaments and tendons.

Rehabilitation should include flexibility exercises to assure full range of elbow motion and isotonic and isometric exercises to maintain maximum forearm muscular strength. It may also be appropriate to direct attention toward technique and equipment, such as size and weight of racquet, tension of strings, and circumference of handle grip. While a lighter weight racquet, lower tension strings, and a larger handle grip may help, the best solution is to combine these changes with a fiberglass or composite racquet that dampens vibrations.

In chronic subacute situations (a common occurrence among tennis players who will play through the injury), the use of an elbow brace or nonelastic band distal to the elbow, which decreases the excursion and stress on the extensor origin, may be extremely helpful. As one who played in many tournaments during an eight-month bout with this condition, I know that the elbow brace can make the difference between having to stop and being able to continue playing. If the condition has persisted for a year or more without any signs of improvement, orthopedic referral for consideration of surgical intervention may be appropriate.

The second most common overuse elbow injury occurs from throwing. The same sports as discussed with the shoulder may produce elbow injury, as the forces moving through the shoulder in throwing or other athletic action are extended distally through the arm to the elbow. The acceleration and follow-through (the final phases of throwing) place tremendous stress on the elbow. The medial side of the elbow is stretched and the lateral side is compressed, as is the olecranon and distal humerus. In the follow-through motion, extreme compressive forces are generated in the concavity of the olecranon and its tip from the pull of the triceps tendon. Pathologic conditions result in these sites in athletes who perform repetitive throwing motion (figures 13–9 and 13–10).

Bony avulsions, injuries to the flexor mass, ulnar nerve inflammation secondary to repetitive stretch and/or subluxation in the ulnar groove, and spurs on the medial edge of the olecranon are the most common problems occurring on the medial side of the elbow from throwing. All of these must be considered, and in the young athlete frank avulsion of the medial epicondyle must be considered as well (figure 13–11).

Figure 13–9   A. Flexor muscle tears. B. Medial collateral ligament rupture.

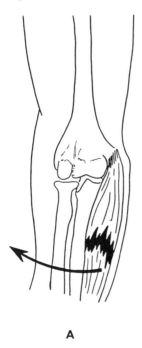
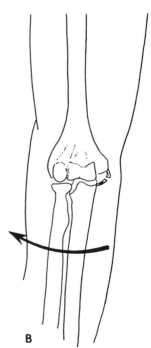

A

B

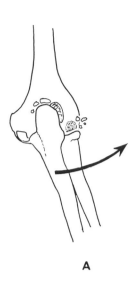

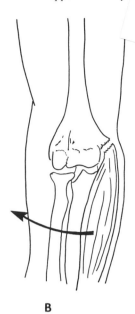

A

B

Figure 13–10   A. Medial epicondylar avulsion fracture. B. Ulnor traction spur and medical collateral ligament attenuation.

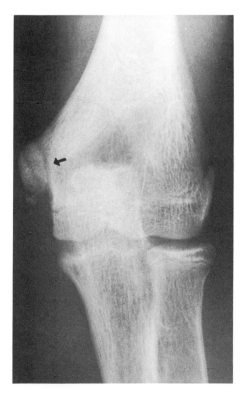

Figure 13–11   Frank avulsion of the medial epicondyle.

The compressive forces on the lateral side of the elbow between the radial head and the capitellum result in a shearing action on the radiohumeral joint resulting in damage to the articular cartilage with progressive fragmentation and formation of intra-articular loose bodies (figures 13–12 and 13–13). In the preadolescent and adolescent athlete, a focal avascular necrosis called Panner disease may be identified in the capitellum (figure 13–14). Furthermore, the compressive force of the traction pull of the triceps impacts the tip of the olecranon against the olecranon fossa of the humerus and may result in articular damage, fragmentation, and loose-body formation.

In the skeletally immature athlete with open epiphyses, the compressive lateral forces may lead to abnormalities of growth, premature degeneration, and long-term intra-articular deformity. "Little League elbow," the nonunion of a stress fracture through the olecranon growth plate, is an example (figure 13–15). While it is impossible to define chronologic age limits as to when a young athlete with open epiphyses with active growth potential should and should not pitch, since this is related to individual skeletal development and maturation, the Little League restrictions for limited pitching are strongly recommended. Clearly, the greater the number of innings pitched by a youth with open epiphyses, the more likely the development of anatomic elbow impairment and ultimate restriction of an athletic career. The curveball and screwball, because of the snap supination, produce the greatest stress on the elbow and should be thrown only by the skeletally mature athlete. The medial epicondyle of the humerus is the last of the epiphyseal centers of the elbow to close, usually after 14 years of age.

The treatment of any of the throwing injuries, whether in the baseball pitcher, gymnast, or tennis player, should involve orthopedic referral if any of the various bone pathologies are visible on x-ray. If ulnar neuritis is present with numbness of the fifth finger and lateral half of the fourth finger, usually without intrinsic muscle weakness or atrophy in the early stages, neurosurgical referral is suggested.

In most instances, the athlete will present with pain, tenderness, and perhaps some local swelling. Treatment should start with rest for 7 to 14 days until all pain and tenderness have abated and should progress through the sequence described for sprains.

Myositis ossificans (figure 13–16) is a chronic condition that may result from any of the acute injuries to the arm or elbow. Treatment consists of rest until pain and tenderness subside. When motion and strength of the affected extremity equal the nonaffected extremity without producing pain or extension of the ossification process as documented by sequential x-rays, return to competition is permissible. To prevent repetitive contusion and extension of the myositis ossificans process, protective .padding should be placed over the affected area.

Forearm, Wrist, and Hand

Most forearm injuries are either fractures, strains, or abrasions. A Colles fracture of the radius and ulna (figure 13–17) results from falling on the outstretched hand or using it to ward off another player. All forearm fractures should be orthopedically referred. Abrasions and sprains can be treated as discussed for the elbow and shoulder.

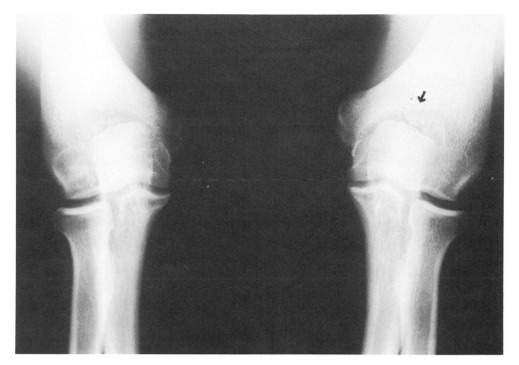

Figure 13–12   Intra-articular loose bodies in the elbow.

Figure 13–13   Intra-articular loose bodies removed from elbow.

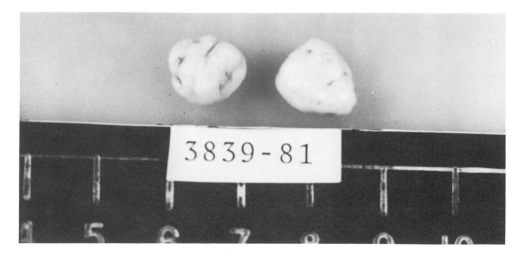

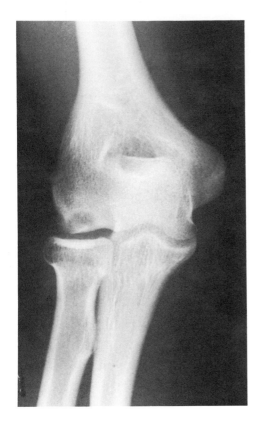

Figure 13–14 Panner disease in the capitellum.

Figure 13–15 Failure of normal closure of olecranon epiphysis. Comparative views of two elbows.

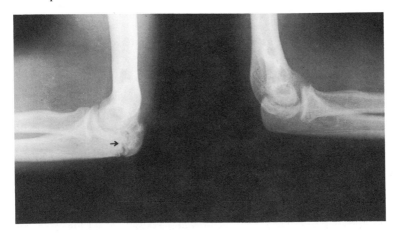

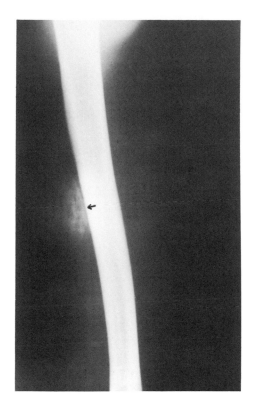

Figure 13–16 Myositis ossificans of arm.

Wrist injuries range from sprains to dislocations that often require open surgical reduction. Major tendon injuries that may terminate careers also occur. The biomechanical requirement through the wrist and intercarpal joints is greatest in activities requiring a wrist snap and/or turnover intercarpal rotation (swinging at an object, as in baseball, tennis, golf, or lacrosse, or release of an object with sudden wrist action, as in bowling, weight lifting, pole vaulting, javelin, discus, or shot put). The forces generated can lead to strains, dislocations, and carpal fractures. There is no area of sports medicine where accurate diagnosis of an injury is more challenging than at the wrist. Occult fractures are common, and it is frequently necessary to obtain comparative views of the noninjured hand, and additional fluoroscopic, tomographic, or nuclear-scan examinations. If initial x-rays are negative but the patient does not respond to the initial sprain treatment, additional x-rays should be taken and/or orthopedic referral made.

The carponavicular joint, the most common site of acute carpal fracture, is often not visualized on initial x-ray. Mal or ununited navicular fracture leads to chronic pain, often requiring surgical intervention for realignment and bone grafting. Fractures of the hook of the hammate can also be very difficult to visualize on x-ray. Avascular necrosis, especially of the carpal lunate (Kienbock syndrome), results in chronic pain and may lead to ligamentous laxity with subluxation from swinging a bat, tennis racquet, golf club,

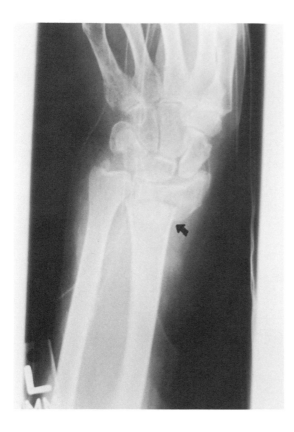

Figure 13-17 Colles fracture of the radius and ulna.

or lacrosse or hockey stick. Treatment of wrist injuries by the team physician should be limited to sprains and abrasions, and if the symptoms of a strain do not resolve by two weeks, orthopedic referral may be prudent.

As with the wrist, sprains, fractures, and dislocations are the most common finger injuries. Orthopedic referral is recommended for all but sprains. Finger fractures that initially appear innocuous may undergo malalignment and malrotation leading to significant disability. Precise alignment and rotational position and its subsequent maintenance is extremely important in the hand. If this cannot be achieved, early open reduction and pin fixation must be considered. Usually resulting from a direct blow to the tip of an extended finger, the Mallet finger injury is one of the most common athletic finger injuries. The blow results in rupture of the tendon at its insertion or avulsion of the tendon with a fragment of bone (figure 13–18). Orthopedic referral is advisable, as open reduction may be required.

Finally, in certain sports where a single digital nerve is subjected to continued pressure, as in bowling, baseball, or swinging any object to contact another object, the compressive force may result in neuroma formation. Rest and/or local anesthetic/steroid injection should be the initial treatment, with prolonged rest as the preferential treatment.

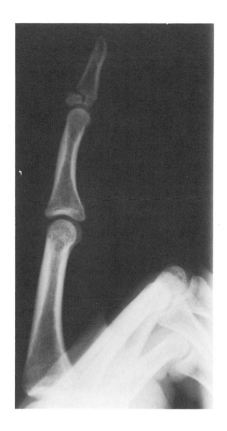

Figure 13–18 Avulsion of tendon in finger with bone fragment.

Failure to respond should suggest referral to an experienced hand surgeon and/or neurosurgeon for neuroma excision.

References

1. Barnes, D. A. and Tullos, H. S. An analysis of 100 symptomatic baseball players. *Am. J. Sports Med.* 6(2):62, 1988.
2. Bennett, G. E. Shoulder and elbow lesions of the professional baseball pitcher. *JAMA*, 117:510, 1941.
3. Bennett, G. E. Shoulder and elbow lesions distinctive of baseball players. *Am. Surg.* 126:107, 1947.
4. Blazina, M. E. Jumper's knee. *Orthop. Clin. North Am.* 4:665, 1973.
5. Fimrite, R. Stress, strain, and pain. *Sports Illustrated.* Aug. 14, 1978, pp. 30–43.
6. Jackson, D. W. Chronic rotator cuff impingement in the throwing athlete. *Am. J. Sports Med.* 4(6):231, 1976.
7. Kennedy, J. C. and Hawkins, P. T. Swimmer's shoulder. *Physician Sportsmed.* 2:35–38, 1974.

8. Kennedy, J. C. et al. Orthopedic manifestations of swimming. *Am. J. Sports Med.* 6:309, 1978.
9. Kennedy, J. C. and Willis, R. B. The effects of local steroid injections on tendons: A biomechanical and microscopic correlative study. *Am. J. Sportsmed.* 4:11–21, 1976.
10. King, J. W., Brelsford, H. J., and Tullos, H. S. Analysis of the pitching arm of the professional baseball pitcher. *Clin. Orthop.* 67:116, 1969.
11. Lombardo, S. J., Jobe, R. W., Kerlan, R., et al. Posterior shoulder lesions in throwing athletes. *Am. J. Sports Med.* 5:106, 1977.
12. MacNab, I. and Rathburn, J. B. The microvascular pattern of the rotator cuff. *J. Bone Joint Surg.* 52B:524, 1970.
13. Neer, C. S. Anterior acromioplasty for chronic impingement syndrome in the shoulder. *J. Bone Joint Surg.* 54A:41–50, 1972.
14. Norwood, L. A., Jobe, F. W., et al. Anterior shoulder pain in baseball pitchers. *Am. J. Sports Med.* 6(3):103, 1978.
15. Pappas, A. M. Injuries of the upper extremities. In P. F. Vinger and E. F. Hoerner (Eds.). *Sports Medicine, the Unthwarted Epidemic.* Littleton, Mass.: PSG Publishing Co., Inc., 1981.
16. Priest, J. D. and Nagel, D. A. Tennis shoulder. *Am. J. Sports Med.* 4(1):28, 1976.
17. Richardson, A. B., Jobe, E. W., and Collins, R. H. The shoulder in competitive swimming. *Am. J. Sports Med.* 8(3):159, 1980.

Suggested Readings

Adams, J. E. Bone injuries in very young athletes. *Clin. Orthop.* 58:129–140, 1968.

Armstrong, J. R. and Tucker, W. E. (Eds.). *Injury in Sport: The Physiology, Prevention, and Treatment of Injuries Associated with Sport.* Springfield, Ill.: Charles C. Thomas, 1964.

Basmajian, J. V. *Muscles Alive: Their Functions Revealed by Electromyography.* Baltimore: Williams and Wilkins, 1974.

Basmajian, J. V. (Ed.) *Therapeutic Exercise.* (3rd ed.). Baltimore: Williams and Wilkins, 1978.

Bateman, J. E. Cuff tears in athletes. *Orthop. Clin. North Am.* 4:721–745, 1973.

Bateman, J. E. *The Shoulder and Neck.* Philadelphia: W. B. Saunders, 1972.

Behling, F. Treatment of acromioclavicular separations. *Orthop. Clin. North Am.* 4:747–757, 1973.

Bennett, G. E. Shoulder and elbow lesions of the professional baseball pitcher. *JAMA,* 117:510–514, 1941.

Brogdon, B. G. and Crow, N. E. Little Leaguer's elbow. *Am. J. Roentgenol.* 83:671–675, 1960.

Brown, R., Blazina, M. E., Kerlan, R. K., et al. Osteochondritis of the capitellum. *J. Sports Med. Phys. Fitness.* 2:27–46, 1974.

Burton, R. I. and Eaton, R. G. Common hand injuries in the athlete. *Orthop. Clin. North Am.* 4:809–838, 1973.

Froimson, A. I. Treatment of tennis elbow with forearm support band. *J. Bone Joint Surg.* 53A:183–184, 1971.

Garden, R. S. Tennis elbow. *J. Bone Joint Surg.* 43B:100–106, 1961.

Goldie, I. Epicondylitis lateralis humeri (epicondylalgia or tennis elbow), a pathogenetical study. *Acta. Chir. Scand. (suppl).* 339:1–24, 1964.

Gugenheim, J. D., Jr., Stanley, R. F., Woods, G. W., et al. Little League survey: The Houston Study. *Am. J. Sports Med.* 4:189–200, 1976.

Hale, C. J. Injuries among 711,810 Little League baseball players. *J. Sports Med. Phys. Fitness.* 1:80–83, 1961.

Inman, V. T., Saunders, J. P., Dec, M., et al. Observations on the function of the shoulder joint. *J. Bone Joint Surg.* 26:1–30, 1944.

Klafs, C. E. and Arnheim, D. D. *Modern Principles of Athletic Training.* (4th ed.). St. Louis: C. V. Mosby, 1977.

Larson, R. L., Swinger, K. M., Bergstrom, R., et al. Little League survey: The Eugene Study. *Am. J. Sports Med.* 4:201–209, 1976.

Linscheid, R. L., Dobyns, J. H., Beabout, J. W., et al. Traumatic instability of the wrist: Diagnosis, classification and pathomechanics. *J. Bone Joint Surg.* 54A:1612–1632, 1972.

Lipscomb, A. B. Baseball pitching injuries in growing athletes. *J. Sports Med. Phys. Fitness.* 3:25–34, 1975.

Middleman, I. C. Shoulder and elbow lesions of baseball players. *Am. J. Surg.* 102:627–632, 1961.

Neer, C. S. and Welsh, R. P. The shoulder in sports. *Orthop. Clin. North Am.* 8:583–591, 1977.

Nelson, C. L. The use of arthrography in athletic injuries of the shoulder. *Orthop. Clin. North Am.* 4:775–785, 1973.

Nirschl, R. P. Tennis elbow. *Orthop. Clin. North Am.* 4:787–800, 1973.

O'Donoghue, D. H. *Treatment of Injuries to Athletes.* (3rd ed.). Philadelphia: W. B. Saunders, 1976.

Posner, M. A. Injuries to the hand and wrist in athletes. *Orthop. Clin. North Am.* 8:593–618, 1977.

Rockwood, C. A., Jr. and Green, D. P. (Eds.). *Fractures.* Volumes 1 and 2. Philadelphia: J. B. Lippincott, 1975.

Rokous, J. R., Feagin, J. A., and Abbott, H. G. Modified axillary roentgenogram. A useful adjunct in the diagnosis of recurrent instability of the shoulder. *Clin. Orthop.* 82:84–86, 1972.

Rowe, C. E. Acute and recurrent dislocations of the shoulder. *J. Bone Joint Surg.* 44A:998–1008, 1962.

Tullos, H. S. and King, J. W. Lesions of the pitching arm in adolescents. *JAMA.* 220:264–271, 1972.

Tullos, H. S. and King, J. W. Throwing mechanism in sports. *Orthop. Clin. North Am.* 4:709–720, 1973.

Weaver, J. K. and Dunn, H. K. Treatment of acromioclavicular injuries, especially complete acromioclavicular separation. *J. Bone Joint Surg.* 54A:1187–1194, 1972.

Wilson, J. C. and McKeever, F. M. Traumatic posterior (retroglenoid) dislocation of the humerus. *J. Bone Joint Surg.* 31A:160–172, 1949.

14 / Lower-Extremity Injuries

Lyle J. Micheli, M.D.

While the range and diversity of sports-related injuries are increasing, reflecting the diversity of sports and fitness activities now available in our society, injuries to the lower extremity still account for the greatest number of sports injuries sustained by the recreational-adult population. The types of injuries seen in this population differ from those seen in high-school or college team sports, and management also differs. Steps that can be taken to prevent these injuries, however, are similar [4].

Mechanism of Injury

There are two ways in which sports injuries occur, either from a single episode of high-impact trauma (single macrotrauma), as in a twisting fall on the ski slope, or from repetitive episodes of lesser trauma (repetitive microtrauma), as in repeatedly striking the foot against the ground in running. Combinations of both these mechanisms can also occur, as in a jump in tennis that ruptures a tendo Achillis previously weakened by an inappropriate running program.

While both mechanisms of injury can account for injuries in recreational-adult athletics, the recurrent microtrauma mechanism is much more common, and the resulting injuries, called overuse or stress injuries, are more frequently encountered. Also, the adult recreational athlete may be more susceptible to injury than his or her counterpart in school or professional sports, because recreational athletes often neglect general conditioning, systematic training, and proper warm-up techniques.

Types of Injury

Understanding the nature of an injury and its subsequent management can be greatly simplified by determining, if possible, the specific structures injured and the type of injury sustained. Lower-extremity injuries involve either the bones, muscle-tendon units, ligaments, cartilage, fascia, bursae, or even the skin.

Bone

Single-impact forces of significant magnitude can cause fractures through the bones and, on occasion, displacement. While fractures are rare in recreational athletics, they do occur, and many a tibial plateau fracture has been confused with an internal derangement of the knee and treated inappropriately. We now know that a twisting fall, involving only a person's own body weight can cause fracture, particularly if the victim is not in condition. Diagnostic x-rays will usually confirm the diagnosis.

Much more common in the recreational athlete, however, are stress fractures. A stress fracture is the result of repetitive activity, such as jumping or running (figure 14–1). Initially, it may be experienced as pain alone, although swelling can also be present. Initial x-rays of the painful extremity are frequently nondiagnostic, and the injury may be misdiagnosed as tendinitis or fascitis [16]. Many cases of shin splints are actually stress fractures. Most stress fractures are the result of inappropriate training techniques, usually with too much training over too short a time [19]. Minor problems of bones or

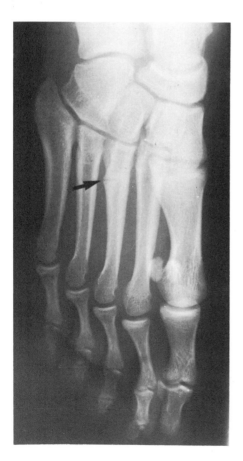

Figure 14–1 Stress fracture of the second metatarsal in a runner, initially misdiagnosed as tendinitis.

joints, muscle imbalances, and even improper footwear or running surfaces can also play a role in lower-leg stress fractures. In certain instances, if training is continued despite persistent pain, or if the pain is masked by cortisone injections or anti-inflammatory medication, a stress fracture can progress to complete displacement.

Muscles

A high proportion of injuries sustained in recreational athletes involves the muscles or their terminations, the tendons (figure 14–2). Muscles can be likened to motorized rubber bands. They have the capacity for contraction and subsequent exertion of force across the joints, but they also have a given elasticity and can be stretched to various lengths and still retain the ability to suddenly contract and exert force. Most recreational sports place demands on both the strength and flexibility of muscles. Unfortunately, emphasis is sometimes placed on strengthening muscles without much regard for improving their

Figure 14–2 The gastrocnemius-soleus and achilles muscle-tendon unit. Injuries may occur in the muscle body (tennis leg), muscle-tendon junction, tendon (achilles tendinitis or achilles rupture), or site of tendon insertion (os calcis apophysitis).

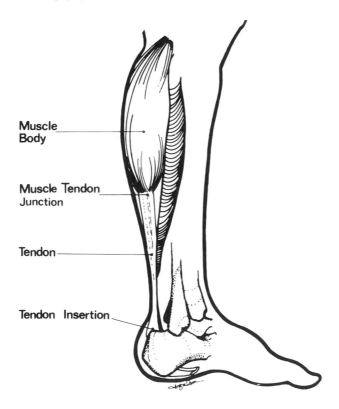

Muscle Body

Muscle Tendon Junction

Tendon

Tendon Insertion

relative elasticity or flexibility [4]. This is particularly true in the recreational athlete, where many injuries are the result of lack of flexibility of muscle groups.

A muscle-tendon unit exposed to excessive force, either as a result of its own contraction or from excessive displacement of the joints it controls, can sustain an actual tear of its substance. These injuries are called muscle strains and can occur at the muscle-tendon junction, midsubstance, or near the sites of muscle insertions. While muscle strains are often called nuisance injuries, they can often cause significant disability and may even require hospitalization or extended crutch support if a major muscle is torn. They often require extended periods of exercise, including both strengthening and flexibility, to return to the preinjury state [2].

Muscles and adjacent soft tissue are also subject to contusions—localized swelling usually resulting from a direct blow with sufficient force to rupture tissues and blood vessels. While often minor in extent and degree of disability, contusions of major muscles such as the quadriceps in the thigh can cause severe pain and prolonged disability. Early use of immobilization, compression, elevation, and icing can dramatically limit subsequent disability. In severe contusions, icing should continue for as long as five to seven days following injury. While the application of heat or the use of warm whirlpools have been recommended in the past to restore flexibility and relieve muscle spasm, use of heat too soon after injury can actually cause a resumption of bleeding and prolong, rather than shorten, disability.

Tendons

Tendons are the terminal extensions of muscle-tendon units. Unfortunately, the diagnosis of tendinitis has fallen into disrepute because of its widespread use in almost any soft-tissue injury where there is localized pain, swelling, and tenderness over a major muscle-tendon unit. We have now learned that while we must respect this inflammatory response, steps can be taken to limit the resultant disability of this injury. The term "relative rest" has been introduced into sports medicine to denote a change in demands on that particular muscle-tendon unit which allows continued use of the extremity and yet allows healing to proceed in a physiological fashion. Thus, tendinitis in the ankle in a ballet dancer can be relatively rested by avoiding jumping or barre work and substituting swimming and a non-weight-bearing range of motion exercises for that particular foot and ankle until satisfactory healing has progressed. Complete rest of an extremity afflicted by tendinitis is often inadvisable, as a pain feedback from the injury to the brain results in inhibition of use to the entire extremity, often with a decrease in the bulk, strength, and endurance of muscle-tendon units not directly involved in the injury. A cycle can thus begin in which the initial muscular or structural imbalance that caused the tendinitis in the first place is further exaggerated by the inhibitory effect of pain.

In this situation, great care must be taken in the use of anti-inflammatory drugs or cortisone injections. Although these may give temporary relief by decreasing swelling or interrupting normal pain pathways, the primary etiologic factors such as relative tightness or imbalance between muscles usually persist. Unless specific steps are taken to alter the weakness and inelasticity of the elements, more serious injury may result. A good example of this is Achillis tendinitis, or inflammation of the tendon of the heel (figure 14–2). This painful injury often results from a single episode of overuse, such as a weekend bike ride. In this situation, the correct initial treatment includes resting the muscle and tendon and using ice compresses and a mild anti-inflammatory medication such as aspirin. When acute stages of injury have subsided and there is a decrease in swelling and pain, corrective measures such as stretching the calf muscles and strengthening the muscles in the front of the leg should be started to improve the primary condition, which is usually a muscle imbalance of the lower leg. If, instead, cortisone is injected into the tendon and no further corrective measures are taken, the medication may mask further small tears in the tendon, which can lead to a complete rupture of the heel cord. Alternatively, repeated episodes of Achillis tendinitis, in which full activity is resumed before complete rehabilitation has been attained, can result in progressive scar formation and adhesions of the tendon to its sheath, to the point where surgery may be required [26].

Joints

The structures comprising any joint consist of the articulating bones, their associated articular cartilage, and the ligaments and muscle tendons spanning the joint. Joint injuries include injury to the ligaments spanning the joint as well as derangements of the structures of the joint surface.

Dislocation is a complete separation and displacement of the bony elements comprising the joint. It is accompanied by serious injury and usually complete rupture of the ligaments and some of the muscle-tendon units spanning the joint. It should be considered a medical emergency. In many cases, dislocation of a joint such as the knee or hip can cause vascular embarrassment or serious injury to adjacent nerves [11]. In the lower extremity, dislocation of the hip, knee, or ankle must be treated as a serious medical emergency, because of the associated threat to the viability of the limb. Even dislocations of toes, however, must not be treated lightly and must always be properly evaluated, since they too can result in permanent disability.

Partial displacement of the joint, which is transient in nature, is a subluxation. While a subluxation may often not be of great significance functionally, resultant injury to articular surface and associated ligaments may cause persistent disability. A subluxing patella, for example, may result in complete destruction of the articular surface of the patella and ultimately require patellectomy, if the imbalance responsible for the subluxation is not corrected [9].

Ligamentous sprains usually result from single-impact macrotrauma and are classified as first,- second,- or third-degree depending on the extent of destruction of the ligaments and the resultant instability of the joint. In a first-degree sprain, there is tenderness and swelling over the ligament, but the joint is stable. In a second-degree sprain, there is some instability in the joint in addition to tenderness and swelling, but the mechanical stability of the ligament is usually sufficient to allow continued satisfactory functioning of the joint. In a third-degree sprain, there is complete tearing of the ligament, usually with loss of stability of the joint on the side of the ruptured ligament.

Third-degree or complete ligamentous tears may often require surgical repair, while first- and second-degree sprains can usually be treated with rest, ice, compression, and elevation, and subsequent rehabilitation of the extremity. The need for specific rehabilitation of the entire extremity must not be forgotten, after even a relatively minor sprain. As an example, a second-degree ankle sprain of the lateral collateral ligaments rarely results in permanent disability if proper rehabilitation exercises, including stretching of the heel cord and strengthening of the peroneal muscles and ankle dorsiflexors, are carried out after the early healing stage [24].

Joints that are relatively stiff and lacking flexibility appear to be particularly susceptible to sprains. Again, the best prevention of these ligamentous injuries appears to be stretching and flexibility exercises that maintain full motion of the joints.

Sites of Injury

Hip and Pelvis

The bony pelvis unites the spinal column—through the lumbosacral joint—with the lower extremities—through the hip joints. In addition, the bony pelvis has three joints of its own that can be sites of injury: the two sacroiliac joints behind and the symphysis pubica in front. Perhaps as important as the joints of the pelvis, however, are the multiple sites of muscle-tendon-unit insertions on the pelvis and in the region of the hip. Many of these muscles are two-joint muscles, with an increased chance of strain or injury, given their increased excursions.

The lumbosacral joint is more appropriately discussed with back injuries. The remaining pelvic joints, the sacroiliac and symphysis pubica, are syndesmotic joints with minimal excursion, which hold the bony elements of the pelvic ring together and allow for stress uptake. Interestingly, we are seeing a new overuse syndrome involving these joints—osteitis pubica (figure 14–3) [13]. This is actually an arthritis of the symphysis pubica joint resulting from recurrent microtrauma. It is seen in distance runners and team-sport players performing on hard surfaces such as synthetic football or soccer turf. It frequently presents as low-grade aching groin pain with onset after running begins. It is associated with a reactive and often dramatic tightness of the groin muscles, with limited hip abduction. Since the public region is the site of insertion of both the rectus and abdominis muscles from above and the groin or adductor muscles, osteitis pubica is often mistakenly diagnosed as a strain of these muscles or a tendinitis of their insertions. Disorders of the genitalia or abdominal wall, such as inguinal or femoral hernia, may also be included in the differential diagnosis. Plain radiographs are often diagnostic in advanced cases, with irregularity of the pubic margins and bony resorption evident. In less severe or early cases, radiographs may be nondiagnostic. Bone scan can be helpful in diagnosing this condition, but recognition is often the result of no more than an index of suspicion and attention to a history of microtrauma.

Treatment begins with relative rest. Sometimes altering the running surface, running on grass instead of pavement, for example, can arrest mild cases. Anti-inflammatory

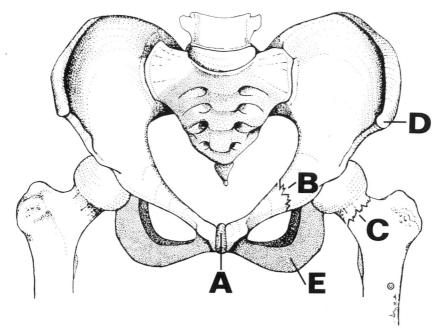

Figure 14–3 The bony pelvis. Overuse athletic injuries can involve (A) the symphysis pubica: osteitis pubis, (B) stress fractures of the pubic rami, or (C) stress fractures of the neck of the femur. Muscle tendon avulsions can occur at (D) the pelvic brim or (E) icheal rami site of hamstring muscle insertions.

drugs can also be helpful. If one type is unsuccessful, a second or even a third should be tried. Additional physical therapy to stretch and strengthen the groin and abdominal muscles must also be undertaken to rehabilitate the athlete after this injury.

Muscle strains and avulsions The most common injuries of the hips and pelvis in athletes are muscle-tendon strains, or even avulsions. The pelvic ring is the site of many muscle insertions: the iliac wing serves as the site of conjoint insertion of the abdominal muscles from above and the gluteal muscles from below; the ischium as the site of origin of the hamstrings; and the pubis and pubic ring anteriorly as the site of insertion of the groin muscles and lesser hip flexors.

Muscle-tendon strain can occur anywhere through the muscle, but adult recreational athletes frequently sustain injury at the muscle-tendon junction, while adolescent athletes can avulse the cartilagenous tendon insertions from the bone itself. (figure 14–4).

Management of these muscle-tendon injuries should be initiated immediately:

(1) Rest: immediately putting the muscle units at rest and minimizing their active and passive contraction or excursion helps to minimize further tissue injury and associated swelling, while allowing torn blood vessels to contract and coagulate.

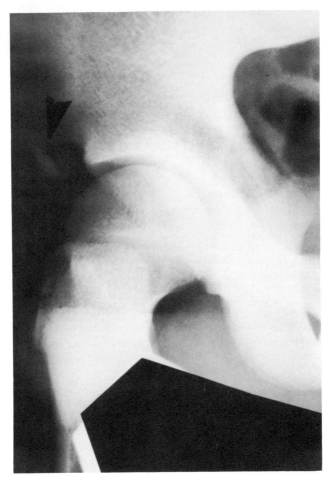

Figure 14–4 Avulsion of the rectus femoris tendon insertion from the anterior inferior iliac spine in a young soccer player.

(2) Ice: immediately applying cold compresses or an ice bag also helps to minimize swelling and additional tissue injury. Chemical coolant bags, while convenient, often have a short period of cooling and may cause skin burns if they leak. Icing should be intermittent, with application for five to ten minutes and then a subsequent interval of five to ten minutes before another application [18].

(3) Compression: most conveniently provided by gentle elastic wraps, but care should be taken to provide a tourniquet effect to the distal extremity. Bandages soaked in ice water are an excellent way to provide compression and cooling.

(4) Elevation: this is the most frequently neglected of the four-fold approach to acute injury but it can be the most effective. Elevation, of course, must be above the level of the heart, in order to provide drainage and blood return. The acronym for these four steps is RICE.

While this initial stage of management has, in the past, been relegated to the first 24 to 48 hours after injury, recent experience has suggested that components of this treatment may have to be continued up to five or even seven days after injury. Hypothermia in particular appears to aid recovery and early rehabilitation, due to its anti-inflammatory and analgesic effects.

The second stage of management of muscle-tendon injuries is progressive return of motion of the affected joints by rehabilitative exercises. The use of local heat at this stage (either wet or dry) can be useful in aiding relaxation of the muscles and promoting blood flow to the area. The type of exercise done may be either isometric or dynamic. It is frequently done without weight bearing of the extremity. I prefer dynamic *resisted* exercises of the affected muscle. The important thing is that the exercises be done without discomfort and certainly without associated recurrence of swelling. Assisted dynamic exercises, while more traditional, run the risk that the assisting therapist may exceed the healing limits of the muscle or tendon, causing pain and recurrent swelling, and actually delaying the healing process.

The final stage of recovery from surgery or injury is the restoration of complete strength and range of motion, and restoration of affected techniques, such as cutting or jumping. A recent addition to sports medicine—the Cybex Isokinetic Dynamometer— permits the most precise measurement of the relative strength, power, and endurance of injured muscles possible. This unit is available in most hospital physical-therapy departments and sports-medicine clinics today [14]. It gives a precise measurement of these muscle qualities and compares them with the opposite uninjured extremity. We no longer have to rely simply on our own manual or visual assessment of an injured extremity to determine recovery from injury.

A brief mention of muscle bulk is important, as muscle strength and muscle bulk are not necessarily directly related. After injury, there can be a dramatic decrease in the circumference of the extremity after only 24 to 48 hours. Subsequently, despite progressive return of muscle strength, the bulk of the extremity may remain decreased. This characteristic is probably a reflection of the integrity of the complete neuromuscular and central cortical reflex loop, and the extremity should not really be considered recovered from injury until this has been restored [8].

Other Injuries of the Hip and Pelvis Injuries to the hips themselves are rare in the recreational athlete. Pain localized to the hip may actually be referred from the back, as a reflection of back disorders. It may also be the result of impingement of adjacent muscle-tendon structures on the hip structures, such as trochanteric bursitis, which is a swelling over the greater trochanter of the hip and actually reflects an impingement of relatively tight fascia lata over this prominence [21].

Trochanteric bursitis can usually be diagnosed by the presence of direct tenderness and, sometimes, swelling over the lateral bony prominence of the hip. Examination of the fascia lata, using the Ober test, usually demonstrates that it is relatively tight [3]. Management includes relative rest and use of anti-inflammatory medication or even corticosteroid injections. Improving the flexibility and strength of the muscles about the hip and, in particular, of the fascia lata, are most important, however.

Onset of hip pain with sports activity can be the first presentation of early degenerative arthritis of the hip. Examination often shows limited rotation of the hips in both flexion and extension, often with loss of internal rotation more than external rotation. Radiographs can confirm narrowed joint space and, sometimes, marginal osteophyte formation. The maintenance of hip motion and strength is very important in the early stages of degenerative arthritis of the hip. Exercises such as biking or swimming, rather than running, are usually recommended.

Additionally, persistent hip pain in association with repetitive microtrauma activities, such as running, may reflect a stress fracture of the femoral neck. Plain x-rays can be nondiagnostic, and radioisotope bone scan may be the only way to confirm the diagnosis [23]. If detected early enough, rest alone is sufficient to manage a stress fracture of the hip. Patients should be placed on crutches, and activities such as swimming, if painless, for a period of 8 to 12 weeks is recommended. Internal fixation or pinning is probably not necessary.

Thigh Problems

Upper-leg or thigh pain in the recreational adult athlete is usually due to muscle-tendon injury. Muscle pulls are muscle strains and must be managed as described for the hips and pelvis. A thigh injury of special concern, and one too frequently minimized, is the thigh contusion known as a charley horse [21]. This can be a minor, moderate, or severe injury depending on the relative disability that results. Minor thigh contusions allow full passive and active flexion of the knee and the maintenance of a fully extended knee against resistance. In moderate injuries, while the knee can be passively extended to neutral, complete active or passive flexion of the knee is not possible but does occur to at least 90 degrees. In severe thigh contusions, there is a dropping of the leg when extension of the elevated leg is attempted and the knee cannot be flexed to 90 degrees. Severe thigh contusions must be treated with great care, and hospitalization may be required to place the extremity at rest. Icing should be continued until passive extension can be maintained, then slow cautious resumption of motion of the thigh should be commenced.

The feared complication of severe thigh contusion is myositis ossificans. This is actual ossification of the resolving thigh hematoma and may be associated with the early application of heat or excessive rehabilitation of the extremity. It rarely requires surgery, although the disability may last up to a year after injury (figure 14–5).

Unsuspected stress fractures of the femoral shaft may also cause thigh or leg pain and should be considered. In addition, referred pain from the lower back and hip region can be confused with local disorders of the leg (figure 14–6).

Knee Problems

Disorders of the knee are the most frequently encountered problems in most sports. In contact sports, cutting injuries or direct-impact injuries can cause severe, and often disabling, knee injuries. Even in running or dancing, however, knee problems can lead the list. While assessment of knee injuries can often be difficult, even for the knee expert, classifying the injuries or problems into three different types—ligamentous disorders,

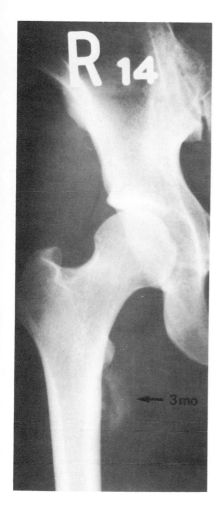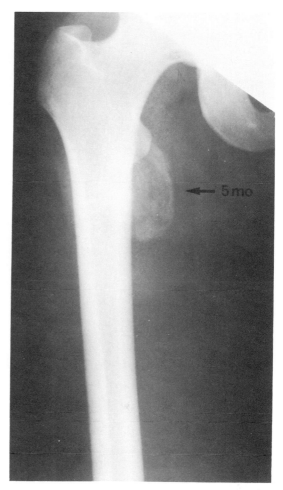

Figure 14–5 A and B. Myositis ossificans in a young gymnast, three months and five months after injury. At five months, the bony lesion has united with the femur, and now will undergo progressive remodeling and reabsorption.

internal derangements, and derangements of the extensor mechanism—is helpful. Combinations of two or even three of these disorders can occur together (figure 14–7). For example, a cutting injury that tears the anterior cruciate ligament may initially appear to be of minor importance after the initial pain and swelling have resolved, and the athlete may actually resume sports in a short time [5]. However, with continued use, the remaining ligaments of the knee may undergo progressive stretching to the point where giving way of the knee—reflecting a rotatory instability—may begin to occur. Straight-ahead running may still be possible without any problem. In addition to the onset of giving way, however, the increased laxity of the knee increases the chance of a tear developing

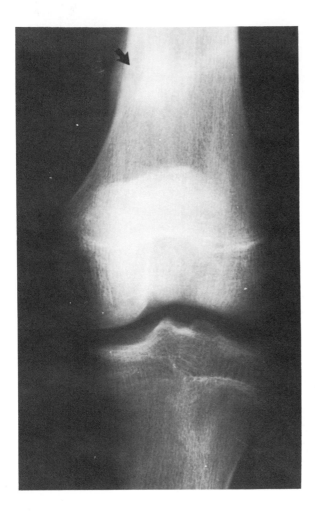

Figure 14–6 Stress fracture of the distal femur, initially thought to be a derangement of the knee.

in the lateral or medial meniscus or, sometimes, in both. Finally, the ligamentous laxity and possible associated meniscal tear can affect the fit and excursion of the patella in its femoral groove. As a result, chondromalacia patella or even subluxation of the patella may subsequently develop.

Similarly, a previous knee injury, with a slight increase in general laxity and a silent meniscal tear, may develop rather typical symptoms of chondromalacia patella when a running program is begun.

Recently, the growing use of the fiberoptic arthroscope as an aid in examining the interior of the knee has dramatically increased the diagnostic acumen and the therapeutic collection of the sports physician [17]. While the solicitation of a careful history and complete physical examination is important, this newer diagnostic technique has dramatically improved our ability to assess and treat knee injuries in athletes.

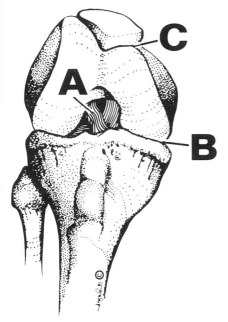

Figure 14–7 Simultaneously occurring disorders of the knee. (A) One initial isolated tear of the anterior cruciate ligament can result in a loose knee, with (B) subsequent tear of one or both menisci. Finally, (C) chondromalacia patella can develop because of the altered tracking of the patella.

Ligamentous Derangements Although our understanding has increased in the past ten years, much remains to be learned about the combination of the ligamentous injuries and the resultant laxities of the knee. The most recent classification divides these ligamentous instabilities of the knee into straight instabilities and rotatory instabilities [10]. The straight instabilities include valgus, varus, anterior, and posterior instabilities.

Valgus instability, reflecting tears of the medial collateral ligament complex, usually results from a blow to the outer side of the knee. This is a relatively benign derangement, and operative repair is no longer considered unless a complete third-degree tear, with associated injury of the posterior capsule, has occurred. Similarly, varus instability of the knee is usually well tolerated and will generally respond to conservative treatment. Isolated anterior and posterior instabilities are rarely encountered.

Of the rotatory instabilities, anterolateral instability, presently thought to be a reflection of the tear of the anterior cruciate ligament, with or without associated tear of the ligaments of the posterolateral corner of the knee, appears to occur most frequently. Anteromedial instability may also result from injury to the anterior cruciate ligament, but with associated injury to medial or posteromedial structures.

A detailed description of the physical examination of the knee will not be attempted in this chapter; the reader is referred to several reviews of this subject [10,12,15,22]. A high index of suspicion, especially for the possibility of anterior cruciate injury, must be entertained in any knee injury occurring in sports in which the athlete recalls a sensation of a pop in the knee, acute onset of swelling in the knee or a sensation of giving way of the knee or transient instability.

The present approach to knee injuries with an associated acute hemarthrosis includes careful assessment, often under general anesthesia, and often by arthroscopy. Studies by DeHaven and others have confirmed the high incidence of major derangements of the knee in association with acute hemarthrosis [6]. In addition, most authorities agree that the results of immediate ligamentous injuries, which have resulted in demonstrable instability of the knee, far exceed late attempts at repair of ligament substitution.

A chronic instability, which may have resulted from injury months or years earlier, is seen much more frequently. In such situations, particularly in the recreational athlete, a thorough rehabilitative program of exercises to restore the strength of the hamstrings, and the possible adjunctive use of a brace such as the Lenox-Hill derotational brace, may be sufficient to allow ongoing activities and prevent further deterioration of the knee. Surgical reconstruction of the chronic unstable knee should be attempted only when there is a progressive functional loss.

Internal Derangements Derangements of the meniscal cartilage are the most common internal derangements of the knee. While the younger player will often present with a locked knee because of an acute longitudinal or bucket-handle tear of the meniscus, meniscal lesions in the recreational adult are usually of the attritional type, consisting of transverse or even longitudinal cracks or fissures in the menisci, which usually present more insidiously. These fissures are often evident as a low-grade ache in the back of the knee with or without associated swelling and sometimes with an associated catch in the knee with activity. True locking is rare, and it can be due to a loose body or joint mouse instead of a meniscal derangement.

Osteochondritis dissecans, although a disease of children and adolescents, can occur in an adult. It consists of a localized death of subarticular bone with or without partial bone absorption and can present as a localized softening of the overlying articular surface, usually of the femoral condyles; it can also result in loose bodies in the joint if the overlying articular cartilage, with or without subjacent bone, detaches (figure 14–8). These symptoms can often be confused with meniscal lesions. [12].

Both the assessment and management of internal derangements have been revolutionized by the arthroscope. In most centers, arthroscopy has replaced arthrography in assessing internal derangements, particularly with the refinement of microsurgical techniques under arthroscopic control. Most internal derangements in the adult athlete can now be diagnosed and treated with the arthroscopic technique [17]. A knee problem that does not respond to exercise techniques to restore motion and strength and that continues to suggest a derangement of the articular mechanics of the knee is now usually considered for arthroscopic evaluation. Arthroscopy can be done under local anesthesia on an outpatient basis, and repair of many of the conditions encountered—such as the presence of loose bodies or tears of the meniscus—can be affected under the same anesthesia, using separate small puncture wounds in the knee and small grasping and cutting instruments.

Extensor-Mechanism Problems Problems of the extensor mechanism are the most commonly encountered knee problems in the recreational athlete [20]. Derangement of the patella, patellar tendon, or quadriceps tendon may occur separately, or in combina-

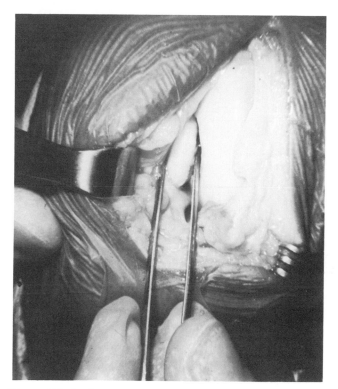

Figure 14–8 Loose osteochondritis dissecans lesion of the medial femoral condyle being removed. This procedure can now be done under arthroscopic control with small instruments and puncture wounds to the knee.

tion. Swimmer's knee, runner's knee, jumper's knee, or biker's knee are terms applied to derangements of the extensor mechanism.

The history is usually diagnostic. A low-grade aching pain, usually activity-related, is described and localized to the front of the knee. Transient episodes of giving way are often described, but these are not followed by locking or swelling of the knee, and immediate resumption of motion is possible. Pain with stair-climbing is often noted, as well as stiffness or aching occurring with prolonged sitting in one position, as with driving or sitting in a movie. There is often an additional history of change in intensity or physical activity preceding the onset of symptoms. Most derangements of the extensor mechanism are overuse injuries and are the result of the recurrent microtrauma of running or jumping (figure 14–9).

Examination will often reveal one or more elements of associated anatomic malalignment of the lower extremity, such as leg-length discrepancy, femoral anteversion, genu valgum, or pes planus. At the knee, an increased "Q" angle is often found, reflecting

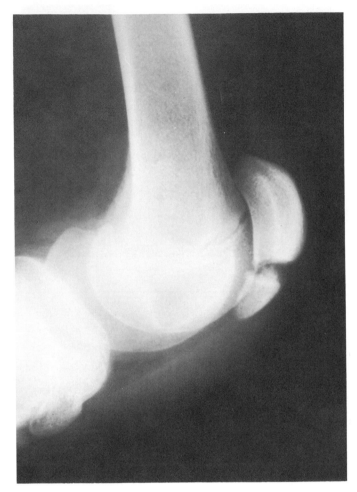

Figure 14–9 Avulsion of the lower pole of the patella in a young
athlete with complaints of knee pain with running, a form of
jumper's knee. Assessment found generalized lack of flexibility
throughout the lower extremities.

the tendency toward lateral deviation of the patella in its groove. Examination of the
muscle-tendon units will often reveal a relatively tight and weak quadriceps muscle, with
the vastus lateralis stronger than the vastus medialis and associated tight fascia lata. The
end result, again, is a tendency toward lateral tracking of the patella in its groove with
resultant asymmetric wearing of the articular surface of the patella and, in severe cases,
frank lateral luxation of the patella. Table 14–1 outlines the associated risk factors that
should be anticipated in an overuse injury such as chondromalacia patella.

Early on, and in relatively mild cases, restoring the balance of strength and flexibility of the muscles of the lower extremity—especially of the quadriceps itself—may be

Table 14–1 Associated Risk Factors in an Overuse Injury

Training errors, including abrupt changes in intensity, duration, or frequency of training.

Musculotendinous imbalance of strength, flexibility, or bulk.

Anatomic malalignment of the lower extremities, including difference in leg lengths, abnormalities of rotation of the hips, position of the knee cap, and bow legs, knock knees, or flat feet.

Footwear: improper fit, inadequate impact-absorbing material, excessive stiffness of the sole, and/or insufficient support of hindfoot.

Running surface: concrete pavement versus asphalt versus running track versus dirt or grass.

Associated disease state of the lower extremity, including arthritis, poor circulation, old fracture, or other injury.

---

sufficient to alleviate symptoms. A program of general lower-extremity stretching exercises, especially for the quadriceps, fascia lata, and hamstrings, and a program of static straight-leg-raising strengthening exercises of the quadriceps should be followed. These exercises are done with the leg in full extension, with weight boot or ankle weights, lifted from the hip while the opposite hip and knee are flexed. This must be a progressive resistive program with increase in the amount of weights lifted as strength improves. A resistance of at least 12 pounds must be obtained, lifted in three sets of ten repetitions, before symptoms are usually relieved. In the average-sized adult, a level of 18 to 25 pounds of resistance, maintained for at least six months, has successfully relieved patellofemoral symptoms in 92% of patients in our sports-medicine clinic.

Additional measures to relieve patellofemoral symptoms may include the use of orthotics in both street and athletic shoes to prevent associated pronation; in severe cases, knee braces may also be useful by helping to distribute the extensor forces across the knee. If these steps do not relieve symptoms over a period of at least six months, simple surgical techniques, such as release of the tight lateral extensor retinaculum under arthroscopic control and the subsequent resumption of extension-type exercises, may be considered. In certain cases, where anatomic malalignment at the knee is extreme, or where lateral luxation or even frank dislocation persists, realignment of the extensor mechanism may be required.

We prefer to call this condition patellofemoral stress syndrome rather than chondromalacia patella, unless frank fissuring and deterioration of the articular surface of the patella can be confirmed either by arthroscopy or arthrotomy. In many cases these symptoms are associated with simple mild softening of the articular cartilage. Intervention with exercises or even surgery in this disorder must be truly prophylactic to be helpful. If this disorder has progressed to the point where extensive deterioration of the articular cartilage of the patella has already occurred, results of subsequent management are usually poor.

Recent interest in debridement of the undersurface of the patella (chondroplasty) has developed because such debridement can now be done using power instruments under arthroscopic control. While these techniques may give symptomatic relief, every attempt must be made to restore the proper tracking of the patella in its groove, since these degenerative changes are secondary to the malalignment or maltracking of the patella.

Lower-Leg Problems

Lower-leg problems in the recreational adult are usually overuse injuries of the muscle-tendon units. Careful assessment and localization must be done to determine the site of pain or tenderness. In particular, one must never be content with a diagnosis of shin splints. Activity-related pain in the athlete subject to repetitive microtrauma activities such as running, may indeed be a tendinitis, but it may also be a stress fracture of the tibia or even fibula, as well as a compartment syndrome of one of the four muscle compartments of the lower leg. Tendinitis and stress fractures have been discussed above, but further discussion of compartment syndromes is indicated.

The major muscles of the lower leg are contained in four different fascial envelopes which are relatively unyielding. They can form a constraining envelope about the muscles that can impair arterial inflow or venous outflow if swelling occurs in the muscles contained in the compartment. These compartment syndromes are usually overuse injuries and are a result of inappropriate training techniques of the muscles involved. While they usually present as a slow, insidious, and activity-related pain in the involved compartment, they can also have an acute onset in association with activity and be a true emergency. If steps are not taken to relieve the pressure within the compartment or restore the blood flow and drainage of the compartment, ischemic necrosis of muscle, tendon, and nerve elements contained within the compartment can occur, resulting in permanent impairment [27].

Again, these lower-extremity overuse injuries are most easily prevented by slow progressive training techniques. If an acute compartment syndrome develops, however, the athlete should be immobilized, and the extremity elevated to the level of the heart, while icing is applied to the involved compartment. If symptoms do not rapidly abate and if pressure measurement of the involved compartment suggests significant elevation of compartment pressure, immediate surgical fascial release should be considered.

Several acute injuries to the lower-extremity musculature can occur in the recreational athlete. One of these, the tennis leg, is actually an acute tear of the medial head of the gastrocnemius from its subjacent tendon. Initiating symptoms can often be very debilitating. The diagnosis can usually be readily made by the localized site of tenderness and swelling and often by the relative elevated level of the involved gastrocnemius muscle belly. Conservative management techniques are satisfactory for this injury, and full return to athletic activities can be anticipated.

The other acute injury that can occur in this area is a rupture of the tendo Achillis. This injury often occurs in racquet sports. The injured athlete often describes a sensation similar to being hit in the back of the heel with a projectile. These ruptures are generally complete, with detachment of the proximal muscles and tendons from the os calcis below. A useful diagnostic test is to have the athlete kneel on the examining table and perform passive squeezing of the proximal musculature. If there is integrity of the gastrocsoleus mechanism, a passive plantar flexion of the foot will occur. If there has been disruption of the mechanism at the site of the tendo Achillis, no passive plantar flexion will occur. This test is important, because associated musculature such as the peroneals can give a false impression of active plantar flexion, even when the tendo Achillis has been ruptured.

Ankle and Foot Injuries

Injuries of the foot and ankle in recreational athletes are common. While many of these injuries are the result of recurrent microtrauma, ankle sprains are a major source of disability in the recreational athlete and are the result of single-impact macrotrauma.

Ankle sprains are generally of the lateral collateral ligaments of the ankle. Localized swelling immediately subjacent to the medial malleolus and over the anterior aspect of the ankle joint or the straight lateral aspect of the ankle joint, as well as swelling and ecchymosis below the site of injury, are common. Physical examination will generally confirm the diagnosis, but it is very difficult to rule out the possibility of an oblique fracture of the lateral malleolus, and x-rays of the ankle should be obtained if there is any doubt as to the extent of injury.

Debate exists as to the proper management of severe ligamentous derangements at the ankle. Most sports-medicine physicians feel that acute repair of ligamentous disruption at the ankle is rarely indicated [25]. Even in severe disruptions of a lateral ankle, as demonstrated by stress radiographs, many physicians will initiate treatment with a period of 7 to 10 days of cast immobilization, followed by early ambulation in a cast brace or special splint that allows flexion and extension of the ankle while limiting inversion and eversion (figure 14–10).

As with any acute injury of soft tissues, rest, ice, compression, and elevation are indicated. It is particularly important in ankle injuries, however, to institute weight-bearing as early as possible in order to prevent progressive debilitation of the entire lower extremity. If heel-toe ambulation is not possible with soft dressings and crutch support, a short leg-walking cast or cast brace should be used until it is possible. Subsequent restoration of the strength and excursion of all the muscle-tendon units about the ankle and, in particular at the tendo Achillis, is important. Persistent tightness of the tendo Achillis after ankle sprain has been shown to be an important factor in reinjury.

In overuse injuries of the foot and ankle, careful attention to localization and diagnostic accuracy is essential. In a dancer, for example, tendinitis of the flexor hallucis longus tendon immediately subjacent to the medial malleolus can be easily mistaken for tendinitis of the tibialis posterior. While management of the two is similar, progressive rehabilitation is somewhat different. In addition, persistent tendinitis and inflammation of the flexor hallucis longus tendon in its bony and ligamentous tunnel under the talus may require surgery in order to prevent serious disability.

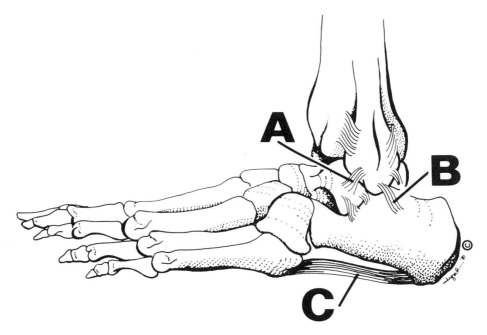

Figure 14–10   The foot and ankle. Sprain of the lateral collateral ligaments of the ankle are common. Less severe sprains involve the (A) fibulotalar ligaments, while more severe sprains involve both this ligament and the (B) fibulocalcaneal ligament. (C) Chronic plantar fascitis can be one of the most difficult injuries to treat, particularly in runners.

In the foot itself, tendinitis and stress fractures can be easily confused (figure 14–10). Stress fractures of the metatarsals, especially the second metatarsals, are common overuse injuries, particularly in the runner.

An injury of particular concern in the runner, and one which can often present dramatic difficulty in management, is inflammation of the plantar fascia of the foot [1]. The plantar fascia is a heavy fibrous structure extending from the base of the metatarsophalangeal joints distally up to the plantar aspect of the os calcis proximally. It appears to be a functional component of the foot and ankle spring mechanism, and relative tightness of the plantar fascia is often associated with relative tightness of the tendo Achillis and other structures at the back of the foot. Plantar fascitis is a tearing of the structure of this fascia, and the subsequent healing and scarring increase its tightness. The end result can be a pain syndrome localized on the plantar and outer aspect of the heel area which can be very debilitating. Improvement can often be attained by the use of orthotics and even taping techniques, which prevent relative pronation of the longitudinal arch. Ultimate management often includes a satisfactory stretching and strengthening program for the small muscles of the foot as well as the plantar fascia. Where conservative techniques have failed, a surgical release of the plantar fascia and detachment of its fibers from the bony os calcis can give relief and allow resumption of activities.

Prevention of Lower-Extremity Injuries

A number of general recommendations should be considered when attempting to prevent, or lessen the severity of, sports injuries to the lower extremity. These include appropriate matching of participant to sport; specific training and conditioning; modification, if necessary, of the rules of the game or playing conditions; and appropriate protective equipment.

Certain physical conditions or anatomic malalignments may suggest that a particular sport or activity is contraindicated for a particular individual. While enjoyment of sports or fitness activities is important, certain people are constitutionally ill-matched to certain sports. Choosing the proper sport to begin with may be the best way to prevent problems. As an example, some people who choose running as their primary technique for fitness lack efficient rotation of the hips or sufficient impact-absorbing qualities in their feet to be able to run distances without experiencing leg problems. High arched, or cavo varus, feet appear to present problems when distance running is attempted. With proper initial assessment, these injuries could be avoided by recommending swimming or cycling as a substitute sport for these individuals.

Prevention of injury by proper conditioning and training has only recently received the attention it merits. Although acknowledged as essential to athletic achievement, conditioning has as often been indicted as causing injury rather than preventing it. In particular, systematic weight training and stretching exercises for the joints and muscle-tendon units are recommended [7]. In both traumatic injuries and overuse syndromes, systematic muscle strengthening and stretching, which overcome muscle imbalances and allow sufficient joint excursion so that excessive stress is not put on these or adjacent muscle-tendon units, are important elements in prevention of injury.

Perhaps the most important step in preventing lower-extremity injuries is attention to the rate and intensity of training techniques. A high percentage of leg-overuse syndromes that I see are associated with too rapid a rate of training or a dramatic change in intensity, such as the sudden addition of hill running by an unprepared runner.

Alteration of game rules and playing conditions can be important in protecting the recreational athlete. Elimination of impact checking in recreational hockey or sliding in recreational baseball are examples.

Finally, attention to proper equipment, including properly designed and fitted running shoes, can be important in preventing injury. It must be added, however, that this is properly placed last on the list of preventive measures, since attention to proper training and conditioning is much more important.

References

1. Anderson, L. D. Injuries of the forefoot. *Clin. Orthop.* 122:18–27, 1977.
2. Brewer, B. J. Injuries to the musculo-tendinous unit in sports. *Clin. Orthop.* 23:32–38, 1962.
3. Brubaker, C. E. and James, S. L. Injuries to runners. *J. Sports Med.* 2:189–197, 1974.

4. Buxbaum, R. and Micheli, L. J. *Sports for Life.* Boston: Beacon Press, 1980.

5. Chick, R. R. and Jackson, D. Tears of the anterior cruciate ligament in young athletes. *J. Bone Joint Surg.* 60A:970–973, 1978.

6. DeHaven, K. E. Diagnosis of acute knee injuries with hemarthrosis. *Am. J. Sports. Med.* 8:9–14, 1980.

7. Holt, L. *Scientific Stretching for Sport.* Halifax, Nova Scotia: Sports Research Ltd., 1979.

8. Hooks, G. *Weight Training in Athletics and Physical Education.* Englewood Cliffs, N.J.: Prentice-Hall, Inc., 1974.

9. Hughston, J. C. Reconstruction of the extensor mechanism for subluxating patella. *J. Sports Med.* 1:6–11, 1972.

10. Hughston, J. C., Andrews, J. R., Cross, M. J., and Moschi, A. Classification of knee joint instabilities. *J. Bone Joint Surg.* 58A:159–190, 1976.

11. Jones, R. E., et al. Vascular and orthopaedic complications of knee dislocation. *Surg. Gynecol. Obstet.* 149:554–55 8, 1979.

12. Kennedy, J. C. *The Adolescent Knee.* Baltimore: Williams and Wilkins, 1979.

13. Koch, R. A. and Jackson, D. W. Pubic symphysitis in runners. *Am. J. Sports Med.* 9:62–63, 1981.

14. Knapik, J. J., et al. Isokinetic and isometric torque relationships in the human body. *Arch. Phys. Med. Rehabil.* 61:64–67, 1980.

15. Marshal, J., et al. Knee ligament injuries: A standardized evaluation method. *Clin. Orthop.* 123:115–129, 1977.

16. McBryde, A. M. Stress fractures in athletes. *J. Sports Med.* 3:212–217, 1976.

17. McGinty, J. B. and Matza, R. A. Arthroscopy of the knee: Evaluation of an out-patient procedure under local anesthesia. *J. Bone Joint Surg.* 60A: 787–789, 1978.

18. McMaster, W. C., Liddle, S., and Waugh, T. R. Laboratory evaluation of various cold therapy modalities. *Am. J. Sports Med.* 6:291–294, 1978.

19. Micheli, L. J., Santopietro, F., Mariani, R., Gerbino, P. G., and Crowe, P. Etiologic assessment of overuse stress fractures in athletes. *Nova Scotia Medical Bulletin.* April/June: 43–47, 1980.

20. Micheli, L. J. and Stanitski, C. Lateral patellar retinacular release. *Am. J. Sports Med.* 9:330–336, 1981.

21. O'Donahue, D. H. *Treatment of Injuries to Athletes.* Philadelphia: W. B. Saunders, 1976.

22. Paulos, L., et al. A practical guide to the initial evaluation and treatment of knee ligament injuries. *J. Trauma* 20: 498–506, 1980.

23. Rosen, P. R., Micheli, L. J., and Treves, S. Early scintigraphic diagnosis of bone stress and fractures in adolescents. *Pediatrics.* In press.

24. Santopietro, F., Micheli, L., and Gerbino, P. Anatomical malalignment associated with chronic inversion ankle sprains: Preliminary study. In R. R. Rinaldi and M. L. Sabia (Eds.). *Sports Medicine Seventy-Nine.* Mt. Kisko, N.Y.: Futura Publishing Company, Inc., 1979.

25. Turco, V. J. Injuries to the ankle and foot in athletics. *Orthop. Clin. North Am.* 8:669–682, 1977.

26. Welsh, R. P. and Clodman, J.: Clinical survey of achilles tendinitis in athletes. *J. Can. Med. Assoc.* 122:193–195, 1980.

27. Whitesides, T. E., Haney, T. C., Morimoto, K., and Harada, H. Tissue pressure measurements as a determinant for the need of fasciotomy. *Clin. Orthop.* 113:43–51, 1975.

Index